DATE DUE

OCT 1 3 2010	
OCT 2 0 2010	
NOV 2 4 2010	

BRODART, CO.   Cat. No. 23-221-003

1816

1816

AMERICA
RISING

C. EDWARD SKEEN

THE UNIVERSITY PRESS OF KENTUCKY

Publication of this volume was made possible in part by a grant
from the National Endowment for the Humanities.

Editorial and Sales Offices: The University Press of Kentucky
663 South Limestone Street, Lexington, Kentucky 40508–4008

07 06 05 04 03   5 4 3 2 1

Library of Congress Cataloging-in-Publication Data

Skeen, Carl Edward.
  1816 : America rising / C. Edward Skeen.
       p.   cm.
  Includes bibliographical references.
  ISBN 0-8131-2271-6 (acid-free paper)
  1. United States—History—1809-1817. 2. United States—Politics and
government—1809-1817. 3. United States—History—War of
1812—Influence. 4. Political culture—United States—History—19th
century. 5. National characteristics, American. I. Title.
  E341.S57 2003
  973.5'1—dc21   2003007863

This book is printed on acid-free recycled paper meeting
the requirements of the American National Standard
for Permanence in Paper for Printed Library Materials.

Manufactured in the United States of America.

 Member of the Association of
American University Presses

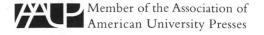

For my daughters,
Marianne and Laura

Contents

Acknowledgments

While the production of a work like this is ultimately an individual project, I am happy to acknowledge the assistance of individuals and institutions. The University of Memphis provided me with a semester's leave to work on the research for this study. The librarians in the microforms department of the Ned R. McWherter Library of the University of Memphis were very helpful. The outstanding collection of microforms in this department was the source of most of my research. Alas, as a sign of the times, due to budget constraints, these librarians have now been replaced by a "self-service" system.

I am also grateful for the assistance of those who read my manuscript and gave encouragement and helpful advice. Foremost was my colleague and friend, Major L. Wilson, who not only read the entire manuscript but also a revision based on his advice. I also received a very valuable reading from Andrew Burstein, whose perceptive advice I gratefully acknowledge. Thomas H. Appleton, Jr., read a portion of the manuscript and gave me the benefit of his expert editorial talents. I also wish to thank Dr. Thad Wasklewicz of the Department of Earth Sciences (Geography), Memphis Center for Spatial Analysis for the preparation of a map for this book. Also, two chapters are revised versions of two articles that appeared in the *Journal of the Early Republic* and are published here with the permission of the editors.

My daughters, Marianne Medlin and Laura Kuns, to whom this work is dedicated, were unfailing in their love and support. My grandchildren, Jonathan and Melinda Medlin, and Matthew and Joshua Kuns, will appreciate seeing their names in print, and I thank them for keeping me young. My wife, Linda, listened patiently and acted as a sounding board for my ideas about this project. Her love and support are greatly appreciated. She knows that she is "okay in my book."

Introduction

A claim could be made that every year is unique and that events occurring each year intertwine with strands from the past to weave a new fabric for the future. There are some years where recognizably great events occurred that had a more profound impact than other years. In American history, the years 1776 (Revolution), 1787 (Constitution), 1861 (Civil War), and 1929 (Great Depression) come readily to mind. A case could also be made that the pivotal importance of some years is not as easily discerned, and the events of that year have had a greater impact than historians have appreciated. This work follows on the heels of two very excellent studies of years in the early nation, by Andrew Burstein (1826) and Louis P. Masur (1831).[1] This study was started before these works were published and before the studies of a single year became fashionable, although there have been many other studies of a single year in history. In fact, in 1914, Gaillard Hunt did a graceful and readable study of 1814 (which is really not so much a study of the year as a broad survey of life in the Early Republic ranging from the American Revolution to the 1830s.)[2] Readers may wish to compare his work, which concentrates much more on the social history of that period than my study.

It is my contention that 1816 was a pivotal year of transition, particularly for the political life of the nation. The United States was "on the cusp" between adolescence and maturity. This was the fortieth year of American independence, and during these years there had been many self-doubts about the permanence of the Union. The War of 1812 was a time of great stress, and the country barely endured the experience, militarily and politically. Americans entered the war with great trepidation and with little harmony. By the end of the conflict, residents of one section of the country were even questioning whether they should continue in the Union. The war was indeed a "Second War for Independence." The happy conclusion of the war, with so little lost, not only assured the survival of the country, it also brought the country together in a way that had not been achieved after the first war for independence. New England's regionalism as evidenced by their opposition to the War of 1812 was already being seen in 1816 as "un-American." For the first time the people of the United States began to conceive of themselves as something more than a collection of individuals in states joined by a central government—not as Virginians, etc., but as Americans—and a nascent nationalism began to develop.

However, this was a barely perceptible development. There were still powerful tensions in American society between liberating possibilities and anxiety about the future, between democratic aspirations and aristocratic reservations, between growing prosperity and fears of debilitating luxury, between bold new social and political experiments and orthodoxy and conformism, and between novelty and experimentation and order and control. Americans also carried the knowledge that their actions could bless or blight their posterity. In short, in the felicitous phrase of historian Fred Somkin, Americans recognized that "democracy was a flaming comet, whose chance of avoiding incineration lay in the development of an internal gyroscope for self-regulating order."[3]

In a sense, Americans, now optimistic about the survival of their "experiment," were setting out on a quest to define themselves. This was particularly true in the realm of politics. The bitter partisan strife that had characterized the early years of the nation now seemed to be momentarily in abeyance, and politicians seemed intrigued by the unique opportunity that presented itself to carry out policies that would set America on a course that would ensure the twin ideas of freedom and the pursuit of happiness that infused all Americans. The Fourteenth Congress was up to the task. A plan for reduction of the national debt was established, and taxes were provided to do so. Order was brought to the financial system and the nation's currency, which were in chaos, by establishing a new Bank of the United States. A tariff measure was passed to protect emerging infant industries, and national security was provided by creating a professional standing army and by raising appropriations for an increase of the navy. The Fourteenth Congress also created a fund for financing roads and canals to bind the nation together, but it was vetoed by President James Madison. In keeping with this dynamic idea that they were doing what was best for America, the Fourteenth Congress also changed congressional pay from a small per diem allowance to a relatively generous salary. This action, however, aroused fears in the American people that the pay raise portended an introduction of luxury and vice into the government of the nation, which would lead to a decline of virtue such as had brought down the Roman Republic. The widespread participation of the average American in this protest foreshadowed the growth of what became known as the "age of the common man."

The progressive measures of the Fourteenth Congress hinted of an emerging market economy, and to many Americans this was an unsettling matter. Prosperity and happiness were not necessarily interchangeable ideas. Virtue undoubtedly led to prosperity, but prosperity could corrupt virtue. The growing prosperity, as well as the physical growth of the United States reflected in the rapid spread of Americans into the Western country, while a source of pride, also bred insecurity and concern about whether the country could be held together. Undoubtedly, the rapid changes taking place in society led defenders of order and stability to strive to uphold the traditional ways and to work to reform what they saw as a declining morality before the society of the "world's best and last hope" fell into decline.

In one respect, however, the year 1816 was clearly unique. The weather of the summer of 1816 was absolutely unprecedented. The combination of cold temperatures and drought blasted the crops of that year. There is no doubt that it created hardships in several parts of the country and offered a reason for many to pull up stakes and move westward. Yet in one sense, it was also a bonding experience. It was a subject of conversation and speculation shared by all Americans. Myriad explanations were offered as reasons for this visitation of nature, but ultimately it was to them an unexplainable freakish occurrence. The weather may have contributed to a minor political uprising over the Compensation Act, but the inherent stability and resilience of American society was shown when the abnormal weather was endured without any great upheaval. Ironically, the thing for which 1816 is best remembered, its weather, is far less significant than many of the other developments of this year.

While the focus is on the political and economic developments that influenced the future, the social trends that were evolving after the War of 1812 have also been examined. One obvious development in 1816 was the growth of voluntary associations and the greater involvement of ordinary Americans in groups attempting to "perfect" their society. This was another manifestation of the sense of nationalism and "coming together" that was a defining aspect of this year. Americans were clearly beginning to think in terms of the country at large and not in the narrow, constricted sense of community that had been the case before the war.

It should be noted that the tensions that have always been present in American life were clearly present in 1816. Thus there was a cautious optimism, leavened by a concern about the path to the future. John C. Calhoun captured this quandary perfectly in a reported speech in Congress, declaring "We are great, and rapidly— he was about to say fearfully—growing."[4] Again, in another context, Calhoun stated the broad proposition facing Congress and the American people in 1816: "whether we are to travel downward, or to raise the nation to that elevation to which it ought to aspire."[5] There were those who wished to press on into the future without fear and those who wished to impose some larger sense of order and direction to the course of the nation. Some of the social issues, such as crime and capital punishment, slavery, and alcoholism, were addressed in 1816. The humanitarian impulse also touched on many other aspects of American life. While this impulse was perhaps born out of a genuine concern for their fellow man, many reformers were also, no doubt, concerned that spreading the blessings of liberty broadly to the masses required that there be an element of social control over them to insure a virtuous republic.

The objective of this study has been to give an overall perspective of America in one year, but necessarily discussion has not been limited to a single year. Some of the events of 1816 had their antecedents in previous years, and the importance of some occurrences in 1816 did not become manifest until the next year or even much later. It may be that some aspects of American life in this year have been slighted—art, literature, and diplomacy, for example. The first two were not developed enough in 1816, in my judgment, and there was little of note to write about, and the last was to some extent subsumed in my chapter on national defense. As to the omission of what is called "social history,"—the life of the ordinary American—coverage would have necessitated a much larger study than here presented, and it did not seem to lend to compartmentalization into a single year or to fit into the scope and focus of the present work.

The material has been organized in a topical rather than in a chronological or thematic way. By doing so, each issue could be more fully and coherently developed. When I began this study, I was prepared to find an undercurrent of division that ultimately played out in the years that followed, namely sectionalism, which became clearly evident with the Missouri controversy in 1820. Instead, I slowly became convinced that the primary guiding principle of this year was good will. For one brief moment, there does seem to have been a period of good feelings, which historians have generally dismissed as a fallacy. This does not mean that there was no ill will in this year, certainly there was, but the prevailing spirit of the American people, the hope and promise of a better life, was never more evident than in this year.

Politically, the implication of this good will was an obliteration of political parties. In their zeal to ameliorate the partisan strife that had marked the last few years, politicians softened their rhetoric and truly took a national perspective on legislation. For the Republicans it often meant supporting measures that had previously been seen as Federalist, and for the Federalists, especially those living in New England, an obliging, conciliatory approach to this legislation was necessitated by fears, conscious or unconscious, that cooperation was better than isolation and persecution, which might have been expected from the victorious Republicans. Federalists had even more reason for trepidation, especially with the growth of the West, which would further marginalize New England politically. With the development of manufacturing in New England, it became apparent to some that government protection would be necessary for growth of industry in that region. By giving up their party, Federalists were welcomed into the fold, and they could have asked for little more. Ironically, the Republican Party, having embarked upon a different course, now lost their bearing. It became evident in the next few years that a new political dynamic was evolving—a new party alignment, a nationalistic-capitalistic wing (which included many former Federalists) and a conservative-agrarian, states rights wing.

Ultimately, this is a story of a more innocent time. The people of the United States were just beginning to expand physically and emotionally. Narrow provincialism was beginning to erode. The strains within American society, particularly the agrarian-capitalist dichotomy, soon disrupted the brief harmony that was happily evident in 1816, and American life fell into the usual struggle between the multiplicity of interests that have marked the course of this nation ever since.

Chapter 1

Year Without a Summer

"We have had the most extraordinary year of drought and cold ever known in the history of America," Thomas Jefferson wrote on September 8, 1816, to his old friend and political collaborator, Albert Gallatin, who was then serving as the United States Minister to France. The Sage of Monticello went on to elaborate in his usual meticulous manner: "In June, instead of 3 3/4 inches, our average of rain for that month, we only had 1/3 of an inch; in August, instead of 9 1/6 inches our average, we had only 8/10 of an inch; and still it continues. The summer, too, has been as cold as a moderate winter." Jefferson was reporting the most extraordinary weather phenomenon in American history, a summer unlike any other in the American experience. This was the "Year Without a Summer," or as some contemporaries dubbed it, "Eighteen-hundred-and-froze-to-death."[1]

Interestingly, the average temperature for the year 1816 was only slightly cooler than normal. February was warmer than usual, and October, November, and December were also above average. The distinguishing characteristic of the weather of this year was the uncommonly cool summer. Even so, the temperatures were not unremittingly cold; there were even periods of very warm, seasonably hot temperatures. The reason for the summer's notoriety can be attributed to three very cold spells, each lasting about a week, one in each of the summer months of June, July, and August. During these periods, typically, strong northwesterly winds set in and temperatures were forced steadily downward, followed by frosts in the Middle Atlantic and upper Western states and by general snows in the New England states.

There were many, often amusing, speculations on the causes of this meteorological phenomenon. Mostly these observations reflected the ingenuity of man in devising explanations for the mysterious works of nature, rather than any solid scientific information. The natural curiosity of the people about this unique summer and their many comments about the weather abounded in the newspaper accounts of the time. While many of the newspaper reports are unreliable and certainly unscientific, frost, snow, sleet, and ice, are observable phenomena, and there is no reason to doubt contemporary statements, even if their thermometric observations may be dubious. The newspapers also revealed the growing concern about crop failures that reached near-hysterical levels by the end of the summer. Surprisingly, much has been written about this summer from the meteorological point of view, but the historical point of view, as well as the social, economic, and even the political consequences of this "Year Without a Summer," have been largely ignored.

The relative coolness and dryness in the spring of 1816 did not at first attract any particular attention. The cool weather persisted later than usual, but frost and snow in March and April were not uncommon in New England and even in some of the Middle Atlantic and upper Western states. A foretaste of the summer ahead, however, was set by the pattern of the spring weather. There were warm, balmy days that spring, but they were invariably followed by a cold spell. The *Richmond* (VA) *Enquirer* reported, for example, that on March 17, "We were melting under the heat of summer. On Monday, visited by a piercing N.E. wind, a hail or drizzling sleet, during the day. On Tuesday morning, the bloom of the apricot and peach trees covered with icicles."[2] In Salem, Massachusetts, on April 16, the weather was a pleasant 74°. Thirty hours later, the thermometer had plunged to 21° and snow was reported in Boston.[3]

By May, a bizarre weather pattern was clearly evident; snow and frost had persisted through the spring. It snowed heavily in Albany on May 14. Planting was delayed or replanting became necessary after killing frosts, and crops were well behind their normal maturity. One traveler to the western country during the summer of 1816 noted on his way that Lake Erie's ice had broken up only on

May 20. On the twenty-ninth there was a frost so hard that it froze water a quarter-inch thick.[4]

Then came the terrible cold wave of June 5–11. At noon on June 5, the weather was warm in New England with temperatures ranging in the 80s. Thunderstorms and a strong wind developed from the northwest, and by the next morning the temperature had dropped into the low 40s—and that was the high for the day. It snowed throughout New England that day, covering the Catskill Mountains in eastern New York and extending even into western New York. One report stated that an elderly man in Peacham, Vermont, age eighty-eight, lost his way in the woods on June 7 in a snowstorm. As a result his feet were frozen and his toes had to be amputated.[5]

Snow fell intermittently the next two days. By noon on the eighth, snowfall ranged up to twelve inches in many parts of New England, while at Cabot, Vermont, it was reported to be eighteen inches deep.[6] The winds continued strongly out of the northwest, and the evening temperatures dipped below freezing in several parts of New England and hovered around 40° during the day. Boston recorded a low of 33° on June 10. The climax came on the following day. Whatever vegetation had escaped the abnormally low temperatures now fell victim to a hard frost. At Williamstown, Massachusetts, where exceptionally good, systematic temperature recordings were made, the temperature read 30.5° on the morning of June 11.[7] Possibly even lower readings were made elsewhere. In Albany, New York, ice was reported on at least two mornings.[8] Then the winds shifted southerly, ending the cold spell.

The effect of this cool weather was not as severe in the Middle Atlantic, Southern, and Western states, but it was harsh enough to destroy the fruit on the trees. At Cape May, New Jersey, hard frosts were reported for five successive nights, terminating on June 11.[9] Farther south, there was frost that damaged crops in Richmond, Virginia, on June 9 and 10.[10] From the systematic temperature observations kept at Charleston, South Carolina, it does not appear that the blustery weather pattern reached that deeply into the South. The coolest temperature recorded for the month of June was 65° at 8 a.m. on June 10. The lowest reading for that day, however, was probably a few degrees cooler.[11] In the West, a hard frost was observed on June 8 in Steubenville, Ohio.[12]

Most of the thermometric observations were, of course, random. There were few places in the United States where systematic, scientific recordings of meteorological data were taken. From the reports given in the newspapers, we have no knowledge of the kind of shelter used or the accuracy of the instruments. At best, most observations were probably only close approximations of the actual reading. Still, as noted earlier, frost is an observable phenomenon. Whether it was a hard or light frost might be a subjective matter, but the effect it had on crops, a cause for much lament among farmers, would tend to verify such claims.

The weather remained erratic during the month of June. In Salem, Massachusetts, the temperature reached 101° on June 22 and 100° the next day. Boston recorded 99° on the twenty-third. Optimism flourished around the country as prospects for crops improved. On June 27, the *Trenton* (NJ) *True American* reported that "agricultural prospects are much brighter than they were a few weeks ago. Wheat and rye in particular, have improved astonishingly." The *Richmond Enquirer* noted on July 3 that the wheat crop was doing fine: "In most places, the quantity is good, and the quality is excellent." The *Norfolk* (VA) *Herald* stated on July 1 that the prospects for farmers were "brightening, notwithstanding the unfavorable appearance of the crops a few weeks ago."[13]

These hopes for good crops were dashed by another cold wave. On July 6 a strong northwest wind set in, and for the next four days New England and the Middle Atlantic states felt the breath of winter weather. In New England temperatures dipped into the 30s and to the lower 40s in the Middle Atlantic states. Killing frosts again gave a check to vegetation as far south as Virginia. The Boston *Columbian Centinel* noted with concern that the weather for the summer appeared to be growing colder. May had been about 4.5° below normal, June was 6° below average, and the first fifteen days of July ranged about 10° below. Vegetation in New England was "languid" and "the fruits of the season, it is said, are without their accustomed flavor."[14]

This second cold spell of the summer was not quite as severe nor as prolonged as the one of a month earlier. The only snow reported in New England was in the mountains of Vermont, and snow was also reported in western New York along Lake Erie. A little farther north, Montreal had not only snow, but ice that formed to the thickness of a half dollar. Reports of frost came from all parts of the Middle Atlantic states, including Chambersburg, Pennsylvania, on July 5; Albany, New York, on July 8; and Trenton, New Jersey, on the ninth, tenth, and eleventh. This time the coolness reached farther south. Richmond, Virginia, had a frost on July 8. In Wilmington, North Carolina, it was reported that on July 9 the weather was so cool that it made thick clothes necessary and even a fire essential. Frosts were also observed in southern Ohio.[15]

This second blow to crops began to raise apprehensions around the United States about a possible scarcity of crops. Adding to this concern was the continuation of a prolonged drought that was affecting all parts of the country. The year had started out very dry, and it was particularly severe in the South. The *Charleston* (SC) *Courier* reported on April 3 that only a little over three inches of rain had fallen in the first three months, and the situation continued into the summer, for the *Courier* related on July 3 that only slightly less than eight inches of rain was recorded for the first six months of the year. At one point during the spring, Charleston went eight weeks without any measurable rain.[16] The Middle Atlantic and New England states were also severely affected. The editor of the *New York Columbian* reported on May 1 that "many farmers in New Jersey are ploughing up their fields of winter grain, which the drought has ruined." He added, "The want of rain is felt everywhere, and is likely to blast the beauties of Spring."[17] Some relief from the drought was felt in May and June in New England and the Middle Atlantic states as far south as Virginia. July was dry and August, by all accounts, was exceedingly dry in every part of the Union. Even a brief shower was considered a blessing. Accounts abound of the "scorched appearance of crops" and of the "fields burned from drought."[18]

By the end of the summer the impact of the prolonged drought was being given prominent attention by the editors. The rivers were very low; many, indeed, were impassable for navigation. The James River was lower than ever remembered; the Schuylkill near Philadelphia was so low that it was said that it could be crossed without wetting your feet.[19] The editor of the *Georgetown* (SC) *Gazette* related early in September, "The oldest inhabitants in the adjoining districts cannot remember that the Pee Dee, Waccamaw and Black Rivers have ever been so low as at present." The Pee Dee was impassable to normal navigation, and the editor asserted that the drought would also account for "the present great scarcity and consequent high price of corn in this market."[20] The editor of the *Augusta* (GA) *Chronicle* noted that not half of the crop of cotton would be made in either Georgia or South Carolina, and he added, "This appears to be generally the state of the season throughout the Southern states, and more generally so, than usual throughout the Union."[21]

As might be expected, the less than auspicious prospects for crops led to speculation and hoarding, particularly in grains, driving the prices upward and further heightening the anxiety of the people. Several editors attributed the increase in flour prices to the demand from Canada. The editor of the *Farmer's Register* in Troy, New York, related on July 23 that "several agents lately came here to purchase up every barrel they could lay their hands on, but not finding anything like the quantity they wanted in this city and its vicinity, have proceeded to New York to drain the market there." He added that "orders from Canada are for upwards of thirty thousand barrels" and that the price was now $11 a barrel, far above the normal $3 to $4 per barrel.[22] The *Albany* (NY) *Argus* also observed that the scarcity of grain was raising "gloomy forebodings of an increased and prolonged scarcity." Grain could not be procured "in many of the interior towns, at any price."[23]

Once again, however, warmer, summer-like weather returned. On August 6, the *Albany Argus* observed that the warm weather and occasional showers for the past four weeks had produced "an astonishing effect upon the crops of grain." The editor was certain that if no additional frosts occurred in the next few weeks, the crops would still be good. But on August 21, the northwest winds set in again, and there were "white frosts" around Albany.[24] Severe frosts were reported that same day in Pennsylvania. For over a week the winds blew with vigor from the north. This cold wave, the third of the summer, was perhaps not as severe as the one in June, but it was felt over a wider area. Snow once more was reported in New England, where the mountains of Vermont were white after a snowfall on August 21. Washington, Kentucky, was hit on August 21 and 22 by a "frost so severe, as in some instances to kill vines in exposed situations," and again by "considerable frost" on August 28 and 29. Cincinnati, Ohio, also experienced frost on August 21 and 22. Petersburg, Virginia, had frost on August 29, prompting one contemporary to remark that it was "a circumstance unparalleled in this part of the country—and what is equally extraordinary, we have had frost every month during the year." Richmond matched that record by having frost on August 29. The *Richmond Enquirer* remarked, "The oldest inhabitants have no recollection of such a prodigy." The frost even reached as far south as Danbury in Rockingham County, North Carolina.[25]

September was ushered in by heavy rains throughout many parts of the United States, which broke the long drought, but as the *Richmond Enquirer* phrased it, "This unexpected visitation from Heaven, added to the severe distress to which the country is otherwise reduced, has infused into the minds of the people generally the greatest apprehension and alarm."[26] The rains may have been from the effects of a hurricane that hovered off the east coast. Severe rain raked the area from Virginia through New England for a week. Albany had sixty-six hours of rain in five days that totaled 7.1 inches.[27] The rains in Virginia did considerable damage to bridges and crops, especially the hay and clover, as well as what corn had escaped the frosts. The weather continued to be cold. Widespread snows were reported in New England in mid-September.[28]

Americans may have taken some consolation in the fact that Europeans suffered through the same kind of summer. The spring, according to one account, was the "latest ever known," and the weather remained exceedingly cold through the summer. Emmanuel Le Roy Ladurie, in his study of European climate since the year 1000, noted that in 1816, "the wine harvests were the latest ever known" and the summer was the coolest "in all the long series of European temperature observations."[29] Europe's weather differed in one major respect, however. While the United States suffered through a drought, Europe was victimized by excessive rainfall, high rivers, and frequent inundations of farm lands. Le Roy Ladurie noted that the wetness was comparable only to the years 1316 and 1675. One contemporary stated that such wine as was harvested in 1816 was "undrinkable," and the bread "damp and sticky."[30] Snow fell in several countries in Europe in June, and there was a snowfall in London on August 30. A correspondent in Paris wrote a friend in America on August 25, "All accounts agree that in the memory of no man living, has a season been so cold—they observe there has been no summer."[31]

Contemporaries, of course, had many explanations for the extraordinary weather. The most frequently cited conjecture was the appearance of exceptionally large sunspots. All along the Atlantic seaboard during early May there were extensive comments about the remarkable appearance of the sun. Large spots were visible to the unaided eye, particularly at sunrise and sunset. A month later, during the last part of May, the sun was reputedly more spotted than before. Again, approximately a month later, another huge spot appeared, which divided into two. More spots were reported in early August and in early October.[32] The coincidence of these spots and the cold weather struck many observers as a plausible explanation for the bizarre weather. There were numerous theories on what caused sunspots: that they were solid bodies revolving about the sun or opaque bodies swimming upon the liquid matter of the sun; that the spots were the smoke and clouds from erupting volcanoes; that the spots were fallen comets, or excavations created by collision with comets; and even that the sun was surrounded by a luminous atmosphere which occasionally parted, permitting glimpses of the opaque body of the sun. There was general agreement that these spots reduced the rays from the sun and thus cooled the weather. Some, however, doubted that the spots diminished the rays of the sun that much, and they noted that the very coldest days of the summer, June 5–11, came during a period when the number of spots had decreased. They also observed, conversely, that the warmest days of the summer, the fourth week of June, were also when the spots were at a minimum.[33]

Many observers were struck by the reports of exceptionally large fields of ice floating in the North Atlantic, particularly east of the Gulf of St. Lawrence, which lingered on throughout the summer. This phenomenon was accompanied by reports that ice persisted in the Great Lakes much later than normal this year. It was believed that the ice absorbed great quantities of heat from the atmosphere, thus lowering the temperatures.[34] Of course, it is the reflection of the sun's rays, not the absorption of heat, that may account for cooling trends. Contemporaries may have mistaken cause and effect, but this speculation was by no means as bizarre as some other theories proposed to explain this anomalous summer.

One interesting idea was that the large number of earthquakes in the years preceding 1816 (including presumably the New Madrid earthquakes of 1811–12, some of the most powerful ever documented), had created an equilibrium of charge between the surface and the atmosphere. Electricity, the great agent of heat when in a state of motion, was presently in balance, and this was evidenced by the lack of lightning. Only when the equilibrium was destroyed, the theory ran, would the quantum of heat necessary for vegetation be generated.[35] Along the same lines, another speculation was that much of the normal heat came from the earth's interior by resistive electric heating and that Benjamin Franklin's lightning rods had upset the natural flow of electricity bringing on the cold weather.[36]

Yet another idea was based on the conjunction of an increase in sunspots and an eclipse of the moon on June 9. One writer conjectured that the moon's gravitational pull, along with the pull of the sunspots, combined to deflect the winds, thus adversely affecting the weather.[37] Finally, it was even speculated that the widespread clearing of the forests and the cultivation of the soil had allowed the heat of the earth to escape into the atmosphere, thereby contributing to the cooler weather.[38]

Twentieth-century explanations for the weather of 1816 have suggested that the most probable cause was the sulphur dioxide injected into the stratosphere from volcanic eruptions acting as a shield from the sun's rays.[39] Several major eruptions throughout the world occurred from 1812 to 1817 which contributed to cooler than normal temperatures. Soufriere, on St. Vincent Island in the West Indies, erupted on April 30, 1812; Mount Mayon, on Luzon in the Philippines, in 1814; and the greatest of all, Tambora, on Sumbawa, Indonesia, from April 7 to 12, 1815. The explosions of this Indonesian mountain were heard nearly a thousand miles away. More than ten thousand persons lost their lives in the eruption, and it was reportedly dark for three days for a distance of three hundred miles. The height of Tambora was reduced approximately 4200 feet, and a vast quantity of ashes and cinders spewed into the atmosphere. Scientific studies have shown that it was the greatest sulphur-producing eruption in the past 750 years, and perhaps ever. The dust girdled the globe.[40]

Some contemporary observations support this hypothesis to some extent. The editors of the Washington, D.C., *Daily National Intelligencer* noted on May 1, 1816 that "the whole atmosphere is filled with a thick haze, the inconvenience of which is not diminished by the clouds of impalpable dust which floats in the air." The

Norfolk, Virginia, *American Beacon* also commented on May 9 that, "the atmosphere is continually impregnated with a fine dust, very injurious to respiration."[41] Also, on July 15, the editor of the Boston *Columbian Centinel* remarked, "The Sun's rays, it has been frequently remarked, have not their usual power." Although he attributed this to sunspots, it may have been the result of volcanic dust, for he further noted, "There appears to be less intensity of light as well as heat." It is possible, however, that the haze and dust were attributable more to dust storms and forest fires kindled because of the drought. Both were common during the summer months. Some other observers suggested that the haze intercepted the rays of the sun and thus contributed to the cool weather.[42]

There has been at least one modern dissent from the consensus view of the volcanic influence upon the summer of 1816. In an article in *Weatherwise* in April 1974, H. E. Landsberg and J. M. Albert disputed the idea that volcanic dust was responsible for the global lowering of temperature. They argued that while it was indeed a cold summer in eastern North America and western Europe, this was "neither unprecedented in either of these areas at the time, nor statistically particularly unique, with similar events occurring also in later years that were not especially distinguished by major volcanic eruptions."[43]

Actually, Landsberg and Albert's evidence does tend to support their contention that later weather aberrations were not necessarily linked to volcanism. They may be correct that volcanism is not a decisive factor in determining weather patterns, but they offer no alternative explanation for the summer of 1816. Their claim that this summer was not "particularly unique" is wrong, however, for it was very definitely a singular weather phenomenon. Nevertheless, their view should serve as a corrective to the common assertion that volcanism was the sole cause for the weather of 1816, which was stated as recently as June 1979 in *Scientific American*.[44]

Almost certainly, volcanism was one cause of the weather of 1816, but probably there were many other factors. Contemporaries who believed the sunspots were behind the bizarre weather were at least partially correct; studies have shown that the earth's temperature is reduced about 0.5° F during sunspot maximums. This drop in conjunction with volcanism, which has been shown to drop the earth's temperature by 1.0° F, could make a significant difference (if sustained over a period of time, it would bring on another glacial age), and it probably contributed to the abnormality of this year.[45]

Another possibility is that the decrease of the surface temperature of the ocean over a large area, influenced by the two previous factors, might have caused a movement of the semipermanent highs and lows, thus altering the track of the moving highs and lows. Le Roy Ladurie noted in his study the unusual barometric observations made in Europe in 1816:"The subtropical high pressures which normally lap over on to Europe during the summer scarcely reached it at all. Low pressures therefore settled over central Europe, and this zone admitted the invasion of masses of cold Polar air which penetrated right to the south." Western Europe thus came under the influence of a high pressure centered over Scotland, directing north winds towards France.[46]

There are other possibilities, of course, that might explain the cause of the abnormal weather of 1816. Very probably it was a unique combination of factors, including volcanism, sunspots, a deviation of pressure patterns, and perhaps others, that all transpired at once to bring about this weather phenomenon.

How did the American people react to this extraordinary summer? There were many supplications to the heavens for relief from the cold and drought. Prayer days and fast days were held, begging for relief and "a more copious outpouring of the Holy Spirit." Other pious people, however, submitted to this judgment from the "Great First Cause," and they quoted from the Bible that said:"By the breath of God frost is given, and the breadth of the waters is restrained."[47]

Several state governors called upon their legislatures to consider measures to alleviate the suffering of their people owing to the weather. Governor Jonas Galusha of Vermont, for example, stated that due to "the uncommon failure of some of the most important articles of produce," steps should be taken to conserve "these articles of provision, most deficient, that . . . we may avoid . . . the foreboded evil of this unparaleled [*sic*] season."[48] Governor William Jones of Rhode Island, noting the "coldness and dryness of the seasons, and . . . the alarming sickness with which many parts of our country have been afflicted," issued a proclamation designating "a day of public Prayer, Praise, and Thanksgiving."[49]

The severity of the drought raised the specter of famine in the land. Jefferson expressed his concern and the apprehension of many in a letter to Gallatin when he noted the scarcity of grains caused by the drought and the frosts. "My anxieties on this subject are greater," he wrote, "because I remember the deaths which the drought of 1755 in Virginia produced from the want of food."[50] Predictably, hoarders and profiteers made their appearance. "A Citizen of Virginia" pleaded in the *Richmond Enquirer* on September 4 for the farmers of Virginia not to sell their corn except within the state. He assured the farmers that they would command as good a price for their products.[51]

Whether it was due to speculation and hoarding or to a natural shortage, or more likely a combination of both factors, a scarcity did develop, and flour prices, normally about $4 per barrel, rose dramatically in the late summer. By fall the cost of a barrel of flour had reached $13 in Philadelphia, $11.75 in Fredericksburg, Virginia, $14 in Baltimore, $12 in Richmond, $15 in Georgetown, Maryland, and Buffalo, and $20 in Charleston.[52] Wheat prices, which averaged $1.30 wholesale for the period 1800 to 1811, rose to $2.45 by 1817. The prices of corn, oats, and rye also rose proportionately, and other crop prices, such as for beans and potatoes, likewise gained dramatically.[53] The commodity price index (base 1860) similarly shows a rise from 111.6 in 1815 to 202.3 in 1816. This was the highest index number for the nineteenth century and was no doubt due to the effects of the weather in 1816.[54]

One interesting by-product of this acute shortage of grain was the effort of temperance advocates to limit the sale of grains to distilleries. No doubt the temperance movement was stimulated by this summer of 1816. The citizens of Otsego County, New York, for example, petitioned their legislature to "cause such restrictions to be laid on the distilleries—as in their wisdom shall be calculated to prevent an undue monopoly of that valuable and necessary commodity."[55] Similarly, a citizen of Virginia who signed himself "A Starving People," not only called upon his state to follow the example of Europe where "the *distillation of grain* has already been prohibited," but added that the legislature should be aware that taxes could not now be paid.[56] There was also support for prohibition in Philadelphia, and the governor of New Jersey called upon his legislature to stop the distillation of grain.[57] In truth, the shortage of grain did not become as severe as many feared. There was scarcity and the prices were high, but there were no reports of starvation, and the speculation in grains began to abate by wintertime.[58]

Another reaction, more tenuous in its relationship to the weather, but nevertheless one worth considering, was what might be termed "taking frustrations out on the politicians." The election of 1816 resulted in the greatest defeat of incumbent congressmen in American political history. In the popularly elected House of Representatives, nearly 70 percent of the representatives in the Fourteenth Congress were not returned to the Fifteenth. The primary explanation for this phenomenon was the Compensation Law of 1816 whereby congressmen doubled their pay and then had the further audacity to accept immediate payment of the increase (see chapter 5).[59] The outrage of the citizenry over this act was undoubtedly fanned by the general malaise created by crop failures and threatened famine. Obviously, there were many other factors involved in these election results, but a pay increase for Congress during this time of trouble did seem totally inappropriate.

It is conjectural how much the weather can affect the mood of the people, but the consequences of the weather certainly can.[60] One obvious result of this summer was the westward emigration of many farmers. New England in particular lost many of its farmers to the West. Other areas also experienced widespread emigration. The *Raleigh Star* reported on September 6, for example, that in the western counties of North Carolina "great numbers are disposing of their property, and preparing to emigrate to the West and South."[61] Many farmers, perhaps, had been contemplating a move westward, and after experiencing the failures of their crops during this summer, made up their minds to go. A report from Lancaster, Ohio, on October 31 observed the movement of people westward almost exceeded belief. The road was nearly covered with wagons. "Last week, it is said, upwards of one hundred moving families passed through this town, and many are daily arriving."[62] The *Zanesville* (OH) *Messenger* noted at the same time "the number of Emigrants from the eastward the present season, far exceeds what has ever before been witnessed."[63]

One additional consequence of this summer was an outgrowth of the natural curiosity to know how this season compared with others. Regular, systematic, and scientific observations were made, however, only in a few places around the country. The editor of the

Albany Daily Advertiser suggested, for example, that "a great mass of useful information might be collected concerning our climate and seasons, if gentlemen who possess the necessary instruments, would be careful to devote a few minutes in each day to mark the state of the weather, and the temperature of the atmosphere." He added that the information thus collected "would be of great and lasting importance."[64]

Perhaps in response to such suggestions, Josiah Meigs, the Commissioner-General of the Land Office, on April 29, 1817, sent out a circular to the Registers of the twenty land offices, requiring them to take tri-daily observations of the temperature, winds, and weather at the various land offices. In addition, the Registers were instructed to make thirteen other observations of such things as the unfolding of leaves, flowering, migration of birds, fish, unusual weather, and other phenomena.[65] The Surgeon-General of the Army, Joseph Lovell, also established a system of meteorological observations at the military posts beginning in 1819. State services for the recording of weather data were established in New York in 1825 and in Pennsylvania in 1837. In the 1840s the Patent Office and the Smithsonian Institution also provided for systematic recording of meteorological observations. The first published weather forecasts were inaugurated in 1849 by the Smithsonian Institution, using reports transmitted daily by telegraph operators in different parts of the country. Although the Civil War interrupted this work, the obvious usefulness of these systematic recordings and the accumulation of meteorological data led eventually to the establishment of a weather service branch of the Signal Corps in 1870. This was the beginning of that venerable and valuable organization, the United States Weather Bureau, now the United States National Weather Service, a division of the National Oceanic and Atmospheric Administration (NOAA).[66]

In retrospect, had poor harvests followed in the next year, it would have undoubtedly created a dire situation. Fortunately, the harvests of 1817 were abundant, making up for the shortfall of crops the previous year. Thus there was no prolonged famine that might have produced a political and social upheaval that was so common in European history. Nevertheless, the summer of 1816 must have loomed large in the minds of many Americans. The clouds of war had just lifted and now God and nature seemed to be punishing them and testing them again. The reactions of the American people are instructive. Their anxiety undoubtedly curbed to some extent the buoyant optimism that was reflected in an otherwise positive year, contributing to an extensive westward emigration and to profiteering and speculation in grains, as well as to a minor political upheaval in 1816. Certainly, the people of 1816 never forgot this abnormal weather phenomenon, and that alone makes the year unique in American history. It continues to hold a fascination as a unique experience in American history. Americans have endured many extremes in the weather, but 1816 remains even today as the only "year without a summer."

Chapter 2

Legacy of the War of 1812

During forty years as an independent nation, Americans had survived two wars with Great Britain, the Quasi-War with France, and various other threats to the Union. The War of 1812, however, had been the severest test yet for the Union, and the country had barely survived the ordeal. The nation's capital lay in ruins after being burned by the British in August 1814, and by 1816, repair of the public buildings still had a long way to go. Other areas of the country had also suffered devastation, not just coastal cities but also interior cities, such as Buffalo, New York. Despite these setbacks, Americans preferred to dwell on the positive. They had survived a war with the world's greatest power and lost nothing in the treaty of peace, which essentially recognized status quo ante bellum. While there had been many embarrassing military defeats, there were also moments of victory. The United States Navy had delivered some stunning blows to the Royal Navy and wounded their pride. Moreover, the war ended with a great victory over the British at New Orleans.

In 1816, in terms of population, the United States was still a small country. The census of 1810 showed approximately 7.25 million, the bulk being clustered along the east coast. No doubt the population reached 8.5 million by 1816. A census taken in New York City in April 1816 revealed that the city had reached a milestone with 100,519 people.[1] While the Western country was growing rapidly (Louisiana was admitted in 1812), migration was slowed somewhat by the Indian wars that erupted in the West during the

War of 1812. Once the war was over, no impediment appeared to check a rapid exodus into the areas of the Ohio and Mississippi valleys. This shift of population to the West was a source of both pride and apprehension to most Americans. Jesse Buel, editor of the *Albany Argus,* had no trepidation. "What a field for splendid contemplation does our western country unfold!" he exclaimed. "When we consider that nature has strewed her gifts with a boun-tiful hand over this vast wilderness, and take into view the benign influence of our government and the enterprise of our population, the mind is lost in the magnitude of the objects which seem rising in futurity."[2]

While certain parts of the East Coast experienced population drain due to Western expansion, many of the new settlers in the West were from Europe. Hezekiah Niles, an influential journalist and a perceptive observer of trends, noted that a heavy tide of emi-grants began arriving from Europe at the end of the war. On Au-gust 17, 1816, he wrote that about 1500 emigrants had arrived in the United States that week alone and that in England there were excited alarms about the "ruinous drain of the most useful part of the population of the United Kingdom." Niles said, "Let them come," and he estimated each individual added at least $300 a year to the national wealth.[3] The editor of the *Boston Recorder* estimated the population of the United States was growing at a rate of three percent per year and doubled every twenty-three years. Using that figure, he calculated (fairly accurately) that the population would expand to 14 million by 1833 (1830 census was 12.8), and to 28 million by 1856 (1860 census 31.5). From there on his estimates ranged too high (e.g., 102 million by 1902; actual, 1900 census 84.3 million).[4] One fact seemed certain in 1816: the United States was destined to become a great and populous country, outstripping even the nations of Europe.

Like all wars, there were bitter legacies from the War of 1812, but for most Americans the apparent prevailing view was to come together and move on. Economically, the end of the war led to a growth in foreign trade. The reports of the secretary of the treasury show that exports rose from approximately $52.5 million in 1815 to nearly $82 million in 1816. Imports that amounted to slightly more than $113 million in 1815 rose to nearly $147 million the following year.[5] The trade imbalance of imports over exports drained specie from the country and led to a crisis when banks south of New England were unable to redeem their paper money with specie. The growing number of banks compounded the problem. In 1801 there were 29 banks in the country, and by 1816 there were 246, capitalized at close to $90 million. The surplus of imports over exports also reflected a policy of the British to sell off their inventories of goods accumulated during the long Napoleonic war at very low prices, and the United States market was also flooded with cheap cotton goods from India.

One particularly significant development during the war was the changing physical appearance of places and people, due to the emergence of the factory system in New England and the beginnings of the industrial revolution in America. The Boston Manufacturing Company had established a power loom at their factory in Waltham, Massachusetts. The factory combined spinning and weaving under one roof, pointing the way to the future development of this industry. Woolen manufacturing also flourished during the war. Connecticut alone had twenty-five woolen factories by 1815. A new fabric, satinette, a blend of cotton and wool, was beginning to revolutionize fashion. Men now wore pantaloons similar to sailors and working-class laborers and abandoned knee britches.[6] The influx of foreign goods, however, threatened these newly established textile manufacturers who pleaded with their government to give them some relief, particularly in the form of higher tariff rates to reduce the importation of foreign goods. Their pleas were couched in patriotic phrases that equated commercial warfare with a continuation of the recently ended military conflict.

Politically, deep divisions had appeared during the pre-war and war years between the Federalist and Republican parties. The future of the country had suddenly appeared uncertain when anti-war New England Federalists gathered at the Hartford Convention near the end of the war to make demands upon the Union. While many feared the result would be a secessionist movement, the Federalists instead only demanded constitutional amendments to protect the interests of their region. Nevertheless, had the war not ended fortuitously a short time after the convention, the eventual political divisions could have torn the country asunder. Bitter partisan rhetoric continued after the war. In April 1815, Republicans in New York reminded electors of the state that a party in the late war had "directed their efforts to prevent the success of loans, to discourage the enlistment of soldiers, and to drain the country of its specie, and thereby produce national bankruptcy and ruin." The Hartford Convention had disseminated "an infamous manifesto . . . [that] vilified your rulers, abused your Constitution, and menaced your government with 'more mighty efforts' in case of non-compliance with their insolent demands." Federalists might be forgiven, the Republicans declared, but they could have "little claim to the confidence of independent freemen."[7]

Orsamus C. Merrill, a future congressman and a highly partisan Republican speaker in Bennington, Vermont, on August 16, 1815, also revealed the lingering bitterness against the Federalists. Opponents of the war, he said, must be counted as public enemies: "A portion of our people gloried in the misfortunes of the country, in times of war, and avowed in legislative bodies they could not rejoice at success." Those enemies, however, were properly rewarded as "The gloomy curtain of mourning they had woven in anticipation for the hearse of departed national glory—was converted to a pall for their dead political monster, and shred to weeds of sadness for their own humiliation." He concluded, "The history of this war will afford us important lessons. The advantage and necessity of patriotism and firmness . . . [and] the peaceful triumph of union, over the fallen depravity of faction."[8]

Contemporary accounts suggest that many Federalists did indeed admire the British system, and the distrust of Federalists may have been warranted in some cases. Former Congressman Ebenezer Sage wrote, for example, to his friend and fellow New Yorker, Congressman John W. Taylor, on January 27, 1816, "I spent a few weeks last summer in Connecticut among my early friends, and the Prince Regent can boast of no such devoted faithful subjects in England, or even Scotland."[9] Federalists, on the other hand, were not certain they could trust the Republicans either. A Federalist political tract written at the end of the war in February 1815 rejoiced at peace, because it delivered the country from the evils the administration had brought upon the people, but it warned that those who expected that peace "would bring internal tranquility and soften the asperities of party spirit" were mistaken. "The termination of the war," the tract continued, "is made by the adherents of administration, a new source of malignant contumely and clamour against their political opponents." Federalists, it said, could expect to "suffer party proscriptions, gerrymandering, etc."[10]

Nevertheless, the circumstances that had threatened a possible divergence of the country into separate societies was now removed. Not until another great struggle over slavery was the Union again threatened. The divisiveness of the war was a sobering reminder to Americans just how fragile their democracy was, and in the aftermath of the conflict, there developed a consensus that party animosities should be quelled and the country brought together. Differences were muted. A book published by an Irish-born Philadelphia publisher late in the war (November 1814) undoubtedly influenced the post-war demand for a healing of party animosities. Mathew Carey's, *The Olive Branch*, insisted that his objective was to dissipate "party rage and rancor." The fault, he argued, lay on both sides of the political spectrum, and he appealed for mutual forgiveness and harmony. Carey was an unlikely candidate to be a healer. He was well known as a violent Irish patriot who, in 1784, fled from prosecution to America, disguised as a woman. He eventually emerged as a leading book publisher in Philadelphia. Among the works he published was the immensely successful biography of George Washington by Mason L. "Parson" Weems (with its tale of the cherry tree), who was also Carey's most successful book peddler.[11] Carey was also well known as a partisan of the Republican Party and, as John Quincy Adams noted, in the *Olive Branch* "all his acknowledgments of faults on that side are apologetic; while all his enumerations of faults on the other side are charges."[12] Nevertheless, by January 1816, Carey's book had reached a seventh edition, testifying to its popularity.

Although Carey faulted both parties for their conduct, Federalists correctly believed he laid his heaviest blows upon them. William Coleman, editor of the Federalist *New York Evening Post*, characterized the *Olive Branch* as "one of the most insidious publications that has appeared in this country." In essence, Carey's work was a long diatribe against political parties. Anti-partyism ran through almost every page. Carey asserted in his preface to the first edition, for example, that "indiscriminate adherence to party . . . *encourages the leaders to proceed to extremities . . .* which the good sense of their followers may reprobate, but from which they have not *fortitude enough to withhold their support.*" In another place he commented,

"No man who has any public spirit, can take a review of our history without feeling the deepest regret at the extent of the mischief this miserable system of conduct has produced."[13]

Carey also argued that Federalist opposition to government measures contributed to causing the War of 1812, because they encouraged Britain to proceed in her outrages against the United States. He attributed the Federalist course to "a few ambitious demagogues in Boston," who had led the nation to the brink of dissolution. His advice to the Federalists was to regard charitably their Republican adversaries as intending to promote the public good. Only by supporting such measures could they ever hope to regain political power.[14]

An incensed New York Federalist, William McKean, wrote a 231–page book "to pluck the mask from the face of hypocrisy." McKean labeled Carey's *Olive Branch*, "a mere collection of democratic newspaper slander against Federalists—a perfect farrago of opprobrium, gleaned from documents, speeches, toasts, and grogshop harangues." He rejected allegations that Federalist conduct provoked British measures that led to war, declaring that Federalists had a "Constitutional and absolute right to complain" about the war, and he denied unequivocally that "any project has been formed, at any time, or that any measures have been taken by any body of men, in the New England states, to bring about a separation of the states."[15]

Other Federalist publications in 1816 also tried to place their opposition to the war in a more favorable light. They noted, alluding perhaps to the Republican riot in Baltimore in 1812, that Federalists never resorted to mob violence or other lawless resistance. In fact, they "submitted with patience to privations, which they felt oppressive and ruinous. They contributed their money and their blood to a war, which they regarded as unnecessary, if not ultimately fatal to the happiness and liberty of their country." Federalist opposition to the war was an exercise of freedom of expression and should not be imputed a crime. Instead, they were being assailed in Republican papers "as the most vicious and traiterous [sic] beings in existence." As one author argued, "Our party divisions have already inflicted deep and dangerous wounds on the republic, to prevent which from rankling into deadly and incurable sores, will require the most patient, lenient and judicious treatment, from those intrusted with its safeguard."[16]

Although Federalists did not fully comprehend the new circumstances, the anti-party rhetoric actually benefitted them. They had
good reason to fear proscription after their conduct during the war,
and many Republicans were in a vengeful mood. Thus the climate of
conciliation reflected in the anti-party literature not only soothed the
political passions, it opened the way for a new political beginning that
invited politicians to reconsider their partisan positions of the past
and look to a future doing what was best for the country, rather than
what was good for the Republican or Federalist parties.

In fact, moderates in both parties were deeply disturbed by the
consequences of partisan behavior, and the decline in party activity
after the War of 1812 showed that many Americans were not willing to accept a permanence in political divisions. The new and growing spirit of nationalism owed much to this feeling. Yet, as some no
doubt recognized, this growing belief that political attachments
should be sacrificed for the sake of union was an illusion. Old passions and party loyalties still persisted, and many publications warned
about the dangers of a partisan spirit. "A Citizen of Vermont," writing
at the end of the War of 1812, declared that the evil of party spirit
was responsible for the present national calamities. It had distracted
public councils, enfeebled the public administration, agitated the
community, kindled animosity of one section against another. A
revolution of public opinion was "indispensable," and he cautioned,
"No republic has ever fallen, without being first torn asunder by
party dissensions."[17]

The pages of the influential *Niles' Weekly Register* reflected the
ambivalence of the American people. Probably the most widely
read paper in the country, it was really a news magazine and is today
perhaps the most important primary source for historians of the
early republic. Niles strove for a neutral partisan stance, but his incli-
nations were strongly nationalistic and pro-Jeffersonian.[18] A September 1815 editorial reflected both the rising expectations of the
country and the lingering distrust of the Federalists. "A high and
honorable feeling generally prevails," he wrote, "and the people
begin to assume, more and more, a NATIONAL CHARACTER."
He continued, however, "In the general prosperity, we behold the
downfall of that faction which would have made a common interest with the British, during the late war ... they are despised by the
people they would have given soul and body to serve ... they are

laughed at by all who consider them too contemptible for serious rebuke." "[They] must be carefully watched," he insisted.[19] Jesse Buel in the *Albany Argus* was similarly ambivalent. He commented favorably in June 1816 on the moderate tone adopted by the newly elected Governor of Massachusetts, John Brooks. "Whether we are to ascribe its mildness to a conviction of the errors of federalism, or to look upon it as a bait thrown out to propitiate republican fever, time will determine."[20]

Others, however, were more forgiving. "The Cogitations of Uncle John," published in the *Otsego* (NY) *Herald* in the spring of 1816, related the tale of the meeting of three travelers including a Republican and a Federalist tavern owner. After their mutually profitable exchange of ideas, the moral was drawn: "There were wise, sincere, and good men in both parties; seeing things in different aspects, but having equally at heart the best interests of our country; and that it was only necessary for the good of both parties to be better acquainted with each other's character and views, to do away a great portion of the party spirit that disturbs the land."[21]

There is considerable evidence that indeed an "Era of Good Feelings" arose after the war and lasted at least into 1817, which was reflected in a growing sense of pride in country and an emerging nationalism. President James Madison set the tone in his Seventh Annual Message in December 1815. He asserted that American arms in the late war had gained a reputation and respect abroad. With a growing population, a productive and extensive territory, coupled with the industrious and fertile ingenuity of its people, the United States was a "highly favored and happy country."[22] The "happy" mood was reflected in the proceedings of the Fourteenth Congress. One of the themes heard early and often in the first session was the lack of party spirit. Perhaps even more surprising is that these sentiments were generally fulfilled in the course of this Congress. William Gaston of North Carolina expressed early in the session his "perfect disposition to cooperate with his associates of whatever political party, in any measures which might promote the public weal." He welcomed a time when "the troubled night of war had departed, and the day-star of peace again beamed on our land, there would be at least a short interval of calm and sunshine, in which all could work cheerfully and harmoniously together."[23] South Carolina's John C. Calhoun, in a speech delivered on January 2,

1816, observed, "Now we see everywhere a nationality of feeling; we hear sentiments from every part of the House in favor of Union, and against a sectional spirit."[24] Samuel W. Dana, a Federalist from Connecticut, told the Senate in March 1816, "The distinction between the two parties which formerly existed . . . was now, or soon would be, merely nominal." Benjamin Huger of South Carolina boldly declared early in the second session, "Party feelings are altogether extinct."[25]

Several congressmen wrote circular letters to their constituents at the end of the session in the spring of 1816 commenting, among other things, on the lack of party spirit. Samuel S. Connor of Massachusetts wrote, "I am happy to inform you, that scarcely any thing of party feeling, or animosity, has made its appearance here this winter." North Carolina's Lewis Williams noted, "among the most auspicious appearances of the times, is the obliteration of party spirit. No question at the present session of congress has been discussed or determined on the ground of party." Another North Carolinian, Samuel Dickens, at the end of the second session in March 1817, wrote, "In Congress . . . party spirit is so far extinct, that the time seems to have passed away, and I fondly hope will never again occur when party measures, ruinous to the best interests of the country, can be carried by the mere force of a name." Dickens added a wry commentary on the political change, "Most of the principles and measures adopted and advocated by Washington and his political disciples, which for a time were unfortunately departed from, are again resorted to and now prevail."[26]

Although partisan rhetoric was noticeably absent during this session, there were occasions when partisan tempers flared. The sensitivities raised over the War of 1812 lingered just beneath the surface. During a debate over additional military academies, Cyrus King, perhaps forgetting the gentlemanly decorum that had thus far been maintained in the debate, launched into a tirade that no doubt reminded auditors of the bitterness of the previous Congress. The Massachusetts congressman questioned the constitutionality of new military academies and asserted the real object of the bill was executive patronage to provide for "the young fry of the Administration . . . and the royal cousins of the Palace." Only sons of the rich and powerful gained admission to West Point, he declared, and only children of the favored few were appointed as midshipmen.

King also attacked references in Congress and in party prints to the glory and success of the late war. In fact, he asserted, a comparison of the supposed causes of the war with the treaty of peace showed that the goals had been "abandoned, surrendered, given up to your enemy." The treaty, he insisted, was "humiliating." The real result of the war was "millions of treasure wasted, and thousands of lives of American citizens, each as valuable as that of your President, sacrificed, in a ruinous, unnecessary, and inexpedient war." He concluded his criticism, "Let the friends and promoters of that war, in future, maintain that humble silence thereon which its solemnity demands."[27]

King's speech brought an angry retort by Richard M. Johnson, a hero of the war and the reputed slayer of the famous Indian leader Tecumseh. While King held the declaration of war in abhorrence, Johnson declared that he held in equal abhorrence "the violent opposition to that war, and that disaffection to the Constitution which prevailed in many parts of the United States, and in none to a more criminal extent than that in which the gentleman resided." Disunion, the Kentuckian asserted, was the chief cause of the calamities, as well as the want of proper military instruction proposed in this bill. "It was this mean, submitting spirit," Johnson added, "united to an incessant opposition to the Administration, the object of which was power, that most of the disasters and evils of the war may be attributed." King, somewhat chastened, explained, and Johnson declined to say anything more.[28]

Rufus King had an interesting observation that is the key to understanding what was happening to the political process in 1816. His analysis of the current situation was extremely astute. As long as the parties were nearly equal in number, the New Yorker argued, moderation and wise policy would be overridden by party considerations. "When the ascendancy of one party is established and the other is so small a minority as to excite little or no apprehension of their being able to overturn their rivals, the counsels of wisdom and experience may be listened to, & the welfare and prosperity of the nation may be consulted without fear of endangering the interests of the Rulers."[29] With no prospect of regaining political ascendancy, Federalists, King implied, could at least expect a tolerable situation with one party dominance that acted more like a no party system. Whether Federalists might expect to gain a share of public offices by acquiescing and accepting the demise of their party was uncertain. As many historians have noted, the long years of Republican ascendancy entrenched a group of federal office holders who further maintained the party's position. Carl E. Prince, for example, noted that between 1800 and 1817 nearly two thirds of the professional party operatives in New Jersey received some appointive office, and he added that "in New Jersey, the Democratic-Republican interest was not a party of yeoman farmers, but a party of office-holders."[30]

The new spirit of pride and optimism that infused the national legislature was also reflected in the annual messages of the governors of several states. While they occasionally engaged in rhetorical flourishes, there is little reason to doubt the sincerity of the views they expressed. Governor William Plumer of New Hampshire declared that the country had "set an example in war, which the nations of Europe cannot fail to admire." Governor William Jones of Rhode Island stated that "from the immense native resources of our country, we may reasonably calculate upon the gradual increase of national wealth and strength." Jonas Galusha, of Vermont, asserted that it was an auspicious time "to correct our errors, to cement our Union." He added, "The constant emigration to this country from under the governments of Europe, is an evidence that we possess privileges and blessings, superior to the other nations of the earth."[31] Governor William Miller of North Carolina concluded that despite its calamities the war, "illustrated the capacity of the United States to be a great, a free, and a flourishing nation. It has put to flight the stale objection of the imbecility of republics for warlike operations."[32] Governor Simon Snyder of Pennsylvania assured his legislature the achievements in the War of 1812 and the recent naval war with Algiers "makes us proud of the name of Americans . . . the late war has done more to secure the permanence of our republican institutions and to establish for us a character abroad, than its most zealous advocates and most sanguine friends could have hoped." Warning against the "baleful consequences of being divided people," he declared, "We must cherish a national spirit and become a united people against all foreign foes."[33]

The opinions of the governors were confirmed by their representatives in Europe. Albert Gallatin, our Minister to France, wrote to Thomas Jefferson in September 1815, that the war had been useful. "The character of America stands now as high as ever on the European continent, and higher than ever it did in Great Britain." He added that we were "generally respected and considered as the nation designed to check the naval despotism of England."[34] John Quincy Adams, who had recently helped Gallatin negotiate not only the peace treaty ending the War of 1812 but also the Commercial Convention, and was now serving as our Minister to England, agreed with Gallatin and the state governors that the war overall "was much more beneficial than injurious to our Country." It had "raised our national character in the eyes of all Europe."[35] Adams also concurred with many Americans and their leaders who considered the Treaty of Ghent ending the War of 1812 only a truce and believed war with Great Britain was certain in the near future. In Congress, the most outspoken were John C. Calhoun and Henry Clay, neither of whom, it should be noted, took to the "tented field" during the past war. Calhoun declared at one point in January 1816, "I am sure that future wars with England are possible, but, I will say more, that they are highly probable—nay, that they will certainly take place. Future wars, I fear, with the honorable Speaker [Clay], future wars, long and bloody, will exist between this country and Great Britain."[36]

One of the many unpleasant incidents that embittered relations between the United States and Great Britain after the war was the so-called Dartmoor Massacre that occurred in April 1815. Dartmoor was the notorious British prison that held approximately 5000 men, many impressed American sailors. Among the prisoners were about 450 African-Americans. Their leader was "King Dick," described as "a black Hercules," who kept order with the assistance of a black preacher named "Simon" and another spiritual leader named "John." When it was reported in the prison that the War of 1812 had ended, the American prisoners naturally demanded their release. However, the British commandant of Dartmoor, Thomas George Shortland, refused to release the prisoners except upon orders from his superiors. When the prisoners attempted to leave anyway, British soldiers fired into the crowd, killing at least seven Americans and wounding many more. Shortly thereafter, the prisoners were officially released. Word of the "massacre" spread, and anger against the British was fanned throughout the United States by the American press. The American government demanded an explanation. The subsequent investigation was inconclusive, but the British expressed their regret and proposed compensation to the families. Secretary of State James Monroe, however, rejected the offer, apparently because it was too little and the explanations were inadequate. For the British, the incident was an embarrassment, and Lord Castlereagh, the British foreign minister, was quoted in response to a member of Parliament on February 14, 1816, that it was "his most ardent wish to discountenance this feeling on both sides, and to promote between the two nations feelings of reciprocal amity and regard."[37]

The reaction in Congress was remarkably restrained. On January 4, 1816, James Pleasants of Virginia moved to have the President lay before the House all of the communications and documents relating to the transactions at Dartmoor. The report was received and laid on the table about four weeks later. Then on February 19, Pleasants, for the Naval Affairs Committee, reported a bill placing the surviving impressed seamen confined at Dartmoor on the list of naval pensioners. The House amended the bill to make the effective date April 6, 1815 (the day the massacre took place), and the measure was passed on March 25.[38] While the memory of the Dartmoor Massacre no doubt lingered in American minds for many years, it was apparently accepted for what it was—a tragic, but unplanned, incident.

Anti-British sentiment was also fanned by supposed slurs cast upon Americans by the *Edinburgh Review*. The editors, in commenting upon the state of literature in the United States in 1816, declared that purity of style and fastidiousness of taste was "not yet to be found we are afraid . . . even among the better educated Americans."[39] This was only the beginning of a prolonged dispute that was further agitated by the aspersions of the Rev. Sydney Smith, Canon of St. Paul's Cathedral and founder of the *Edinburgh Review*, in the years that followed. His dismissive statement in 1818, "Literature the Americans have none," spurred Robert Walsh to write a vigorous book in 1819 defending American literature and culture.[40]

One of the ironies of the American experience is, as North Carolina's Governor Miller noted, that anti-foreign sentiment has always been part of the national spirit, yet Americans are uniquely a blend of many foreigners. There has also always been a certain ambivalence about welcoming new arrivals from foreign shores. John Randolph may or may not have been expressing the views of his fellow Virginians when he stated in a speech in Congress in the spring of 1816, that Europeans coming to America must have no share in our government, and in order to protect freedom in the United States "you must endeavor to stop this flood of foreign emigration."[41] It is likely that the prevailing sentiment of Americans was represented more faithfully by the Shamrock Society of New York, which published in 1816 a little pamphlet giving hints to emigrants from Europe. The authors gave an overview of the government of the United States, including comments on political parties. They asserted that Republicans were attached to popular government, while the Federalists were "thought to have a leaning towards aristocracy." New immigrants were advised to observe and make their own judgments before plunging into politics. They were also informed that the practical result of the liberty practiced in the United States was that "the poorer classes in this community are more civilized, more polite and friendly, though not so submissive, as persons of the same fortunes in Europe." New York City held at that time approximately 12,000 Irish, and an equal number of other foreigners. All were strenuous supporters of the government, and the laws were made by the majority for the good of the greatest number.

The pamphlet also advised that between the thirty-seventh and the forty-second degrees latitude was the most congenial for Europeans. The authors also noted, without passing censure, that some white men in the South "think it disreputable to follow the plow." Much useful information was included—and some dubious (for example, one should not drink cold water when very hot). The pamphlet is instructive about revealing what the writers thought of their country. They quoted Benjamin Franklin, for example, that America was a land of labor and that idlers would be shunned by decent people. Americans did not inquire, "*What is he*? but *What can he do*?" The new arrivals were admonished not to linger in seaports but to go inland and learn agriculture. Seaport towns were more expensive and had more temptations, such as drink. Despite evidence that suggested Americans were consuming more and more alcoholic beverages, the authors insisted, "In few countries is drunkenness more despised than in this." Americans also preferred to purchase and work on their own land, rather than live on wages. The authors also gave a representative sampling of wages in New York City for several occupations, such as stonecutters and bricklayers ($2 per day), carpenters ($1.87 per day), and ordinary laborers ($1 to $1.25 per day). Other opportunities for Irishmen included preceptors (or teachers).

The authors also characterized the land as bountiful and rich in natural resources. They even expressed sentiments that would later be called "manifest destiny": "In time our settlements will reach the borders of the Pacific." Pennsylvania was deemed a suitable place for Irish to settle, and there was still plenty of good land. Western New York also had fine land, but its value would increase greatly when the canal to Lake Erie was completed. They also identified ways to travel to the West, noting that the National Road was not yet completed. From Pittsburgh, however, a traveler could descend the Ohio River into Kentucky or Indiana, to the Mississippi River, and thence up to St. Louis or the Illinois Territory.

Contrary to the words of Randolph, prospective immigrants were assured "nowhere in the world is a well-conducted foreigner received into the bosom of the state with equal liberality and readiness as in America." Finally, they added, "The extraordinary characters which the United States have produced may be, in some measure, ascribed to the *mixed blood of so many nations flowing in our veins*; and . . . will carry, in this country, all the improvable faculties of human nature to the highest state of perfection."[42]

Not only immigrants were attracted to the West; another consequence of the War of 1812 was to unleash the pent-up desire of many native Americans to head west in search of a better life. If nothing else, the War of 1812 was a successful Indian war. The Tecumseh Confederacy was broken in the Northwest by Gen. William Henry Harrison, while Gen. Andrew Jackson crushed the Creek Confederacy in the Southwest. Numerous treaties with the Indians followed ceding their territory in the West to the United States and opening up farmlands to new settlers. The census in 1820 showed that the United States grew by 2.2 million over the decade (to 9.6 million); more than half (about 1.2 million) found their way into the Western country, which led to the rapid admission of four new states, Indiana, Mississippi, Illinois, and Alabama, before the decade was over. Nearly all of this movement, due to the war, occurred after 1815. The editor of the *Buffalo Gazette*, for example, observed in August 1815 that scarcely a day had passed without witnessing the movement of "several families from New England, through the village for the state of Ohio."[43] There is little doubt that the pace of this westward migration accelerated in 1816, as was noted earlier, due to the bizarre cold weather which blasted crops and caused many farmers to seek a more temperate climate, as well as a new beginning in the West.

However these immigrants traveled west, they found horrible roads, which had been made abundantly evident during the late war. Due to the British blockade, the government was forced to transport goods by land on indifferent roads, which greatly hampered the war effort. At war's end there were renewed calls for the state and federal governments to finance internal improvements, or at least to invest in the stock of various road and canal companies. Fortunately, by 1816, there was a growing interest in improving travel and trade with the West. The National Road from Cumberland, Maryland, to the Ohio River, begun in 1811, was pursued with new vigor after the war, and several states, most notably New York, were approving canal projects.

Interestingly, by 1816, the symbol of the United States, its flag, was in need of alteration. Congressman Peter Wendover of New York pointed out in December 1816 that the original flag had one star and one stripe for each state. When two additional states entered (Vermont and Kentucky), two stars and two stripes had been added. Since then, however, four additional states had been added, but the flag remained unchanged. Thomas B. Robertson of Louisiana apparently did not see the problem. He suggested that the president be given power to alter the flag upon the admission of new states. John W. Taylor of New York saw the problem, but he was equally unhelpful. He stated that he had been told by seamen that our flag could be recognized at a great distance. If more stripes and stars were added, it "would become less distinct to distant observation." He preferred to return to the original flag with thirteen stars and stripes. Wendover's motion was referred to a select committee, which he headed. On January 2, 1817, he reported and moved a bill to alter the flag. His report explained the need for a change and gave a history of the flag, noting the Act of January 13, 1794, that had added two more stars and two more stripes. It was inexpedient to add more stripes, he contended; his bill proposed to return to the original thirteen stripes and to add additional stars when new states were admitted.[44]

The House failed to act upon Wendover's bill, even though he claimed "the flag proposition is almost universally approved of." In the next Congress, however, Wendover's persistence paid off. On March 25, 1818, the House approved his bill substantially as written. The title was changed from "alter" to "A Bill to Establish the Flag of the United States" and sent on to the Senate, where it was approved. President James Monroe signed the bill into law on April 4.[45]

In retrospect, the War of 1812 did not bring about a significant transformation in American life, such as the Civil War and World War II did. Its influence might be compared, perhaps, to the transitional aspects after World War I, and the legacies of the War of 1812 were mostly positive. The asperity of the political dialogue prior to and during the war was clearly being replaced by a decline of partisan rancor and a growing sense of nationhood and pride in being an American. Prospects facing the United States in 1816 were auspicious, notwithstanding the failed crops caused by an anomalous summer. Development of manufacturing gave indications that Americans were on the threshold of a market revolution. Rather than a divided country after the war, the people were more optimistic and unified than ever before. Nowhere was this new solidarity more evident than in the workings of the Fourteenth Congress.

Chapter 3

The Fourteenth Congress Begins

When Congress convened in Washington for the first session of the Fourteenth Congress on December 4, 1815, the city still bore the scars of the British torching of the capital in August 1814. Congress, in fact, was meeting in the cramped quarters of the Patent Office, the only public structure spared by the British. A new building had been erected at a cost of $30,000 to accommodate Congress until the Capitol was ready for reoccupation. The owners asked Congress to contribute $5000 and an annual rent of $1650. Both houses quickly accepted the offer, and the transfer of the sessions to the new quarters took place on Wednesday, December 13.[1] The building was located on First Street, N.E., on part of the site now occupied by the Supreme Court Building. Occupied from 1815 to 1819, it was thereafter referred to as the "Old Brick Capitol." During the Civil War it was used to house prisoners.

Congress also had to find a space for their library. To replace the books burned by the British, they had recently purchased former President Thomas Jefferson's personal library for $23,950. The expense of packing and transporting the materials cost nearly $1000. Even temporary lodging for the books was difficult to find on Capitol Hill. The owner of the only house that might have been adequate, however, asked an annual rent of $1000. Instead, Thomas Monroe, the superintendent of public buildings, fit up a library room in a building occupied by the Post Office, which cost over $1500 for supplies, furniture, and labor costs. A House Library Committee report in January 1816 argued that a permanent place in the Capitol needed to be found for the Congressional Library. (In fact, a suggestion was made in the Senate in February 1817 to build a Library of Congress on Delaware Avenue, north of the Capitol, but the idea was rejected.) The Library Committee also proposed an annual appropriation of $10,000 to purchase books and maps, and they recommended raising the annual $1000 compensation for the Librarian, the Russian-born George Watterson, who would have to devise a new catalog based on Jefferson's classifications, which were not always classed correctly or under any heading.[2]

Work on the Capitol proceeded through 1816. Benjamin Henry Latrobe, the architect in charge of the project, reported progress to the House of Representatives early the following year. The hall of the Representatives, he related, "was so ruined that, although the columns and the vault they supported still stood, it was inevitably necessary to take them down, so as to clear the whole area of the principal story of the former work." New plans called for the areas of the House and gallery to be enlarged considerably. However, no work, except externally (windows and doors repaired), had been accomplished on the hall in 1816, due to problems in getting freestone from the quarries. The Senate wing lay in a much more ruinous state. The intense heat had burst the walls, burned the marble columns in the Senate chamber, and found a vent through the windows and up the private stairs, damaging the exterior of the wing materially. What work that had been done was halted when the Senate recommended extensive alterations and improvements. This entailed taking down the vaults which had been reconstructed. Enlargement of the Senate chamber also required the great dome and its semicircular wall be entirely removed, and the arches and walls of the two committee rooms and the lobby adjoining the chamber had to be demolished also. As of February 1817, work was progressing on the committee rooms, the vault, and walls of the Senate chamber. The changes, Latrobe maintained, would "render the building much more strong and durable than it was before the conflagration."[3]

Samuel Lane, the Commissioner of Public Buildings, reported to Congressman Lewis Condict on January 31, 1817, that he expected both the House and Senate chambers to be ready by the autumn of 1818. Lane attributed the delay to the rearrangement of the House and Senate buildings, which had produced the loss of one season's labor and part of another "undoing what had already been done."[4]

Congressman John W. Taylor of New York believed the delay in repairing the Capitol was due to Latrobe. He wrote his wife in late December 1816 that Latrobe was "a man notorious for his extravagance in every work in which he has been employed." He hoped that President James Monroe would fire him. Taylor continued that as long as Latrobe "receives a salary for superintending the building, I have little hope of seeing the work completed."[5] Taylor got his wish; Latrobe was forced to resign in November 1817 due to criticism of cost overruns. Charles Bulfinch replaced him in January 1818, but the reconstruction and redesign of the Capitol would not be completed for another dozen years.

James Hoban, charged with the repairs to the president's mansion, also reported on December 3, 1816, on the progress on that building. The roof had been framed and covered with shingles. The chimneys had been rebuilt and were about to be covered with copper. Extensive stone and brick work had been undertaken, as the injury to the exterior walls was found to reach much deeper than first thought. The walls on the north front, east of the center, as well as on the east end of the building south of the center had to be taken down and rebuilt. Seven Ionic pilaster capitals had been cut and set, and the windows had also been rebuilt and finished. Inside, the doors had been framed, and the ornamental decorations on the doors and mahogany trimmings of the windows were "in a state of forwardness." On December 12, apparently in response to an inquiry, Hoban stated that it might be possible to have the house ready for the president by October 1817. At least the center and west end "might, with considerable exertion, be got ready."[6] In fact, the President's Mansion, soon dubbed the "White House" because of its new white exterior to cover the burn stains, was ready for occupation by September 1817. During the interim period, President Madison had taken up residence at the so-called "Octagon House," owned by Col. John Tayloe, at the corner of New York Avenue and Eighteenth Street (which is still standing today). The new President, James Monroe, remained at his residence at 2017 I Street until the presidential residence was ready.[7]

A recapitulation of the disbursements for repairs to the Capitol, the President's House, and other government buildings showed a balance of about $114,600 left from the congressional appropriation of $500,000 in 1815. Lane estimated in February 1817 that Congress would need to authorize approximately $275,000 more to finish the task.[8] These estimates proved to be sanguine. The work continued for several more years, and the expenses continued to mount.[9]

After the two houses were organized, with the popular Henry Clay elected Speaker of the House of Representatives, President Madison submitted his annual message to Congress. His report was very positive and pointed the way to a nationalistic congressional agenda. He cited the "successful termination" of the Algerian War, led by Commodore Stephen Decatur, which forced the Dey of Algiers to relinquish all pretensions of tribute. "Subsequent transactions" with Tripoli and Tunis offered the "prospect of future security from Barbary cruisers for our commerce." In keeping with this theme, Madison called for strengthening the military establishment, improving the organization of the militia, enlarging the Military Academy, and construction of a larger navy. He also recommended a higher tariff to protect manufacturing so as to relieve the country from dependence on foreign supplies; new national roads and canals; consideration of a new national bank; and a national university.[10]

In short, Madison laid out a program that reflected the growing optimism of the times (some said highly Federalist), and it met with favor in the Fourteenth Congress. As Henry Adams noted, "Under the stress of war the people had selected as their representatives the ablest and most vigorous men of their generation." He also declared that they, "for ability, energy, and usefulness, never had a superior, and perhaps, since the First Congress, never an equal."[11] The roster of the Fourteenth Congress included two future presidents, two vice-presidents, five secretaries of state, a secretary of the treasury, three secretaries of war, two postmaster generals, a secretary of the navy, and an attorney general. The roster of outstanding men in the House included Henry Clay, John C. Calhoun, William Lowndes, Richard M. Johnson, and Peter B. Porter, all of whom had been prominent war leaders. Anti-war leaders included Timothy Pickering, Daniel Webster, John Randolph of Roanoke, Thomas P. Grosvenor, and Richard Stanford. Other distinguished members were William

Henry Clay, engraving after Charles Bird King. National Portrait Gallery, Smithsonian Institution, Washington, D.C.

Pinkney and Samuel Smith from Maryland, Philip Barbour and Henry St. George Tucker from Virginia, Joseph Hopkinson, Samuel D. Ingham, and John Sergeant from Pennsylvania, John Forsyth of Georgia, John McLean of Ohio, and Henry Southard of New Jersey. Other notables soon to join the House were John Tyler of Virginia and William Henry Harrison of Ohio.

The Senate also claimed a distinguished group of members. Gone were some of the more divisive characters of the previous Congress, such as William Branch Giles of Virginia, Michael Leib of Pennsylvania, David Stone of North Carolina, and Joseph Anderson of Tennessee. Newly elected members to the Senate included Jonathan Roberts of Pennsylvania, George W. Campbell of Tennessee, Robert G. Harper of Maryland, Nathaniel Macon from North Carolina, and George M. Troup from Georgia, who joined with sitting members including Rufus King of New York, who had been a member of the Constitutional Convention, James Barbour of Virginia, Samuel Dana of Connecticut, and Jeremiah Morrow from Ohio.

After taking care of some preliminary business, a dozen standing committees as well as eight select committees were organized. The chair of the important Committee on Ways and Means, perhaps the second most important position in the House, was given to William Lowndes, the tall (six feet six), dignified, and highly respected South Carolinian. Another South Carolinian, the immensely talented John C. Calhoun, also rising to national prominence, was placed as Chair of the Committee on a Uniform National Currency. The Foreign Affairs chair was given to young John Forsyth of Georgia, who was eventually to serve as secretary of state under both Presidents Andrew Jackson and Martin Van Buren.[12]

In early proceedings, the House quickly became bogged down in a prolonged debate over the Commercial Convention of July 3, 1815. The treaty, negotiated for the Americans by John Quincy Adams, Albert Gallatin, and Henry Clay, which essentially established reciprocal trading rates on American and British goods collected in each other's ports, evoked very little excitement. William Coleman, editor of the *New York Evening Post*, for example, informed Rufus King that Bostonians were "perfectly indifferent about the treaty, contrary to your expectations." King's former Senate colleague, William Branch Giles of Virginia, also wrote, "it scarcely has excited any attention in this part of the country. It is generally supposed, that it will have the effect of increasing the competition for carrying our tobacco to market, and so far exempt the planters from the high charges of freight &c."[13] On the other side of the Atlantic, British shipowners were described as liking the treaty "very well," were "glad of the opportunity of running with us upon equal terms," and happy to accept nominal freight rates to letting their ships remain idle.[14]

At issue in the House was not the treaty itself, which was ratified by the Senate in late December. Essentially, the question was whether the treaty had officially revoked the tax laws or whether the House, by legislation, needed to modify these laws to conform to the terms of the treaty. The debate evolved into a constitutional discussion not only of the meaning of the treaty-making power and the role of the House in this process, but also of the relative roles of the legislature and the executive branch. When John Forsyth, chair of Foreign Relations, introduced a bill on December 29 to carry out the provisions of the treaty, William Gaston of North Carolina objected, arguing that as the treaty had been ratified, it was the law of the land. Speaker Clay, one of the negotiators of the treaty, explained its details, but he declined to enter into a discussion of the treaty-making power. The proposed bill, he added, could be either harmless or necessary according to one's point of view. Forsyth responded that passage was "indispensable."[15] Philip Barbour of Virginia stated the position of the bill's advocates: the Constitution vested all legislative power in Congress. Because the treaty repealed congressionally levied duties on British goods, a legislative power, then such duties must be repealed by an act of Congress.[16]

As the debate progressed it became clear a strong majority favored the bill. Calhoun created a stir when he declared a treaty was "paramount to laws made by the common legislative powers of the country;" and a "contract between independent nations." He agreed, however, that treaty-making had limits; no treaty could alter the fabric of government or take steps inconsistent with the Constitution.[17] Calhoun's speech drew John Randolph into the debate, not that the Virginian was ever shy about expressing his opinion. Randolph had long before established himself as a maverick who could not belong to any party. During the Jefferson Administration he had briefly served as a party leader, but that was uncongenial to his personality. After his break with Jefferson, Randolph led a fac-

John Randolph (of Roanoke), by John Wesley Jarvis. National Portrait Gallery, Smithsonian Institution, Washington, D.C.

tion sometimes called Old Republicans. He was a harsh critic of Madison's foreign policy and an outspoken member of the anti-war faction during the War of 1812. Randolph represented a strong states-right point of view, and he undoubtedly considered himself more principled than his opponents. Certainly he spoke more often in debate than any other member of the Fourteenth Congress. One contemporary stated that "He is truly a man of astonishing powers of mind. His manner of speaking is the most forcible I ever witnessed, and his language elegant beyond description." He added, "Notwithstanding all this he is certainly a very useless member."[18] Another observer called him a "phenomenon amongst men," and noted, "Popular opinion has ordained Mr. Randolph the most eloquent speaker now in America. He amuses by his striking and graceful delivery, and by the most original combinations of thought, and ludicrous imagery."[19] Although he considered the bill trivial, he added his "little rill to swell the torrent of debate to which this bill had given rise." He denounced Calhoun's claim that a treaty was above the legislative power, and argued the president and Senate had never possessed the power, by treaty, of repealing any law of the land or enacting any law in its stead. He characterized Calhoun's views as "highly federal doctrine," which would subvert the Constitution of the United States and all free government.[20]

Opponents of the bill worried the House was trying to exercise powers not granted to them by the Constitution and that their interference would anger the other branches of government. Nevertheless, the bill was ordered to a third reading by a vote of 86–69, revealing a distinct party division. Only a few Republicans joined Federalists opposing the bill.[21] Calhoun's position was attacked more than once. Albert Cuthbert of Georgia dubbed it "fallacious," and Henry St. George Tucker from Virginia called it a "monstrous construction." He asserted that the treaty reduced taxes, "which the legislative body alone can impose, and alone can abrogate."[22]

At this point, Maryland's William Pinkney, considered by many as the most outstanding member of the American Bar, and who had recently served (1811–14) as the attorney general of the United States, took the floor. Pinkney was also counted as one of the leading orators of the country. His delivery, one observer said, was "vehement . . . characterised by the most irresistible impetuosity; it is a conflagration ravaging the earth."[23] Pinkney stated bluntly that he did not view the treaty as "the still-born progeny of arrogated power," nor did he believe it needed "the filiation of Congress to make it legitimate." Useless legislation was vicious legislation. The president and Senate had been given exclusive control over diplomacy, and if the consent of the House had been intended, it would have been stipulated. The Constitution explicitly stated that treaties, regularly made, had the force of law. He considered the House bill an assault upon the treaty-making power and the Constitution, "alien to its theory and practice."[24]

In the meantime, the Senate sent the House a bill declaring the commercial acts contrary to the provisions of the treaty "of no force or effect." Forsyth opposed. The House bill proposed to repeal explicitly the statutes by law. He admitted the probability the Senate would reject the House bill, but he wished to throw the responsibility of rejecting the bill on the Senate, instead of the House. Former secretary of state, Timothy Pickering, expressed his hope that the Senate would reject the House bill as interfering with their exclusive power to make treaties, while Thomas B. Robertson of Louisiana marveled at the phenomenon of House members ranged against their own body and supporting the extravagant pretensions of the Senate.[25]

William Lowndes contended that rejection of the Senate bill without consideration might create a bad public impression and prompt the Senate to reject the House bill. A better strategy would be to postpone the Senate bill and pass the House bill. If the Senate rejected it, the House could then amend the Senate bill to fit the House position. If the Senate rejected it again, the blame for the double rejection would be theirs; and the House could not be accused of acting in haste or passion. Pickering, however, argued that if the Senate would not accept the House bill, it would be better not to send it to the Senate at all.[26]

John W. Taylor, a future Speaker of the House, denied treaties were the law of the land in the sense of a law of Congress. The hierarchy was the Constitution, then laws of Congress, and finally treaties (in their limited sphere). The view that legislative power granted to Congress by the Constitution might be usurped by the president and Senate was an "enormous political heresy." There was no guarantee the presidency and Senate would always be occupied by honorable men. If the Senate rejected the House bill, the latter would be required to erect barriers against the tyranny of Senatorial usurpation.[27] John G. Jackson from Virginia warned that the opposition's desire to enhance executive power would "bind the nation hand and foot to the car of the Executive."[28] Joseph Hopkinson regretted hearing arguments based on suspicions and jealousies of the Senate's power.[29] Finally, the bill was passed, 86–71, and sent to the Senate.[30]

In the upper chamber, James Barbour pointed out the obvious, that the House had not acted on the Senate bill but had sent one differing materially and "wanting in that courtesy which should be perpetually cherished between the two Houses. It would have been more decorous to have acted on our bill . . . to reject or amend it." The issue, he noted, involved whether or not the treaty repealed laws of Congress. He argued that the Constitution (Art. VI) declared all treaties the supreme law of the land, and all municipal regulations under its provisions "must *ipso facto* be annulled." There could not be two supreme laws of the land, he contended, and no law was necessary to execute the treaty.[31]

Eligius Fromentin of Louisiana asserted the Senate had a duty to resist encroachments on its rights.[32] Other Senators, however, such as David Daggett of Connecticut, Jeremiah Mason from New Hampshire, Nathaniel Macon, and Jonathan Roberts, supported the House bill. Roberts stated simply, "the treaty-making power is not a law-making power," and the supreme law of the land clause was qualified by the words, "under the authority of the United States," which included the legislative authority.[33]

The Senate rejected the House measure 21–10.[34] The House reluctantly took up the Senate bill. A motion to postpone indefinitely was defeated, and a motion to reject by Forsyth was withdrawn.[35] Forsyth was determined not to yield on this measure. A Princeton educated lawyer from Georgia, Forsyth was first elected to the House in 1810. He quickly emerged as a leader. Called by his admirers the "best off-hand orator in the world," he had not yet developed the traits of tact and diplomacy that marked his future career.[36] On February 4, Forsyth moved to strike the whole bill and insert the House bill passed earlier. He condemned the Senate for attempting to deprive the House of its powers in relation to the origination of public revenue measures.[37] Asa Lyon of Vermont, on the other hand, blasted the House's effort to inject itself into the treaty-making process. After more than twenty years operating under the Constitution, he asked, "Are we yet ignorant of the duties assigned, and the bounds set to our authority?" The safety of the Government depended on each branch knowing and performing its particular duty.[38] Nevertheless, the House passed Forsyth's amendment, 81–70, and sent it back to the Senate.[39]

In the Senate, Rufus King's motion to postpone (effectively to kill the bill) was barely defeated, 18–17.[40] They then rejected the House amendment. The House insisted on its amendments and asked for a conference. The Senate appointed King, Barbour, and William W. Bibb of Georgia as their managers. Forsyth headed the managers for the House. The Senate managers stated they did not believe legislation was necessary in this case, but they would agree to a measure provided no precedent was established. The Senate managers wanted to retain "declared," which the House managers accepted. As King explained the Conference Committee report to the Senate, the word "declared" imparted the character of declaratory law. Forsyth's explanation of the Conference Committee report was that declaratory words were viewed "as mere surplusage not changing or impairing the force of the act."[41] Some House members objected that their managers had yielded the ground taken by the House, but the overwhelming approval of the report by a 100–35 vote suggested that most members simply wanted to get the issue out of the way and go on to other business.[42]

Thus the dispute between the two houses over the Commercial Convention, which Rufus King called "the fruit and trophy of the late war," was finally reconciled. While the Senate had defended its exclusive role in the treaty-making process, it had yielded enough to allow the House managers to claim a small victory. No doubt House leaders understood they had pressed their position too far and welcomed an opportunity to retreat. Interestingly, among those in the House who voted against accepting the report were Calhoun and Pickering, who no doubt believed the Senate had conceded too much to the House, while others, such as Randolph and Cyrus King of Massachusetts, voted against it in the belief the House yielded too much to the Senate.[43]

Another issue brought before Congress, aid to widows and orphans of soldiers killed in war, was subsumed in the debate over relief for disbanded officers and for Canadian refugees who fought on the American side during the War of 1812. Both issues were brought up in mid-February, with the Canadian refugee relief discussed first. It stimulated an animated and interesting debate. Opponents claimed the proposed bill would reward treachery. John W. Hulbert of Massachusetts was particularly outraged by the proposal, which he characterized as inconsistent with morality and justice. Rewarding "faithless foreigners," he declared, confounded all notions of right and wrong. While we had seduced and armed our enemy's subjects, he warned in future our enemy might in turn incite our slaves to treason and rebellion. He noted that the House had rejected several pleas of good Americans who had lost property in the war and added, "Let it not be said that these traitors . . . are faring sumptuously at the national table, while your own citizens . . . are left, like dogs, to pick up the crumbs that fall from the same table."[44]

Nevertheless, despite strident opposition, several members spoke on behalf of the character of the Canadian refugees. Robert Wright stated he was sorry to see an indisposition to compensate volunteers invited to join the American standard. While he admired, in abstract, Hulbert's principles, the question was whether the Government would fulfill its promises made to them. When Daniel Webster's motion directed at killing the bill was supported by only about twenty-five members, it expressed the House's sentiment and foretold the eventual outcome. A motion by Philip P. Barbour to substitute a bounty of land according to rank and not on losses in Canada, passed, 77–49. The House adopted a bounty running from 960 acres for a colonel to 320 for non-commissioned officers and privates and accepted a proposal to locate the bounty lands in Indiana Territory. Despite further efforts to derail the bill, the question was finally passed on February 21 by a vote of 89–54.[45]

The House also clashed over providing a bounty of land for disbanded officers of the late war. Objections were raised that the bill only included regular officers, not soldiers or militia officers. Proponents argued that soldiers had already received bounties of approximately ten million acres as part of their discharge. Bounties under this law would amount to less than one million acres, but including militia officers would require at least fifty million acres. Oliver C. Comstock of New York argued that the government had a legal obligation with the soldiers, and it had been met. There was no such obligation owed the officers to provide further compensation. The bill also excluded meritorious officers retained in service, and he disliked the discrimination between regular and militia officers. Micah Taul of Kentucky argued that passage of the bill would disgust the militia and do great violence to public sentiment. A motion to strike the section passed, 74–60.[46]

Several constitutional amendments were offered in the Fourteenth Congress. One of the most interesting was by North Carolina to divide each state into the number of districts equal to the number of electoral votes each state was entitled. Each district would choose an elector for president. As was the custom of the time, North Carolina submitted their proposal to the states, as well as having it submitted in Congress. Several states rejected the proposed amendment, including Massachusetts, although its legislature submitted an "improved" version that would require all districts to be as equal as possible in numbers and redistributed after each census reapportionment.[47] Only the Senate discussed this proposal at length in the first session, and it was the Massachusetts version, introduced by Senator Joseph B. Varnum. Rufus King favored the amendment, arguing that the election of president was no longer the process contemplated by the Constitution. The mode of election should be uniform throughout the country, he asserted, and "no particular addresses could be made to the special interests and particular men of particular sections of the country."[48] Opponents, however, worried that the use of districts instead of the at-large (winner take all) ticket would diminish the power of large states. Thus New York, with twenty-nine electoral votes, and Virginia, with twenty-five, might be evenly divided and carry only a weight of one, where Delaware, with three electors, might have a weight of three to one over New York or Virginia.[49]

The amendment for electoral districts was dropped by the Senate, but the North Carolina proposal was brought up again in the second session in the House. The amendment received some editorial support in various parts of the country. Jesse Buel, for example, supported it in the *Albany Argus*. "The time seems to have arrived," he wrote, "when no party considerations forbid the permanent establishment of the uniform system proposed; when party spirit has lost its asperity; and the ascendancy of republican principles seem fixed upon a solid basis."[50] Many of the same arguments advanced in the first session were repeated, but there was greater support. Advocates saw the amendment as a much-needed reform of the election process, but opponents, including John Randolph, saw it as an infringement on states rights. He would not tamper with the Constitution, he said, "We are very well as it is." Nevertheless, proponents of the measure to create uniform election districts prevailed in the first vote, 86–38, meeting the two-thirds requirement of the Constitution. Randolph professed to be more surprised by this vote than any he had ever witnessed in the House. He had not imagined the House was serious. If the amendment passed, he warned, "I would not give a button for the rights of the states."[51] The vote on the second part of the amendment, to choose electors for president in each district, failed to carry a two-thirds margin. The vote was 86–51, and the House, rather than prolong the debate, tabled the whole measure and did not take it up again.[52]

Other amendments offered in this Congress included one from Georgia that would have lowered the terms of senators from six to four years. It received little support. In fact, it was voted down in the Senate by a three-to-one margin.[53] Another amendment proposed by Senator Nathan Sanford from New York would make all United States court judges subject to removal by the president and a two-thirds vote of both houses. Rufus King and Eligius Fromentin, in particular, attacked the proposed amendment as a threat to the independence of the judiciary. It was eventually postponed indefinitely by a substantial margin.[54] An amendment offered by Charles Atherton of New Hampshire to establish a National University was briefly considered and rejected, 86–54.[55] Finally, Barbour of Virginia advanced the amendment first proposed by James Madison (but not approved) in the 1790s which stated: "No law varying the compensation for the services of the Senators and Representatives shall take effect until an election of Representatives shall have intervened." Despite the unpopularity of the Compensation Act, or perhaps because of a residual anger in Congress against the popular reaction, the amendment was not acted upon. The Madison amendment, however, because there was no time limit established, remained before the country for two centuries, and it was eventually added to the Constitution as the Twenty-seventh Amendment in 1992.[56]

A motion on January 19 by Richard Stanford of North Carolina to expunge "the previous question" generated a heated debate

over the rules and orders of the House. He regretted "such an abomi-
nable badge of slavery should have found its way into the regulations of any free deliberative assembly." It allowed a tyranny of the
majority over the freedom of debate. Stanford was supported by
John Randolph, who characterized the rule as a "gag law." It began
as a way to stifle a member who "was a nuisance" (Randolph himself), but it was "perverted into an engine to intercept fair discussion, and prevent the sense of the House from being taken."[57]

Speaker Clay defended the previous question and the right of
the majority to make it. He insisted it was not resorted to until
abuse of debate rendered it necessary, some members speaking
twenty-four hours without stopping. He also said the majority should
not be controlled by the minority. William Gaston, however, declared the previous question "hostile to every principle of our Government, inconsistent with all notions of correct legislation, and
without a precedent in the annals of any free deliberative assembly." He had hoped that with the return of peace and "a spirit of
mutual forbearance between the political parties of the House," it
would be a good time to get rid of this rule. If Clay's ingenuity and
zeal could offer no other defense than he had just heard, it could
not be defended. Gaston traced the rule through British and American examples to show it had not been used to stifle debate, but since
February 1811 it had been used in that manner, and at least six
times in the last session.[58]

Burwell Bassett from Virginia moved to postpone the order indefinitely. John G. Jackson and another Virginia member, Henry St.
George Tucker, preferred to meet the issue directly. Stanford at least
wanted the yeas and nays on his motion to show who was for and
who against this rule. The vote, ayes 56 and 31 nays, indicated a
quorum did not vote, which simply reflected that the House did
not want to take up the issue. Stanford and Bassett successively withdrew their motions, bowing to the wishes of the House.[59]

The oratorical flourishes in the first session of the Fourteenth
Congress had revealed the outstanding quality of the members of
this Congress, and the general good will displayed in the debates
suggested that the issues confronting Congress would be dispas-
sionately discussed and perhaps resolved without the usual intru-
sions of partisanship. Congress had yet to tackle the really important
issues relating to regulation of tariffs and revenue, as well as banking

and currency questions. These issues would not only test the new sense of unity in Congress, their success in deciding these economic issues would help determine the future strength and stability of the nation.

Chapter 4

A Tariff and a Bank

Perhaps the most serious questions facing the Fourteenth Congress were in the financial field. The country had emerged from the war with an accumulated debt of $127 million, which needed to be repaid, and the currency was also in disarray. All of the banks south of New England had suspended redemption of their bank notes in specie (gold and silver). The Treasury received notes for payment of taxes that were greatly depreciated from their face value. Congress was faced with the task of encouraging, or forcing, banks to redeem their notes in specie, and there was a strong sentiment that another Bank of the United States should be established to cope with the problem. Further, although the value of American exports increased greatly after the war, imports did also, and textile manufacturers, new fledgling industries, complained bitterly about cheap British exports flooding the market and undercutting their profits They and their representatives in Congress demanded protection. Some members wished to develop a greater degree of self-sufficiency, while others, for patriotic reasons, believed the British should not be allowed to stifle infant industries in America. The Fourteenth Congress set about resolving these problems.

On January 9, William Lowndes, for the Committee on Ways and Means, reported twelve resolutions intended to guide legislation relating to the debt and taxes. Lowndes was perfectly suited to shepherd this difficult measure through the House. First elected to the Twelfth Congress in 1810 as a war hawk, his intelligence and his calm, dispassionate demeanor quickly established him as one of the leaders of the House. Unfortunately, he was afflicted with poor health, inflammatory rheumatism, which weakened him and eventually led to his death at the age of forty in 1822. Undoubtedly, but for his health he would have become one of the leaders of the American nation. He was projected by some to be a future president.[1] His report assumed an annual revenue of about $25.5 million, and included a proposal for a sinking fund to reduce the debt by allocating $13.5 million annually to pay interest and principal on the national debt.[2] As might be expected, basic issues like taxes ignited a prolonged debate dealing with many aspects of American society, most importantly the relationship of the government to the people and the direction the government should take. Topics discussed were the need for protection of manufacturing, the retention of wartime taxes, the maintenance of a strong military and navy, the extent and duration of the direct tax, and the question of which section of the country benefitted or suffered from the current revenue system.

The first resolution proposed to continue double duties until June 30, or until a new tariff act was passed. The salt tax and related bounties and allowances, duties on sugar, and stamp taxes on bank notes were continued, but the additional duty on postage was abolished. There was grumbling about the phrase "new tariff" in the first resolution, but the resolutions were approved on January 19. Lowndes then presented the remainder of his report, which called for retention of the direct tax (but reduced by half to raise $3 million). It was justified as needed to pay the public debt.[3] Henry Clay approved the committee's proposals, but he preferred reducing the direct tax (a tax on land and slaves) to $2 million and relying on a tariff on foreign imports as the chief source of revenue for the government.[4] Lowndes countered by proposing an amendment to reduce the wartime double tariff rates and set the rates at 42 percent after June 30 (i.e., regular duties plus 42 percent). Clay moved to insert 50 percent, which would add $1 million to revenues and allow that much to be taken from the direct tax. His motion, however, was defeated, 80–64, as were several other attempts to amend the bill.[5] Of the remaining measures, only the salt tax excited extensive debate. Eventually all of the committee recommendations were passed to a third reading.[6]

Benjamin Hardin, a new congressman from Kentucky, whose unpolished oratory was characterized by John Randolph as "a carving knife whetted on a brickbat," observing "an unconquerable indisposition to alter, change, or modify anything reported by any one of the Standing Committees," nevertheless moved to repeal the direct tax altogether. This tax, he asserted, was calculated to enhance the power of government, "oppress the people and destroy the republican form of government." The real object of the excessive revenue was to squander it on "flatterers and favorites," who might be removed from office by reduction of expenses, and to give the heir apparent, James Monroe, popularity by repealing these odious laws.[7]

This led to a discussion on the inequality of the direct tax. The tax rate varied in many states. For example, in Massachusetts it was 21 cents per $100; in Vermont, 30 cents; Rhode Island, 16 cents; and Connecticut, 13 cents.[8] Clay followed with a long speech, which this debate seemingly invited. He was a popular and influential leader. Although a Virginian by birth, he had migrated to Kentucky and emerged as a spokesman for the West. He served briefly in the United States Senate, but he entered the House of Representatives in 1811 and was immediately chosen Speaker of the House. He led a group of "War Hawks" that helped impel the country into war in 1812. He also served on the peace commission that wrote the Treaty of Ghent ending the war. As Speaker of the House in the Fourteenth Congress, Clay spoke frequently and pushed his nationalist views. The cry of retrenchment might be popular, he said, but it was not proper. The nation should not disarm itself regardless of impending danger. The government would be bankrupt in three years if the taxes were not continued. He also earnestly recommended internal improvements to bind the country together and a protective tariff to insure self-sufficiency, views that later came to be known as the "American System."[9]

Joseph Hopkinson of Pennsylvania observed the anomaly of the majority differing among themselves as to the measures to be pursued. If this movement succeeded in embarrassing the government, he said, let it be remembered that it was not due to the Federalist opposition. In fact, he was inclined to support the taxes: "It is better that unfit men should have the means necessary to govern, than that the Government should perish for want of means." Moreover, without the land tax the South and West would pay little to extinguish the debt.[10]

Contrary to Hopkinson's contention, a Federalist, Cyrus King of Massachusetts, launched into a diatribe against the "oppressive taxes" and the "overgrown, expensive" military establishment. He also injected sectionalism into his argument, suggesting that New England's lumber and other staples had been sacrificed in the Commercial Convention to the cotton growers of the South and West. Reflecting the doctrinal confusion of this session, King complimented Randolph for his efforts upholding true Constitutional principles.[11] James B. Reynolds from Tennessee condemned King's partisanship, but he also had a problem with the inequality in levying the direct tax, which affected Tennessee as well, and he hoped that could be corrected.[12]

Calhoun, who was, like Clay, in a nationalist mode, captured this moment and the opportunity that confronted the Fourteenth Congress when he observed "there were in the affairs of nations ... moments, on the proper use of which depended their fame, prosperity and duration." He hoped the measures of Congress would be divested of the character of parsimony. The country was growing rapidly and the government should encourage domestic industry, improve transportation, and lay taxes wisely and moderately.[13] Randolph rejoined that these measures would "prostrate the State governments at the feet of the General Government."[14]

Henry St. George Tucker complimented both the "frank, manly, liberal, and comprehensive remarks" of Calhoun and "the watchful sagacity" of Randolph. He observed the direct tax bore most heavily on the populated sections and was favorable to the South and West where population was dispersed and whose lands were not estimated at its intrinsic worth. In Virginia, he said, the tax on an estate of $5000 would be $7, hardly odious or oppressive.[15]

Hardin's motion for an immediate repeal of the direct tax lost, 88–69. On February 3, Clay's motion to limit the tax to one year so as to bring the tax annually before the House passed, 109–16. Nevertheless, opponents in the House continued their assault on the direct tax. Richard Stanford of North Carolina declared that the doctrines heard in debate were "unrepublican," and he accused some Republicans of surpassing the Federalists.[16] He was joined by Randolph, Wright, John Ross of Pennsylvania, and Samuel McKee of Kentucky, while the tax was supported by Joseph Desha of Kentucky, John Burnside from Pennsylvania, William Gaston of North Carolina, and William Woodward from South Carolina.[17]

North Carolina's Israel Pickens tried unsuccessfully to reduce

John C. Calhoun, (attr.) Charles Bird King. National Portrait Gallery, Smithsonian Institution, Washington, D.C.

the direct tax from $3 million to $2 million. A motion to reconsider launched yet another debate. Charles H. Atherton of New Hampshire declared he was for disbanding the army of tax collectors. "Do not enervate the American Hercules," he concluded, "by steeping him in the hot-bed of Executive patronage."[18]

Alexander Hanson of Maryland regretted to see Federalists departing from the principles and maxims of their party, but he was pleased to see many gentlemen on the other side converting to the principles of Washington and Federalism. He commended Calhoun's "manly frankness and independence," and he pledged to cooperate to heal the wounds inflicted upon the country. Why should Republicans be disowned or renounced, he asked, if they had learned the country could flourish and grow great by following Federalist principles? The vote to reconsider was defeated, and continuation of the direct tax of $3 million for one year was passed and referred to the Finance Committee to bring in a bill.[19]

On February 7, the committee recommendations on the remaining taxes were upheld except that the capacity tax on stills was reduced from 100 percent to 50 percent.[20] A week later, the engrossed appropriation bill was passed and sent to the Senate. The Senate made a few non-substantive amendments and sent them back to the House, which took them up on March 4. The House agreed to the Senate amendments and passed the bill.[21] Appropriation bills usually were a pro forma process after the real decisions had already been made on the laws they were funding, but this was an extraordinary period, and decisions had to be made first on how to manage the large debt raised by the war. Once that decision had been made, Congress could then address the current needs of the country.

Closely related to revenue measures was foreign trade, and intertwined with it was domestic manufacturing and agriculture. What was beneficial to one sector of the economy was not necessarily favorable to another. During the debate over revenues, Southerners had raised the argument that would be heard often in the years to come against the tariff, that it would hurt their agricultural constituents to benefit "the interest of the merchant and manufacturer."[22] John Randolph observed that the party that had supported the principles of Thomas Jefferson was now adopting "old Federalism, vamped up into something bearing the superficial appearance of

Republicanism." The tariff would take money out of the pockets of the hardworking cultivators of the soil, he said, to give bounties to manufacturers to encourage them to do what they would do anyway. He wondered why he should pay more to have his own cotton worked into clothing, "when by selling my raw material, I can get my clothing much better and cheaper from Dacca."[23] Congress had to balance the demands of the new manufacturing interests with the traditional needs of agriculturalists and shipping interests in the first session of the Fourteenth Congress.

The British were well aware of the growth of American manufacturing in the post-war period, and with large inventories and a desire to reestablish their former levels of export of manufactured goods to the United States, began emptying their warehouses and undercutting the prices of American manufacturers. Cheaper British goods, particularly textiles, led to demands by industrialists for congressional action to restore a balance of competition. Hezekiah Niles, a strong supporter of the tariff in his *Niles' Weekly Register*, declared that the manufacturing interest was in the "precise relation of an infant to its mother." He estimated about $100 million capital was invested in manufacturing in the past few years. For cotton, more than a half million spindles consumed 100,000 bales @ 300 pounds, or 30 million per annum. These spindles produced 90 million yards @ 90 cents per yard, or $27 million, and employed 100,000 people.[24] On the other hand, Southern farmers, buoyed by rising cotton prices, which reached twenty-nine cents a pound in 1816, were expanding cotton farming and were content to continue the status quo. New England shipping interests engaged in the carrying trade were also loath to engage in restrictive systems or commercial warfare.[25]

American shippers did complain about the British policy of exclusion, which closed their possessions in the West Indies to American trade. Cyrus King observed in the House on February 4 that our vessels were permanently excluded from her colonial ports, while we threw our ports open to her. Until the British were disposed to trade on the most perfect reciprocity he would reject their commerce and encourage the produce and manufacturing of the United States. He moved to instruct the Committee on Foreign Relations to consider excluding from the ports of the United States all foreign vessels touching any British possession in the West Indies, from which American vessels were excluded, as well as excluding or increasing the duties on any goods brought from these possessions.[26] Fears were raised that King's proposition might start a new commercial contest between the two countries. William A. Burwell of Virginia pointed out that the Convention of 1815 applied only to British vessels arriving from Europe, and former laws that discriminated against British navigation in our ports still applied. King's resolution was passed, but no action was taken by the committee. Undoubtedly, it was felt that the intent was subsumed under the broader tariff policy adopted by Congress.[27]

Petitions calling for protection flooded Congress early in the session and were submitted almost daily. On February 13, Speaker Clay laid before the House a letter from the controversial Secretary of the Treasury, Alexander James Dallas. Jamaican born, a man of great talents and enormous energy, he had drawn up a list of suggested tariff duties on imported goods. That same day, Thomas Newton Jr., of Virginia, Chair of the Commerce and Manufacturing Committee, to whom the memorials and petitions had been referred, proposed protection of infant industries from British competition by increasing the ad valorem taxes (percent of the value).[28]

The tariff debate opened on March 20. The Dallas proposals were read through and taken up by sections. Perhaps the most controversial suggestion was the 25 percent ad valorem on imported woolen and cotton products. In committee of the whole, Clay attempted to try the sense of the House by advancing the rate on cotton to 33.3%. He assumed the question was not whether to adopt protection but by how much, and his preference was ample duties.[29]

Clay's motion was defeated (51–43), as was Timothy Pickering's effort to tax all cotton cloths (except nankeen) costing below twenty-five cents as if they cost twenty-five cents per square yard. Clay next tried to set the duty at thirty percent. Samuel D. Ingham of Pennsylvania, a member of the Ways and Means Committee and a future secretary of the treasury, spoke at length defending the tariff. He denied it would harm navigation or was partial to the Northern and Middle States and not the South. Higher rates would stimulate competition at home, and a similar opportunity would not likely come again.[30]

Clay's motion carried, 68–61. This was just the beginning of attempts to adjust the rates. Benjamin Huger's proposal to reduce the duty on brown sugar from four cents to two and a half cents per pound aroused the ire of Thomas B. Robertson from Louisiana. Agriculturalists, he argued, were as deserving of protection as manufacturers. If Louisiana was to be taxed to augment the wealth of other parts of the country, they asked for reciprocal sacrifices. He worried the manufacturing interest was being favored to raise revenue, "whatever ruin be brought on the maritime industry, however much the agriculturalist suffer."[31] He was supported by Calhoun, who stressed the need to establish self-sufficiency at home, but others argued that the tax pressed too heavily on the poorer classes. Eventually the rate was set at three and a half cents.[32] During the debate, Randolph made some remarks about the tariff and the state of Louisiana that incensed Robertson, who was angry enough to challenge Randolph to a duel. Randolph refused, stating that "he was not disposed to sport with his *precious* life."[33]

An item that excited considerable debate was the duty on imported cottons. Daniel Webster, who was at this time tied to the shipping and not the manufacturing interests, moved to hold the rate on imported cottons at 30 percent for two years, 25 for two years, and then to 20 percent, which engendered yet another debate. Lowndes agreed 20 percent was sufficient protection, and was "a return of correct principles." Erastus Root of New York and John Ross argued that if 20 percent was correct it should be established now. Ross feared manufacturing "would prove destructive to the liberties of this Republic," and he added, "There was already a great necessity for a strong country party to withstand the manufacturing and commercial parties here." Webster's motion prevailed by a large majority.[34]

Ross's observation about the appearance of a manufacturing and commercial faction in Congress was premature, but he was correct that such a faction was forming which would grow ever stronger in the years to come. At this point in 1816, appeals to patriotism outweighed the fears of those who only dimly perceived the dramatic changes that would be wrought by the industrial and market revolution.

The duties on several other items were adjusted.[35] Perhaps the most substantive motions were by Lowndes to allow piece goods imported from India that arrived after June 30 to be reexported

with benefit of drawback to June 30, 1817, and by Ingham to reduce the number of ad valorem grades.[36] The House then took up
the committee of the whole report. A motion by Forsyth to reduce
the duty on imported cottons to 20 percent from June 30 failed,
despite support from several members. Robert Wright injected an
interesting issue when he offered a resolution that would bar members having a proprietary interest in a cotton factory from voting.
The blatant suggestion of conflict of interest was objected to, and
Wright withdrew his resolution.[37]

Supporters of higher duties on cotton goods fought hard, but a
motion by Benjamin Hardin to establish the rates at 25 percent for
two years, then revert to 20 percent, carried 84–60. Among the nays
was John C. Calhoun.[38] Thomas Telfair of Georgia, an opponent of
protection, denounced taxing, not for the coffers of the country,
but to go "from the pockets of consumers to those of the manufacturer." Agriculturalists were being sacrificed to benefit the manufacturers. Thomas R. Gold of New York admitted he had a concern
in manufacturing, but he feared "the inundation of foreign fabrics . . .
[would lead] to their destruction." The East India Company had
ruined English cotton manufacturing by underselling. Samuel Smith
of Maryland did succeed in amending Hardin's motion to extend
the 25 percent duty to three years.[39]

A few other minor modifications of the committee of the whole
recommendations were made by the House, the most important
being a motion by Pickering to admit all India importations within
one year after June 30 on their paying 25 percent in addition to the
usual 20 percent. It was approved by a large majority.[40] Randolph,
not at all happy with the progress of the tariff measure, characterized it as "a scheme of public robbery . . . levying an immense tax
on one portion of the community to put money into the pockets of
another."[41] Calhoun replied that it was good policy to protect manufacturing. It would strengthen the security of the country in the
event of war and make us more self sufficient. He also called for a
system of internal improvements to bind the country together to
"form a new and most powerful cement far outweighing any political objections that might be urged against the system."[42]

On April 8, the engrossed bill was read a third time. Randolph
made a final effort to postpone, but the sentiment of the House was
revealed when his motion was defeated, 95–47. Randolph, Wright,

and Telfair occupied several hours of the House's time opposing the tariff, then the final vote on passage was taken and approved, 88–54.[43] The bill was then sent to the Senate where the mood was strongly for protection. Several attempts to amend the bill, such as reducing the tax on woolen goods and salt were easily defeated, and a motion by Robert Goodloe Harper of Maryland to postpone (and thus defeat) was soundly rejected, 27–3. The Senate then passed the bill on April 19, 25–7, and sent it back to the House.[44] The House approved minor amendments made by the Senate and passed the bill, which was approved by the president on April 12.[45]

Several Southern politicians voted for the tariff, including Calhoun and Lowndes. Both undoubtedly did so, as they informed the House, for patriotic reasons. Not only were they reacting to the avowed British policy of dumping to stifle the development of American manufacturing, they were also concerned that Great Britain still offered a military threat to the United States. They may also have entertained the view that the South might soon establish infant industries and benefit as well. Another factor that may have influenced some was the undeniable need for revenue after the war. In fact, Southerners had succeeded in cutting the direct tax by half, a tax that was generally detested in the South. While there is no direct evidence of any bargain, some Southerners may have promised to support the tariff in return for Northern votes to reduce the direct tax.[46]

Overall, the average rate of the Tariff of 1816 was 20 percent, but higher duties (25 percent) were granted on the item of most interest, cotton textiles, but only for a period of three years. The tax on textiles and woolens fell to 20 percent after 1819. Perhaps the most important feature of the law was the minimum duty on cotton goods. All cotton cloths costing less than twenty-five cents would be considered as costing that amount and taxed accordingly at 25 percent. This was the first minimum valuation proviso, which became more important in future tariff laws. The Tariff of 1816 has been characterized as the first protective tariff in American history, but the higher rates are explained primarily by the need to pay the war debt. It properly belongs to the series of acts from 1789, rather than the consciously protective tariffs of 1824, 1828, and 1832.[47] Nor should the Tariff of 1816 be considered a powerful stimulus to textile manufacturing. The greatest stimulus was the war, which gave far greater protection from foreign competition. Nevertheless, the Tariff of 1816 should be remembered as the first tariff to apply the principle of protecting "infant industries."

Some recognized that the United States was on the threshold of a new era and questioned whether encouraging manufacturing was a wise policy. One anonymous pamphleteer in New York wondered if capital would be diverted to speculation in manufacturing and away from agriculture. He pointed out that there was still so much land untouched, and he wondered whether, with the high price of labor, the United States might not be at a disadvantage. He also worried that manufacturing would bring about ranks in society which was incompatible with republican institutions. Finally, he questioned whether our population was sufficiently dense to justify "withdrawing a material portion of it from the honest, and moral, and manly pursuits of agriculture—supposed to be the true and incorruptible nursery of freemen."[48] The last mentioned argument, that able-bodied men would be withdrawn from much needed labor for agriculture, was often met, as Hezekiah Niles did in October 1815, that children could be usefully employed in manufacturing. Niles asserted that children up to the age of fourteen rendered "little service to their parents," and that they could be utilized as workers in cotton and woolen works. By paying them ten cents a day, or about $2 per month, a large sum would be derived "from a class of citizens who have generally yielded little or nothing to the community."[49]

From a different perspective, the tariff was greeted with enthusiasm. The Norfolk, Virginia, *American Beacon* wrote on July 1, 1816, "The new tariff going into operation today, we anticipate the pleasure of seeing our port crowded with arrivals from all parts of the world. We understand that many vessels have been off the coast some time, awaiting this new state of things, so advantageous to the importer."[50] This statement reflects that the rates were actually lowered on many items from the double duties that had prevailed.

Oliver Wolcott of Connecticut, a former secretary of the treasury, observed to Rufus King that the tariff, particularly on cotton manufactures, was "entirely right," given the state of commerce, the demand for revenue, and the manufacturers' interest. New England, he wrote, manufactured a sufficient supply of common and coarse fabrics to meet the country's consumption. Prosperity was threatened, however, by the want of a uniform currency. "[It] is severely felt here & I believe generally in the Eastern States." He hoped that the national bank would be adopted.[51]

Madison's annual message in December 1815 merely stated that "a national bank will merit consideration." Treasury Secretary Dallas, however, presumably with Madison's approval, wrote Calhoun, Chairman of the Committee on Uniform National Currency, on December 24, 1815, detailing a national bank plan with a capital of $35 million. One fifth of the capital ($7 million) and one fifth of the twenty-five directors would be provided by the national government.[52] On January 8, 1816, Calhoun reported a bill to establish a Bank of the United States (BUS). Clearly, the bill was based on Dallas's letter, including a $35 million capital, a twenty-year charter, and one-fourth of the capital would be specie. It was also specified the bank would pay a bonus of $1.5 million for its charter.[53]

The Republican Party had allowed the charter of the first Bank of the United States to expire in 1811, but as a consequence state banks proliferated during the War of 1812 and paper money more than doubled. Congress had clearly failed to provide a uniform currency. The Coinage Act of 1792 created a gold and silver bimetallic currency system, but the ratio established (15 to 1), undervalued gold below the market value which meant that it hardly circulated. The lack of specie (gold and silver) forced the growing economy of America to rely increasingly on a variety of paper currency ranging in value from five cents to $10,000.[54] Without adequate specie to back these paper notes, every bank south of New England was forced to suspend specie payments within two years of the start of the War of 1812. Consequently, paper money fluctuated wildly in value and the federal government faced bankruptcy. Congress struggled with this issue in 1814, and they eventually passed a bank recharter bill, but it was vetoed by President Madison, who objected more to the inadequacies of the proposed bank than because of any constitutional differences.[55]

The task of pushing through a national bank bill was given to one of the ablest and most respected members of the Fourteenth Congress. Calhoun was still a very young man, only thirty-four years old, but he had impressed everyone with his intellect and his intensity. He had entered Congress as a war hawk in the Twelfth Congress and had quickly emerged as one of the leaders of that faction. He was a tower of strength for the administration during the War of 1812. Calhoun had managed to be a partisan leader without being abrasive, and his strong post-war nationalism was admired by individuals in both parties. A contemporary, a prominent citizen from Maine, James C. Jewett, related that he was told that Calhoun had "the most weight" in the House of Representatives. He described Calhoun as an "elegant speaker." "He confines himself closely to the subject, which he always understands, and enlightens every one within hearing; having said all that a statesman should say, he is done."[56] This would be an asset during the struggle to establish a national bank.

Calhoun, who had taken part in the earlier debate and was well aware of the pitfalls confronting him, explained the bill in detail when it was taken up on February 26 in committee of the whole. He passed lightly over the constitutional issue, noting that question had already been freely and frequently discussed. Rather, he argued that the extremely depreciated state of the circulating currency opposed a principle of the Constitution. The power to regulate the currency was given to Congress, but in fact it was in the hands of the banks. He distinguished between banks of deposit and banks of discount. The latter had grown from one to 260, and their capital had increased from $400,000 to $80 million. These institutions, he asserted, now continued in violation of their contract to redeem notes in specie, and worse, they controlled the currency through bank notes. "The right of making money—an attribute of sovereign power, a sacred and important right—was exercised by two hundred and sixty banks, scattered over every part of the United States, not responsible to any power whatever for their issues of paper." The solution was to force these banks to redeem their notes in specie and restore uniform value. The depreciation of paper was caused by the vast increase of bank notes in circulation since 1811, from about $80 million to more than $200 million. Gold and silver had been drained out of the United States, but it would return if it became again the basis of bank transactions. Calhoun denied the banks were insolvent; indeed, "they were never more solvent." Bank stockholders had lately realized twelve to twenty percent on their stock. The present state of things would not cure itself, and a national bank was needed. By paying specie itself, it would make specie payments general. It would not take paper notes from banks that did not pay specie. Calhoun warned, "The evil grows, whilst the resistance to it becomes weak."[57]

John Randolph, whose hostility to state banks was well known, rose to say that he "was glad to see a cause so important in hands so able." While he might not agree with the mode of remedying the evil, he would support an adequate remedy for this enormous evil. Others, like Jonathan Ward of New York, admitted the evil but opposed the remedy. He believed a better way would be for the government not to accept notes of banks refusing to pay specie. This mode should be tried before considering establishing a national bank.[58]

The general mood of the House favored the idea of a national bank, but there were many varied objections. Some wanted a less complex plan, others were hostile to government control, a few opposed the use of treasury notes to form part of the capital, and still others opposed giving the bank power to authorize suspension of payments in specie.[59] The strongest opposition, however, came from state bank supporters. John Sergeant, although from Philadelphia and well aware of the advantage of having the BUS headquartered in that city, nevertheless moved to reduce the capital of the bank from $35 million to $20 million. Politically, the bill would "create a vast machine of incalculable force" and should be approached with great caution. State banks had a claim to public consideration. Their predicament was due to loans to the government for defense and to a run on the banks that occurred after the capture of Washington, forcing a suspension of specie payment. State banks needed more time to correct their situation instead of relying on a very doubtful experiment. Sergeant questioned whether the BUS would acquire sufficient specie to become a specie bank, and in any event it should not be allowed to issue more in paper than it actually possessed in specie.[60] Several members agreed with Sergeant, arguing that limiting the capital would narrow to some extent the power of the bank. Others, however, contended that new and growing countries needed more, not less capital, and high interest rates suggested the demand for more capital.[61]

Daniel Webster, surprisingly, considering his later staunch support for the BUS, registered his opposition. The evil was due to banks issuing more paper money than they could redeem. Instead of establishing a bank, the government should interdict the paper of banks not paying specie from being received at the custom-house. A national bank, he contended, should not be used to rectify the present state of the currency, but to aid the government in the exercise of its power over currency.[62] Another Federalist, Joseph Hopkinson, while stating that he believed a national bank was necessary, opposed this new system which abounded in new ingredients, many of which were known to be unsatisfactory in the judgment of many of the best friends of a national bank. He added that the greater the amount of capital, the greater the danger the BUS could "crush the State banks."[63]

It soon became clear that Federalists comprised the main opposition to the bank, although even they did not form a united front. The size of the majority that voted against the Sergeant motion, 74–49, gave an indication of the strength of the bank supporters. Nevertheless, a multitude of potent arguments were raised against the BUS, many of which were raised again during the recharter debate of 1832 leading to Jackson's ultimate destruction of the BUS. The problem for proponents of the measure was to avoid getting bogged down in details. As Calhoun stated at one point in the debate, "It was a fate peculiar to great measures to fail in their details."[64]

Among these details was an effort to eliminate the government subscription to one-fifth of the bank stock. Opponents of the BUS argued that government stock would be an irresistible power in the hands of any administration, while proponents contended that ownership would be profitable to the government and would do no injury or mischief. The motion was defeated, 61–38.[65] Motions to exempt Treasury notes as a mode of payment for government stock and to make the government shares receivable in stock bearing interest of five percent were accepted.[66]

An attempt to strike the provision that the president and Senate appoint five directors excited considerable debate. Opponents argued the BUS in the hands of government might endanger the country; that the bank should be managed without government interference; that it would increase executive patronage; that the government appointees would be political and not men of business; and that government would have enough power over the bank without directors. On the other side, it was urged as necessary to guard the interest of the public and was used in state banks without abuse; that the twenty directors appointed by stockholders would be competent to control the government's five; and that the government's appointees would be persons of wealth and respectability. Henry Clay found the opposition arguments to be strange. Could the government not be trusted to appoint five directors who had no salary? The government should have influence over the BUS, he asserted. In addition to one-fifth of the capital, there would always be fifteen to twenty million in government deposits in its coffers.[67]

The main motion to exclude government directors failed, 79–64, but several amendments were made that affected directors. Among them were provisions that government directors must hold bank stock; that no more than three of the five could be from the same state; and that the choice of president of the BUS was to be made from any director and not be confined to directors chosen by the president and Senate.[68] A motion by John Randolph to add the word "native" in the choice of government directors was accepted, but when Luther Jewett of Vermont proposed adding "native" in choosing branch directors, Calhoun opposed it as an "odious and unprecedented" discrimination between native and naturalized citizens. The motion was eventually rejected without a division, but not before Randolph vented his spleen against foreigners generally.[69] Randolph's amendment was later deleted.[70]

Clay apparently felt compelled to explain his present support for the new bank and his seemingly contradictory actions in the Senate in 1811, when he voted against the renewal of the BUS. He had been instructed by his constituents to oppose rechartering the BUS in 1811. Also, constitutional questions influenced him. A bank did not seem necessary then, but now one did. Suspension of specie payments had shaken the confidence of the public. The fluctuating value of paper around the country meant that taxes were no longer uniform, and a national bank was necessary as a counterpoise to state banks.[71]

The House accepted Wright's amendment to strike the clause making the charter forfeitable in case of non-payment of specie, leaving only a penalty of ten percent on their notes if not paid. Randolph's effort to raise the penalty to twenty percent failed. Webster's motion to designate "state courts" in the clause that the bank may sue and be sued "in all courts whatsoever," met objections that Congress did not have power to grant jurisdiction to state courts, but it was accepted also.[72]

One interesting motion, in view of developments in the next session, was a proposal by Bolling Hall from Georgia to apply the bonus to internal improvements. Calhoun approved the object but feared this amendment might drive away some supporters. Hall thought it might gain some support. Thomas P. Grosvenor of New York hoped a majority of Congress would be friendly to internal improvements in a separate bill, but he opposed attaching it to this bill. Hall's motion was rejected by a considerable majority.[73]

Also interesting, considering later developments in the 1830s during Andrew Jackson's presidency, was a motion by Lewis Condict of New Jersey to substitute New York City for Philadelphia as the location of the BUS. Calhoun opposed the motion, but it was approved by Robertson and Oliver C. Comstock of New York. Wright supported the motion, but he urged the claims of Baltimore and Washington. The vote on the transfer to New York, surprisingly, passed, 70–64. The following day, March 13, however, a motion to reconsider passed, 81–65, and the House then struck New York and inserted Philadelphia.[74]

Throughout the debate there was great sensitivity to the constitutional question. When Kentucky's Alney McLean moved to prohibit the establishment of branches in any state without their permission, he raised not only the question of a state's ability to protect its investment in state banks, but the constitutionality of the BUS as well. Calhoun expressed a wish to avoid this subject, and McLean's motion was defeated.[75]

Old details were raised again, particularly by Federalists seeking to derail the bill. Timothy Pitkin of Connecticut proposed to strike the appointment of five directors by the president and Senate, which lost, 91–54. Pitkin then tried and failed, without debate, to reduce the capital of the BUS from $35 million to $20 million. Charles Goldsborough from Maryland moved that if the government sold its stock, it should cease to have the right to appoint directors, which also failed. Finally, the House rejected Webster's proposal to increase the value of the shares to $400 and diminish the number to 87,500.[76] On March 14, the bill was read for a third time and passed, 80–71. Most of the opposition was Federalist (38), but thirty-one Republicans and two no-party members, Randolph and Stanford, joined them.[77]

The House bill was sent on to the Senate, where debate began on March 25. Jeremiah Mason of New Hampshire and Rufus King complained that the amount of specie to be raised in the initial subscription was too small. William W. Bibb of Georgia objected that any amendment "would certainly endanger or defeat its passage, and that upon its fate depended, more than any other measure to which the attention of Congress could be drawn at this moment, the welfare and prosperity of the country." The regulation of the currency at that moment, he argued, had been "wrested from the hands of the Government by petty corporations and swindling individuals," and the BUS was the correct way to deal with the problem.[78]

Bibb was supported by James Barbour of Virginia, who agreed that the BUS was necessary to correct the evils of the mass of paper in circulation. Mason countered that if it was the opinion of the Senate that it would be dangerous to amend the bill, it would be better to save the labor and decide the question at once.[79] Nevertheless, a few minor amendments were adopted. A hostile motion by Mason that would have allowed Congress to repeal the act and abolish the bank if it suspended or refused specie payment for its notes was defeated, 17–14, which confirmed the Senate's majority sentiment in favor of the BUS.[80]

The Senate raised many of the same issues discussed in the House. For example, a move to strike the appointment of five directors by the president and Senate was defeated, as was an attempt to reduce the number of government directors proportionately if it sold its stock, as well as an amendment to require government directors to hold a minimum of $10,000 stock in the BUS.[81] Finally, Delaware's William H. Wells's motion to postpone consideration until the first Monday of December (effectively to defeat) was soundly defeated, 29–6.[82]

Further efforts to amend the bill brought similar rebuffs. However, a motion by David Daggett of Connecticut to authorize Congress to establish a committee to examine the books of the BUS and bring suit if it believed the charter was violated was adopted, 27–6, with only hard-core pro-bank supporters demurring. After all amendments were approved, the bill was read a third time on April 3, passed, 22–12, and sent back to the House.[83]

The next day, Calhoun noted the Senate amendments were not important, and he hoped that they could be dealt with all together.

Randolph objected to the haste and got the House to agree to postpone consideration until the following day. When the BUS was taken up on the fifth, opponents of the BUS resorted to delaying tactics. Motions to postpone one week and an indefinite postponement were beaten back. Randolph, calling the BUS unconstitutional, inexpedient, and dangerous, declared this bill and the tariff would make the present session be looked back upon as "the most disastrous since the commencement of the Republic." Calhoun, trying to avoid a debate over the constitutionality of the BUS, argued that it was unnecessary to go into this subject; the present task was to consider the Senate amendments.[84]

Thomas P. Grosvenor argued that the bill was not passed improperly. He noted that 200 state institutions had put great pressure on members. It required "something more than common firmness, it required boldness to urge the bill," he said. If the bill did not pass now, it never would. The constitutional question had been "long since put to sleep by the repeated decisions of all the proper authorities, after mature reflection, and ought never again to be revived."[85]

Randolph declared that if the bill passed he would buy the stock, because it would create a great privileged order, and he would rather be a master than a slave. If he must have a master, he would prefer "one with epaulets, something that he could fear and respect, something that he could look up to, but not a master with a quill behind his ear."[86] Others added their protest against the BUS. Interestingly, many Federalists explained their vote for the bill, among them Grosvenor, Wright, and John W. Hulbert of Massachusetts, who stated that he would not part with friends unless they cast him off, but he "would prefer parting with friends to parting with his conscience." Finally, the House concurred in the Senate amendments, and President Madison signed the bill into law on April 10.[87]

There was still another matter to be dealt with, and Calhoun brought in a bill on April 6 to require banks to resume specie payments on December 31. The government would not deposit any money in banks that did not redeem their currency in specie. Punitive provisions were later withdrawn by Calhoun, no doubt to speed the measure to passage. In the committee of the whole, however, objections were raised about the timing of specie resumption. Henry St. George Tucker noted that only absolute necessity induced Congress to establish the BUS, now it remained to be seen whether Congress would give the BUS powers to be effective. He argued the government had a right to dictate the medium which it would be paid. Banks, from self-interest, opposed resumption. They formed "a colossal power which it was difficult to resist," but he added, "the longer we delay, the more seriously is that influence to be apprehended."[88]

Motions were made to delay resumption to March 1, 1817 and then to February 1, 1817. It was argued that undue haste could harm the whole business community. Others asserted that banks were making large profits and were certainly capable of resuming specie payments. Further delay would only bring down the full weight of banking influence on Congress in the next session.[89] These motions were rejected, but supporters of the bill revived efforts to add punitive provisions. Although the bill escaped from the committee of the whole unamended, Calhoun felt compelled to add a proposal to authorize an issue of Treasury notes (he intimated he would ask for $15 million) to meet the possible deficiency of circulating medium that might be created when banks called in their notes. The bill was then referred back to the committee of the whole.[90]

Calhoun's motion to fill the blank with $15 million, was rejected, 59–55, as was a motion by Thomas Newton to fill it with $13 million. Finally, Tucker's proposal of $10 million carried (ayes 66).[91] On April 24, on the House floor, Calhoun withdrew the Treasury notes amendment. Other amendments designed to defeat the bill were rejected by substantial margins.[92]

When the bill was read for a third time the next day, Wright accused Congress of wreaking vengeance on friendly banks that saved the credit of the nation during the war. Now they were to be "sacrificed on the altar of ingratitude." He was joined in opposition by Root, Randolph, and Gaston, while Telfair, Grosvenor, Robertson, and Webster supported the bill. The bill was rejected 60–59.[93]

The defeat of the bill reflected that several supporters were absent when the vote was taken, rather than a rejection of the principle of specie resumption. The next day, Webster offered a joint resolution that would require the secretary of the treasury not to accept any medium (bank notes, Treasury notes, or notes of the

BUS) not redeemable in specie as payment after February 1, 1817. Webster noted the unfairness of the situation where paper money fluctuated so much in value, and some sections of the country paid much more in value than others. Taxes ought to be equal, and the government should not accept paper of varied and uncertain value. "If it cannot collect its revenues in a better manner than this," he concluded, "it must cease to be a Government."[94]

Webster's resolution sparked a lengthy and warm debate. Samuel Smith's motion to strike February 1, 1817, and insert March 1, 1817, was barely defeated, 53–52, but the House accepted Timothy Pitkin's motion to set the date at February 20, 1817. Other attempts to amend the resolution were rejected. By a 71–34 vote, the resolution was read a third time and passed. The House approved amendments made by the Senate on April 30, and passed the resolution, 68–23.[95]

Banks, particularly in the Middle States, were reluctant to resume specie payments because they would be forced to contract their notes in circulation. Treasury Secretary Dallas issued a warning to these banks in July 1816 that the Treasury would comply with the resolution of Congress to collect only specie or its equivalent after February 20, 1817.[96] A convention representing banks of the Middle States was held in Philadelphia on August 6, 1816, to discuss the situation and their response. They declared they needed more time to comply, and in any event, they could not attempt resumption until the BUS was in operation. A formal resolution was adopted that the banks should resume specie payments on the first Monday of July 1817.[97]

Secretary Dallas, exasperated with the banks, did not wish to do them a favor, even if the request was not unreasonable. In fact, a contraction of paper had already begun, and Dallas had the power to enforce his warning. He issued instructions to hasten the opening of the BUS to January 1, 1817. In fact, the bank subscription was filled in August, and a board of directors was chosen in October. Dallas renewed his warning in September that he intended to comply with the congressional resolution after February 20, 1817. In November, former Secretary of the Navy William Jones was elected President of the BUS, and the bank began operations in January 1817.[98]

Once the BUS was established, there was an effort in the House to investigate whether the directors had complied with the charter by not meeting the specie requirement of the second installment. The question was whether the BUS could receive its own notes for the second installment. Calhoun stated that the specie capital was not expected to exceed the amount of the first installment. It was brought out that the directors had sent to Europe to obtain a large supply of gold and silver to insure payment of specie. Eventually, due to the end of the session, the inquiry was indefinitely postponed.[99]

The banks from the Middle States held another convention on February 1, 1817, and they basically surrendered to Secretary Dallas. The currency opened at par on February 20, 1817, and the BUS had fulfilled the most sanguine views of its supporters. Even before the opening of the BUS, citizens in Lexington, Kentucky, were already petitioning the directors of the BUS to establish a branch of the bank in their town. Moreover, many state laws enforced compliance with specie resumption by levying fines on any bank that failed to redeem its notes in specie.[100]

Despite skeptics who said that it could not be done, Congress had confronted a serious currency crisis and had taken appropriate action to bring the currency back under the control of the federal government. Unfortunately, the BUS made some early missteps that contributed to an economic downturn known as the Panic of 1819, which aroused anger and distrust of the BUS in the West.[101] Congress had also established the revenue on a sound footing. Also, while taxes were reduced somewhat, Congress was mindful of the debt and had set up a sinking fund plan to retire the debt, which actually occurred in 1836. Finally, a tentative step had been taken to protect American manufacturing, but this action was only the beginning of a century long debate on the wisdom of such a policy. Despite the significant achievements of the Fourteenth Congress to safeguard and even improve the financial condition of the country, however, this Congress gained even greater notoriety by their ill-fated attempt to improve their own financial situation with the Compensation Act of 1816.

Chapter 5

Compensation Act
of 1816

One of the most neglected aspects of early American political history is the transition from the deferential politics of the first party system to the popular politics of the second party system.[1] We know that the second party system began to take form sometime after the War of 1812 and before the election of Andrew Jackson, and that it was characterized by being more democratic than deferential in orientation, but historical treatments have lacked precision as to when this shift occurred. William Nisbet Chambers, for example, wrote that the first party system fell into decline, and "sometime around 1817 or 1819, it was no more." Richard P. McCormick stated vaguely the first party system "deteriorated after 1815, and in a loose sense came to an end in 1824." Walter Dean Burnham arbitrarily set the end of the first party system as 1820, and Ronald P. Formisano simply concluded, "the matter of timing remains as a source of confusion."[2]

A little noticed event, however, greatly accelerated the shift from deferential to popular politics—the Compensation Act of 1816. Widespread public outrage resulted in the ouster of an unprecedented number of incumbents in the congressional elections of 1816 and gave dramatic evidence of declining deference to public officials. The public reaction forced Congress to beat a humiliating retreat and repeal the law in the second session of the Fourteenth Congress. In doing so, however, they engaged in one of the most remarkable debates in the history of Congress. At issue, literally, was the question of *vox populi, vox Dei*—whether the voice of the people is the voice of God. It involved an intense discussion of the right of instruction and the nature of a representative of the people. Clearly, politicians learned from this that a new era was dawning, that those who would survive politically must pay keen attention to popular sentiment.

The democratization of American politics began almost as soon as political parties first formed. Both the Federalist and Republican parties shared fundamentally the same precepts of Lockean liberalism, but with one important difference. "The Jeffersonians," as Lynn Marshall observed, "envisioned a locally established intellectual elite handing down great humane theories from on high, a conception that differed from the Hamiltonian only in the assumption that the theories would, if worthy, necessarily receive ratification from an enlightened populace." This is a crucial distinction. As William Nisbet Chambers noted, "the Republican outlook developed in terms of leaders not only acting on their following but also interacting with it."[3]

Reliance upon appeals to the people became a force that could not be denied. David Hackett Fischer has shown that many young Federalists sought to imitate the successful tactics of the Jeffersonians by assuming stances popular with the people. The change in American society between 1800 and 1816, he observed, was a movement "from deference to political democracy, but most of all from open to covert elitism."[4] The transition to a broader participatory politics was slow, perhaps even imperceptible to some politicians, but it was undeniably occurring.

Many factors were involved in that change, such as a liberalized franchise, a diffusion of the political base through the physical growth of the country, improved transportation and communications, and changing concepts of party. As Michael Wallace noted, individuals of lower status or no connections could aspire to power and influence through the party organization.[5] With the steady decline of deference, with an increasingly egalitarian political system, and with no established center for court politics, the one constant for ambitious individuals or interest groups was an appeal to the electorate for support. As Chambers observed, where conditions produced "regular patterns of mass participation which must be reckoned with in the distribution of power . . . means to power will be sought by politically active elements through mobilization of mass public opinion or a mass electorate."[6]

Within this framework of development from deferential to democratic politics, the popular response to the Compensation Act constituted an important milestone. Having been told repeatedly that they were the ultimate repository of power, the public was confronted by an issue that energized them. While the issue may seem trivial (and perhaps was), it transcended partisanship and enlisted broad participation. In a sense, the popular response was a new phenomenon in American politics that created its own inner dynamic. Once the force of public opinion was displayed, it took on a new meaning. It may even be said that American politics was never the same again.

The Compensation Act arose out of a perceived need to raise the pay of Congress. For years congressmen had complained that their $6 per diem was inadequate. Their pay had not changed since 1789, while the cost of living was estimated to have doubled. Modern studies suggest that there was some truth to that perception. One study indicates that the consumer price index, which was 108.9 in 1789, spiked to 211 in 1814 and was still 185 in 1815.[7] While prices gradually declined (the consumer price index was 169 for 1816), congressmen also complained that they were further victimized by receiving their pay in depreciated currency worth only 75 percent of par. In early 1815, a House resolution to inquire into the expediency of raising Congress's pay was defeated overwhelmingly (99 to 8) on grounds that it was inappropriate in wartime.[8]

No such impediment appeared before Congress in 1816. Timothy Pickering asserted the people could afford to pay their congressmen. The nation's population had doubled since 1789, wealth had tripled, and the cost of living had increased greatly. Hezekiah Niles, editor of the influential *Niles' Weekly Register*, endorsed the need for a congressional pay raise in January 1816, and he asserted that fifty percent "would hardly be equivalent to the increased expenses." Joseph Gales in the *Daily National Intelligencer*, agreed. He estimated that money in 1789 "was worth at least fifty per cent. perhaps an hundred per cent. *more* than it now is." The *Baltimore American* also endorsed a pay raise.[9] Richard M. Johnson, a popular representative from Kentucky and a war hero, apparently agreed to bring into the public arena a subject which, according to one congressman, had long been "the daily topic of conversation at the fireside, and in every circle." On March 4, 1816, he suggested a salary in lieu of the per diem should be established: "nothing extravagant, nothing prodigal," perhaps comparable to the pay of a clerk in the executive branch. He claimed that efficiency would improve; congressmen would attend more punctually and sessions would be shorter.[10] After cursory debate, the resolution passed without opposition. On March 7 a committee headed by Johnson recommended a salary of $1,500 per year which, Johnson submitted, was less than the salary of twenty-eight government clerks.[11]

John Randolph, the erratic and eccentric Virginian, supported the measure, but he moved to suspend its operation until the next Congress. Speaker Clay and the old Federalist Timothy Pickering insisted the new system should take immediate effect. It was suggested that Randolph's provision would not remove the Senate from the same objection and the House would be accused of "false delicacy." Randolph withdrew his motion, but it was renewed by Richard Stanford and "negatived by a large majority."[12] This action, it later developed, was a fatal mistake.

Benjamin Huger, a Federalist from South Carolina, opposed the bill. Acknowledging that he was independently wealthy, he charged in the committee of the whole that the salary feature was a scheme to "render the thing palatable, and make it go down with the people." While the committee estimated the salary amounted to a new daily average of between $9 and $10, Huger insisted it came to between $14 and $17. Commenting upon Randolph's observation that congressmen were paid no more than day laborers, less than $1 per hour (in fact, it was more like $1 per day for common laborers and $2 for skilled workers), Huger noted that congressmen were in fact "day laborers," and he added that he remembered when economy, frugality, and simplicity were as much the cry and watchword as "dignity, and living like gentlemen." He conceded, however, that money had depreciated and living costs were higher.[13]

Huger's remarks obviously touched some sensitive nerves. Randolph suggested that Huger's arguments were better calculated for the "*stump*, than for this Committee," and he predicted the people would sustain the majority. Pickering stated that he "had never in his life taken time to think whether an act would make him popular or otherwise, and he should disregard such a consideration on this occasion." Robert Wright agreed. He argued that congressmen could not live in the style of gentlemen. He noted that Richard M. Johnson even had to sell his horse and servant to make accounts. He then added comments that would haunt him later: that in the old days Maryland delegates "lived like gentlemen, and enjoyed a glass of generous wine, which cannot be afforded at this time for the present compensation."[14]

Efforts to trim the salary figure to $1,100 and $1,000 were defeated easily. Supporters of the bill, such as Thomas P. Grosvenor, a Federalist, argued that it was never intended that congressmen should "come here to live on hominy and molasses in hovels." There should be enough compensation to enable the poorest man to come to Congress; otherwise it was anti-republican and would bring only the wealthy to Congress. John C. Calhoun agreed, and he expressed his preference, as had Randolph, for a salary of $2,500.[15]

In a mere four days, Johnson's proposal went to committee, through three readings, and was passed by a vote of 81 to 67. The close vote revealed only that many congressmen, certain the bill would pass, and perhaps facing tough reelection battles or lacking the courage of their convictions, chose the safe side. In the committee of the whole, only about twenty opposed the measure. In the Senate, several members worried about the retrospective feature of the bill, but others noted the need for a pay raise and argued that they should follow the lead of the House, which as the purse holders of the nation was considered more immediately responsible to the people. With even greater haste, the Senate speeded the bill to passage in three days on March 14 by a vote of 21 to 11. The vote was not sectional. In the House, the Middle Atlantic and South opposed the bill; New England and the West voted for it. Dividing along the Mason-Dixon Line and the Ohio River, the North was 49–35 in favor, and the South split 32–32. In the Senate, the North was 9–8 in favor, and the South favored it 12–3.[16]

Undoubtedly, most members of Congress acted out of pure motives. Congressman John W. Taylor of New York, for example, wrote to his wife that he and other congressmen would now be able to bring their families with them to Washington. "My objection to political employment," he stated, "has been owing chiefly to the absence it required from all the endearments of domestic life. . . . The hope of not being again necessitated to endure so long a banishment from your arms enables me with more fortitude to bear present inconveniences."[17]

President Madison signed the bill into law on March 19, and congressmen received $1,500 for the first session and began to draw salary for the second session. A debate arose, however, over the manner of drawing compensation. The act referred to "annual" salary of $1500 in the manner heretofore used. William Lowndes, in accordance with his understanding and a ruling from the attorney-general, moved a sum to cover up to March 4, 1816. Clay disputed that interpretation and moved a sum to cover through the calendar year, arguing the public interest would be unaffected. Clay's interpretation was upheld. The House did show a sensitivity to public opinion when it accepted Richard M. Johnson's motion to deduct from the salary an amount for member absences.[18]

There is a suggestion that members of Congress expected some public reaction, which was revealed in other debates. During the discussion of the Post Office bill in early April, there was opposition to a Senate amendment limiting the franking privilege. John Randolph alluded to the clamor against the Compensation Act, and stated he "could not agree to the practice of stripping the members of Congress of a necessary privilege, like so many livery servants." Daniel Webster argued that if it was proper during the session, it was equally proper during the recess. However, when the vote was taken, a strong majority (apparently mindful of public opinion) voted to accept the Senate amendment, 80–51.[19]

There is little reason to believe that members of Congress expected the hysterical reaction that followed. Public outrage was first awakened by partisan newspaper editors. William Coleman, editor of the staunchly Federalist *New York Evening Post*, immediately attacked the salary law, calling it a Republican Party measure. Pickering cautioned Coleman that two-thirds of the Federalists had supported the bill. Coleman admitted that the compensation of Congress was inadequate, but he recalled how Republicans had used the issue of economy against President John Adams. "Is it not permitted to us," he asked, "to fight our enemy with his own weapons?" He asserted, in a gross misapprehension of the force he was unleashing, that the people would blame the majority and would never inquire how a particular Federalist voted.[20]

The Republican newspapers, however, cited the fact that a higher percentage of Federalists voted for the salary law than Republicans.[21] Only the administration organ in Washington, the *Daily National Intelligencer*, generally approved the Compensation Act. On the issue of how much congressmen had actually increased their pay, editor Joseph Gales published a letter from "A Private Citizen" who calculated, using the average length of all sessions of Congress from the beginning to that time, that the new daily average compensation was $9.37.[22] Others, however, maliciously using Republican arguments that the law would shorten the sessions of Congress, concluded the new daily average would amount to fifteen, or even seventeen dollars. The general consensus of the editors and other spokesmen was that Congress had doubled its pay, to about twelve dollars per day.

Public indignation, fanned by the press, was aroused to such heights that according to contemporaries it was without precedent in the history of the early republic. The phenomenon, moreover, transcended partisanship. Richard M. Johnson said in the aftermath that "the poor compensation bill excited more discontent than the alien or sedition laws, the *quasi* war with France, the internal taxes of 1798, the embargo, the late war with Great Britain, the Treaty of Ghent, or any one measure of the Government, from its existence." Ex-President Thomas Jefferson observed that "there has never been an instant before of so unanimous an opinion of the people, and that through every State in the Union." He predicted "almost the entire mass [of congressmen] will go out, not only those who supported the law or voted for it, or skulked from the vote, but those who voted against it or opposed it actively, if they took the money; and," he added, "the examples of refusals to take it were very few."[23]

Opposition to the law was manifested in many ways. Public meetings, invariably attended by "several hundreds of persons of both political parties," were held in all parts of the country to denounce the salary law. They adopted indignant resolutions, usually between a half-dozen and a dozen, which were forwarded to newspapers requesting that they be printed. The available lists of members of the committees that drafted these resolutions do not confirm congressional allegations that they were staffed by interested politicians.[24] These resolutions virtually exhausted the arsenal of arguments against the act and undoubtedly taxed the ingenuity of the resolution writers and their store of adjectives to avoid redundancy.

One protest, for example, assailed the salary law as "high-handed and arbitrary," "a wanton sacrifice of *our* interest to their own private emolument," "wrong and unjustifiable," "reprehensible," and "criminal." Another set of resolutions characterized the law as "a daring and profligate trespass against . . . the *morals* of the *Republic*," "wanton extravagance," "dangerous," and "pernicious."[25]

The law was denounced in presentments of grand juries, and members of Congress were burned in effigy in Georgia. Several state legislatures specifically condemned the salary law and instructed their representatives to work to repeal the law. The New Hampshire legislature even reduced the salaries of its principal officers. Finally, at Fourth of July celebrations, the young republic's favorite holiday, usually given over to celebrating the virtues of the nation, this year was partially reserved to condemn the odious salary law.[26]

The resolutions indicate the nearly hysterical reaction of the people had its foundation in fears that the Compensation Law was antithetical to republican virtue and would open the door to corruption in the nation's legislature and crowd the House of Representatives with venal, corrupt, and mercenary individuals.[27] It was argued that $6 per diem was a liberal allowance and $1,500 was a wanton extravagance; the law ignored the high taxes imposed upon the people and the high national debt; and that others were more deserving, particularly the disbanded soldiers of the late war.[28] Americans were also warned repeatedly that if these corrupt and extravagant ways were continued, the United States would follow the example of Rome, "and like her sigh over the extinguished embers of republican simplicity and republican manners."[29]

Undoubtedly, this event also contributed to the declining prestige of public figures. There was a strong undercurrent in the protests of a sentiment that Richard Hofstadter called "The Decline of the Gentleman."[30] Public opinion would not accept the premise (as it was given to them) that common decency required a higher style of living for public men financed by the people's money. Such distinctions between public men and the private man did not have the right sound to a people who were learning to see dignity as a function of humanity, and not of privilege. Admittedly, the people responded to untruths, half-truths, and blatant appeals to their prejudices, but they acted from deeply and sincerely felt motives.

There was virtually no support for the Compensation Law. One rare exception was "Yankee," who warned in the Ballston Spa (NY) *Independent American* that if Congress received no pay, then only the rich would go to Congress. Needy men, he noted, would be paid in favors from the government and sell their independence. He cited the British Parliament where places were sold, and where members were not paid. "Take care brother Jonathan," he warned, "false economy is very dear to your purse, and very dangerous to your liberties; it is your *national weakness.*"[31]

Joseph Gales of the *Daily National Intelligencer* was the only editor to give the salary law even lukewarm support. The act, he noted, was "sustained by strong arguments."[32] What amazed Gales, and many others, was the almost total preoccupation of the public with this topic, while virtually ignoring other seemingly more important issues. Gales noted in the early summer of 1816 that he sampled the views of some three to four hundred editors with whom he exchanged papers, and the Compensation Law was "the *leading* topic of discussion." Other ostensibly controversial and more important measures passed by the same Congress, such as the Second Bank of the United States and the protective tariff, he observed, "pass almost without remark of approval or disapproval." Even the presidential election, he added, "calls forth few pens."[33]

Others were equally mystified by the depth of the popular response. The editor of the Philadelphia *True American* marveled that the people had been "thrown into convulsions" by the Compensation Act, "when others of infinitely deeper moment, of far more disastrous influence, pass unregarded."[34] Along these same lines, John Randolph asked his fellow congressmen when they reconvened in the fall, who would have believed that the American people, who had borne the privations and losses of the War of 1812, a swollen national debt, saw the presidential election taken out of their hands by the caucus, and borne quietly every other sort of abuse—that these same people, "the great Leviathan, which slept under all these grievances, should be roused into action by the Fifteen Hundred Dollar Law?"[35]

What was unique about this public reaction was not only the depth of the feelings but also the breadth of participation, which became a hallmark of popular politics in the years to come. Gales gave an indication of this when he noted that the Compensation Law had "not only pointed the pens of some of our ablest writers, but has inspired those with eloquence who never spake before."[36] Similarly, Congressman Oliver C. Comstock of New York noted the salary law aroused not only those habitually involved in politics "but also many who had seldom if ever been seen before on the political theatre."[37]

As Jefferson predicted, the wrath of the people fell on both Federalists and Republicans and upon all congressmen regardless of how they voted, on the supposition that "the receiver is as bad as the thief."[38] In New England, the Republican legislature of New Hampshire and the Federalist legislatures of Rhode Island and Massachusetts instructed their representatives and senators to work for repeal. Daniel Webster, then a representative from New Hampshire, declined renomination, but he took a bitter swipe at the Federalist legislatures, particularly of Massachusetts, which showed no appreciation for the labors of their Federalist members, "who came here to be kicked and stoned and abused," in her behalf. "No respect for talents, services, character, or *feelings*," he added, "restrained her from joining with the lowest democracy in its loudest cry." He concluded disgustedly, "I pity the *mass*, who meaning right, have not knowledge enough to know what right is—the rest I despise."[39] Timothy Pickering, fearing defeat, declined to run rather than defer to popular sentiment. "In voting for the Compensation Law, as in every other act of my public life," he declared in a widely published letter, "I did not take time to consider whether it would be popular or unpopular; but simply whether the measure was right and just and calculated to promote the public good."[40]

In the Middle Atlantic states, three quarters of the New York representatives were not returned. In Pennsylvania there were many public gatherings and resolutions condemning the salary law. William Duane's Philadelphia *Aurora* led the way in attacking the act. In New Jersey, Congressman Lewis Condict said the law was not just "a two-edged sword, aimed at the throats of both friends and foes," but "a sort of triangular weapon. I have been dismissed for voting for the bill; one of my colleagues for voting against it, and another one for not voting at all on either side."[41] In Federalist Delaware, the two representatives who had voted for the law were not renominated, creating a bitter rift in the Federalist Party in that state.[42] One of them, Thomas Clayton, in a public letter, complained that he had been persuaded to sacrifice his lucrative law practice to run for Congress, and he was now rudely rejected by some of the very people who had persuaded him to make that sacrifice. He added, "I did vote for it, and I voted for it conscientiously, believing it to be right. . . . If you wish to engage men of talents in your service you must pay them."[43] In Maryland, the popular and powerful Samuel Smith, who voted for the law, won reelection only after declaring his intention to vote for repeal at the next session of Congress. Former Governor Robert Wright, whose comments in Congress that a pay raise was necessary to enable the members to live like gentlemen was quoted unceasingly by opponents of the law, was not renominated to embarrass the people of Maryland again.

Southerners also reacted strongly. In Virginia, many congressmen who had voted against the law were still obliged to promise their constituents that they would vote for repeal. John Randolph declined renomination because of his health, but the popular reaction against his vote for the act may have influenced his decision. In South Carolina, the reaction was strong enough that John C. Calhoun was challenged by three opponents. He was reelected, but Benjamin Huger, the heroic defender of the purse, was defeated by a Republican opponent in a largely Republican district. Five other South Carolina representatives who voted for the salary law were defeated. All six of the Georgia representatives voted against the measure, but only one survived. (Voting against the law was not enough. Representatives were expected to humble themselves, pledge to work to repeal the law, and even return the money they had taken.) Senator William Bibb, who voted for the law, came under such harsh attack that he wrote plaintively to his Georgia constituents "whether a single error should outweigh a whole life of zealous and faithful devotion to the public interests?"[44] His plea was unavailing, and he resigned on November 9, 1816. Georgia Congressman Richard H. Wilde was less apologetic. He refused to run, declaring that when it became necessary "to course through the country in pursuit of votes, to fawn and creep, and wriggle into favor, and to insure temporary caresses by deserving permanent contempt, he, for one, must be contented to forego them."[45]

In Kentucky, opposition threatened to tumble Henry Clay and Richard M. Johnson. Both were reelected after stiff battles. Johnson stated that every office-seeker, from constable to Congress, had to declare his opposition to the law.[46] Several of the representatives declined to run again. Benjamin Hardin explained he "could not have been elected without going the rounds, and begging pardon for what I do not consider to have been incorrect."[47] The reaction was strong in Ohio, Tennessee, and even the Indiana Territory, soon to be granted statehood, where the legislature instructed its delegate to work for repeal of the salary law. This prompted a New York representative to remark later, "this is not the first time we have heard of an infant making a great noise, before it was introduced to the other members of the family to which it belonged."[48]

Nearly two-thirds of the Fourteenth Congress, about twenty percentage points above the usual high turnover rate, were not returned to the Fifteenth Congress. Sixty-four percent of congressmen in the Fifteenth Congress were serving for the first time, compared to 48 percent in the Fourteenth Congress, and 47 percent in the Sixteenth Congress. Only fifteen of the eighty-one members (18.5 percent) who voted for the law were reelected, and thirty-one of sixty-seven (46 percent) who voted against the bill survived. By sections, only two of fourteen western congressmen who supported the bill were reelected; only four of twenty-seven from New England; six of twenty-two in the Middle Atlantic states; and three of eighteen from the South.[49] A very large number of incumbents, perhaps as many as half, declined to run or were not renominated to face the wrath of the voters.[50]

John McLean of Ohio was among those who did not run for reelection. Although he had been elected to the Ohio Supreme Court, he voted for the bill, as he stated in a published letter to a friend, because he believed it was "necessary to maintain the principles of representation in their purity."[51] Able young men of moderate means could not continue in public life "at a pecuniary sacrifice." No pay raise, he added, would cause the House of Representatives to fall, "sooner or later into the hands of the wealthy." Nevertheless, McLean concluded that if he were to vote again after the people had expressed their opinion on what they were willing to pay, he would gladly vote for repeal. He was also certain that those who had voted for the bill would be the first to recommend such a repeal.[52]

Election returns reported in the newspapers of that time are scant and not easily interpreted, at least to determine whether popular participation in meetings and other forms of protest were translated into an exceptional voter turnout. Such reports as there are appear to indicate that while the vote was large, it was not a record. The size of the vote would not necessarily be a decisive factor, however, for large turnouts are usually reflective of bitter partisan battles, and this election might be considered a protest vote.

Despite their efforts to turn the Compensation Law to their advantage, the Federalists suffered proportionally more than the Republicans. Only nine of their fifty-two representatives were returned, and their number dropped to thirty-five in the Fifteenth Congress. More importantly, the caliber of men lost in this election from both parties was never replaced. Historians have cited Federalist opposition to the War of 1812, capped by their role in the Hartford Convention, as the major reason for their decline, but clearly the Compensation Act of 1816 was also a factor. The Federalist *Columbian Centinel* in Boston acknowledged, "a number of members of Congress, as has been the case almost universally, had made themselves extremely unpopular in joining democracy in its most obnoxious proceeding—the Compensation bill."[53]

A chastened Congress assembled for the lame duck session of the Fourteenth Congress in December 1816. Many suggested reasons for the outburst of the people, but clearly they had no answers. Some congressmen attributed the public response to the malevolence of the press, or as Wright of Maryland phrased it, the "false clamors in circulation by the typographical gentry." Richard M. Johnson expressed an opinion that was reiterated by many of his colleagues, that the reaction arose from "the misrepresentation of designing men, and from a misunderstanding of it by the virtuous, the faithful, the honest, yeomanry of the country."[54] Party rivalry was also cited. Thomas P. Grosvenor lamented that the salary law had become "the very foot ball of the parties," and the "scapegoat of all political offences." Henry Clay thought the form of the pay increase, a salary, was the chief problem.[55]

Some offered the explanation that public opinion was affected by the lingering wartime taxes and hard times occasioned by a severe drought and exceptionally cold weather during the summer of 1816 which threatened crops and the ability of farmers to pay their taxes. Indeed, resolutions cited the "precarious times" and the "inauspicious season," and newspapers reported farms being sold for the non-payment of direct taxes to satisfy "Madison's tax gatherers."[56] In truth, however, as Lewis Williams of North Carolina pointed out, the burden upon the people was being reduced. The direct tax and other taxes had actually been lowered in the last session.[57] Also, the evidence indicates that the postwar years were generally prosperous.[58] Nevertheless, the appearance of hard times undoubtedly contributed to uncertainties and a general malaise. The congressional pay raise was very poorly timed.

Faced with the overwhelming demand for the repeal of the Compensation Act, Congress was forced to act. It became clear during the debate that a majority still believed the people were wrong. Ultimately, the question revolved around whether the people and legislatures could instruct their representatives to vote against their consciences. State instructions was an unsettled doctrine, but four states allowed the people to instruct their representatives in their original constitutions (North Carolina, Pennsylvania, Massachusetts, and Vermont). The right of instruction had been proposed as one of the original amendments in the First Congress, but it was rejected. Still, the question had arisen from time to time, for example, in the Virginia legislature in 1812 over the refusal of Senator Richard Brent to obey instructions from the legislature.[59]

Undoubtedly, as some congressmen pointed out, the idea of instructions came from the practice of legislatures under the Articles of Confederation when state delegates served at the pleasure of the legislatures and were regularly instructed on how to vote. The Constitution, however, made the representatives agents of the people, and even the senators, although elected by the state legislatures, were not recallable by the legislatures and presumably were also agents of the people. It was a matter of dispute, of course, how congressmen and senators were to determine the will of the people or be instructed by them. In 1816, not only was Congress instructed by state legislatures and by resolutions of citizen meetings, it was also alleged that the widespread public outcry against the Compensation Act constituted an implicit instruction to Congress to repeal the law.

Richard M. Johnson was again appointed to head a committee to recommend whether to repeal or modify the salary law. His committee report on December 18, 1816, reputedly written by Daniel Webster, was a ringing defense of the law but concluded by recommending repeal. The per diem and travel pay figures were left blank, however, to be filled by the committee of the whole.[60] The debate lasted for two weeks in January 1817 before a packed gallery.

At first, several congressmen paid obeisance to the will of the people. Richard M. Johnson was the first to raise the issue of instructions. He argued that "*vox populi, vox Dei* has its controlling influence," and he added that even if they should be "carried away by a momentary impulse . . . the presumption is, that the people are always right."[61] A fellow Kentuckian, Joseph Desha, who had been reelected after pledging to work for the repeal of the law, said that "to deny that the people have a right to instruct their agents, is striking at the very nature of our Government." Henry Clay joined his colleagues by also affirming that "instructions given by the people are obligatory on the Representatives."[62] Cyrus King noted that he, like others, had not been "solicitous as to the impression which that law might make on the public," and he and half the members of the House had felt the effects of that decision. Regardless of the merits of the law, it was odious to the people, and "Public wisdom, on some occasions, must condescend to give way to popular *excitement.*"[63]

John N. Hulbert, also a Massachusetts Federalist, disagreed. "Shall the senseless clamor which we have heard make us give up our opinion and oppose the dictates of our own consciences?" Robert Wright, once dubbed by John Randolph as "a Wright always wrong," declared that he was devoted to the people and would always bow "with submission to their will," but he doubted the clamors in the newspapers represented their will. He counseled his colleagues to postpone action until the next Congress when the will of the people would be correctly known.[64] It was also disputed who had the right to instruct representatives. Samuel S. Connor of Massachusetts declared he would obey the instructions of his constituents to vote for repeal of the salary law, but he would pay no attention to the instructions of his state legislators. His colleague from Massachusetts, Albion K. Parris, however, stated that he was under no instructions from his constituents, but he would accept the legislature's instructions.[65] Timothy Pickering stated emphatically to Massachusetts Governor John Brooks that he did not admit the right or propriety of legislatures to instruct the state's representatives in Congress. They would become "no more than attorneys," and he declared, "I would never be a representative on such a footing."[66]

Much of the debate revolved around the questions posed by Hulbert and Wright, namely whether a representative was bound to obey the will of his constituents in violation of his conscience, and whether the instructions truly represented the will of the people. On the former question, Calhoun made a dramatic impact when he rose on January 17, 1817, to decry the talk of instructions. "Have the people of this country snatched the power of deliberation from this body? . . . This doctrine of implied instructions, if I am not mistaken, is a new one, for the first time broached in this House; and, if I am not greatly deceived, not more new than dangerous." He added, "Are we bound in all cases to do what is popular?" He asked how that would differ from "the mere trimmer, the political weathercock?"[67]

Future president John Tyler of Virginia accused Calhoun of indulging in "theoretical speculations," and he asked how a representative could set his opinion at variance with the people he represented, for if he did, he was representing only himself. He deduced that "from the very meaning of the word representative, the obligation to obey instructions resulted." William Henry Harrison of Ohio, also a future president, declared that he was an agent of his constituents and was bound by a "moral obligation to execute their Will."[68]

Thomas P. Grosvenor denied, however, that the voice of the people could be determined in the toasts and harangues of the Fourth of July meetings, or the "indecent resolutions" which demagogues persuaded knots of partisans to adopt, or the "officious intermeddlings of State legislatures upon a subject with which they have no Constitutional concern." He warned Tyler not to mistake "the importunate clack of a few ephemeral noisy insects of his district, for the voice of the real tenants of the soil." He expressed his satisfaction at Calhoun's speech and declared, "to those who surrender their conscience, their judgment, and their independence, at the shrine of popular caprice and clamor, he shall finally hold the same relation, that the eagle in his towering flight holds to the groveling buzzard." Rather than sacrifice his judgment, reason, and conscience to the clamor of prejudice, ignorance, and deception, he would rather "be a dog, and bay at the moon."[69] Grosvenor's words carried conviction, but they were a death rattle of the old politics, and the frankness of his words would rarely be heard in Congress again.

The weight of opinion, if not the most solid arguments, was clearly in favor of instruction. Joseph Hopkinson of Pennsylvania sought to show near the end of the debate, however, that there was almost no difference between the two opposing doctrines. Even the most extreme advocates of instruction, such as Tyler, reserved the right of disobeying instructions if in their opinion the instructions violated the Constitution. The other side, in essence, agreed the people might instruct their representatives, but they reserved the right of judging for themselves whether to obey or not.[70] It was thus a matter of degree, no unimportant matter, but there the question rested.

Alney McLean of Kentucky groused after hearing the debate, "We are sent here to legislate and pass laws, not to discuss mere abstract principles."[71] Nevertheless, this remains one of the most remarkable debates in the history of Congress, when the very nature of representation was debated by one of the most outstanding group of men ever assembled in any Congress.[72]

In the debate, as McLean noted, the main object of repealing the law was secondary. Although it was readily agreed the law should be repealed, there was disagreement on whether a new per diem rate should be established. Richard M. Johnson proposed that repeal should be effective at the end of the session and the responsibility for fixing the per diem should be left to the next Congress, "four-fifths of whom were elected to regulate this matter."[73] John Randolph, however, believed that like the law, the repeal should be retrospective in operation. His motion was decidedly unpopular and was voted down, 101–61.[74]

After an effort to restore the $6 allowance was defeated (91–81), successive attempts were made to fill the blanks with $10, $9, and $8, all unsuccessfully. Finally, unable to agree, the House on January 23, 1817, by a vote of 138 to 27, merely repealed the law as of the end of the session and left the question of setting a compensation to a subsequent Congress. The bill passed the Senate on January 31, 1817, with almost no debate, 27–7.[75] Members of the Fifteenth Congress eventually established their compensation at $8 per day and $8 per 20 miles of travel.[76]

Afterwards, Federalist Senator Christopher Gore of Massachusetts wrote cynically to his colleague, Rufus King, that "both parties made it the occasion of catching a little popularity by addressing the mean passions of the mob."[77] The *Daily National Intelligencer*, however, believed the Representatives of the people had been taught "a lesson of accountability, which will not be soon forgotten."[78] The lesson apparently was that representatives were indeed "day laborers," hired by the people. As one historian aptly put it, "The old conception of the elected representative as a sort of quasi-magistrate, already unmercifully savaged by the democratic doctrines of the revolutionary and Jeffersonian eras, was finally put to rout by the idea that the representative was the servant of the people and owed humble obedience to them."[79]

No doubt the incident further eroded the respect and the deferential attitude many people still had for their representatives. The Compensation Act also undoubtedly tended to confirm fears that the politicians of the new generation were not worthy of their fathers, the revolutionary generation. Many of the protest resolutions found the congressmen not only unacceptably elitist but also accused them of intrigue and corruption. Whether the decline in the caliber of men in Congress was real or not, the prestige of Congress was undeniably declining. Egalitarian doctrines clearly were replacing the patrician style of politics. Many protest resolutions, for example, in a mean-spirited way typical of the new politics, suggested that congressmen were not worth more than six dollars per day. When Hezekiah Niles wrote in his *Niles' Weekly Register* in December 1817, that the compensation law was "objected to on account of its manner than for the amount," and that every reflecting man believed that the six dollars per diem "was insufficient to command the talents of any gentleman who had business of his own to attend to," he was met with an indignant letter to the editor which strongly disagreed and declared that six dollars was quite enough.[80]

The future belonged to those politicians who had learned the lesson of the Compensation Act and discerned the changing attitudes of the people toward their representatives. Erastus Root, a member of the Fourteenth Congress, candidly admitted he had learned the lesson. During salary debates in the New York constitutional convention in 1821, he declared, "I will admit that I vote for popularity," and he advised "members that are calculating on a reelection, will generally be cautious how they vote for higher wages, on account of their popularity."[81]

Ezekiel Bacon, a former Massachusetts congressman, expressed his disgust, however, at "that ball of popularity which was ever bandying about between the rival parties of the state, on the subject of salaries and compensations." He noted salaries and compensation had been "made the hobby horse of ambitious demagogues, and piddling politicians." When one party nominated a candidate, he said, they "took care to put in something about the wages of members; the other party equally cunning, and about equally sincere . . . were sure to bait their trap with the same catching topic." Although both candidates were pledged to lower salaries, "this was most generally the last of it, until another year, when the game was played over again."[82]

Bacon's comments vividly illustrated the legacy of the Compensation Act of 1816 and described how politicians applied the lessons learned in that affair. Many factors were subtly eroding the authority of the established politicians and preparing the way for the "reign of the common man," but no event was more symbolic of these changes than the Compensation Act of 1816, which taught the representatives of the nation the lesson of "*vox populi, vox Populi.*"

Even in the face of the controversy over the Compensation Act, the Fourteenth Congress still had work to do. In addition to the call for greater economic security through protective tariffs and a uniform currency, many also called for growth of the nation's transportation system in the form of internal improvements such as canals and roads.

Chapter 6

Internal Improvements

Just as the federal government was called upon in 1816 to foster and protect infant industries by their tariff policies, it was also urged to facilitate domestic trade and commerce through internal improvements. However, with the major exception of the Cumberland or National Road, the federal government, rather than initiating public works programs during these years, preferred to participate with private enterprise in various road and canal projects. State governments likewise encouraged private enterprises by granting charters, buying stock in canal or turnpike projects, or lobbying for federal support for state internal improvements. Frequently, the issue of state versus federal power was raised, particularly when improvement schemes reached beyond a single state. Rarely were road or canal projects narrowly confined to state boundaries; often they crossed several state lines. Beyond the local and state jealousies, the concern about federal participation was not just an economic consideration, it also aroused fears of federal consolidation or centralized control.

On the other hand, some saw internal improvements as countering the centralizing tendencies of the federal government. Roads and canals allowed people to spread across space and thus preserve liberty and the union. The Republican Party and its leaders, Jefferson and Madison, reflected this ambivalence about internal improvements. They generally favored systematic development under the auspices of the federal government, but they were constrained by their constitutional scruples to preserve state sovereignty and local autonomy. Alexander Hamilton did not develop a proposal for a national system of internal improvements, largely because he understood that Republican states' rights sentiments would oppose any such plan.[1]

Interestingly, as historian John Larson has noted, despite Republican hostility to centralized power, the federal government under Jefferson "took bolder steps toward a national system of internal improvements than Hamilton ever had dared."[2] In his sixth annual message to Congress in December 1806, Jefferson called for adding to "the constitutional enumeration of Federal powers" regarding internal improvements. Such projects, he added, would improve communication and dissolve the lines of separation between the states, as well as cementing the union "by new and indissoluble ties."[3] Jefferson's encouragement spawned a host of proposals before Congress petitioning for assistance to finance local projects. The need for a coherent plan was obvious, and it was filled by the famous report of Secretary of the Treasury Albert Gallatin in 1808. Among the things he called for were four connections: between the Atlantic seaboard and Western waters; canals connecting the Atlantic and the St. Lawrence River; canals from the north and south along the Atlantic coast; and interior feeder lines of roads and canals.[4]

Travel in 1816 was still very primitive. The quickest way was on horseback, although along the East coast there were some passable roads permitting stagecoach traffic between the major cities. From Philadelphia to New York City, for example, travel and expenses for the 100 mile trip by stage and steamboat took thirteen hours and cost $10. Steamboats ran regularly from New York City to Albany, a distance of about 160 miles, on a Monday, Wednesday, Friday, Saturday schedule, leaving Albany on those days at 9 a.m., and from New York at 5 p.m. The trip took about twenty-four hours and cost $7.[5] Travel over longer distances, such as from Washington to Boston, about 460 miles, took about a week over very indifferent roads. From Washington to New Orleans took nearly a month.[6] During the War of 1812, while the coast was under a blockade, the movement of troops and supplies was greatly impeded by bad roads. Americans were reminded that ancient Rome had better roads, and that such roads held their empire together. If the Americans expected to reach the greatness of the Romans, they too must invest in better roads.

In fact, the government had already embarked on the first federally planned and funded highway project, the Cumberland or National Road, to connect Cumberland, Maryland, at the head of navigation on the Potomac River, to the Ohio River at Wheeling, Virginia (now West Virginia). The need for such a road was long felt, particularly after the admission of Ohio in 1803. Congress passed an enabling act on March 29, 1806, and funding for surveys was provided in 1808. As an indication of the sensitivity of those along the path of the road, the entire congressional delegation from Pennsylvania sent a memorial to President Madison in December 1810 objecting to the proposed route. They noted that Pennsylvania gave its permission to run the road through their state in April 1807, but the commissioners had laid out a road that did not pass through Uniontown or Washington, two of the populous and wealthy towns in the western part of the state. The proposed route, they said, would have "ruinous" consequences particularly for Pittsburgh. The memorialists noted that the road would not have been laid out without Pennsylvania's permission, and its consent would never have been given "had the consequences that now threaten us have been foreseen and considered."[7]

Eventually, a compromise was worked out that ran the road through these two towns. Construction on the road, which connected with the Frederick Pike that ran from Baltimore, began in 1811. Progress, however, was slow due to the War of 1812, a shortage of labor, and indifferent funding from the federal government ($143,000 through 1812). Only about twenty-four miles were completed by 1813.[8]

By the end of 1815, approximately forty miles were built or nearing completion from Cumberland to the Big Youghiogheny River, and additional contracts had been let to continue the work over the next thirteen miles to Uniontown. David L. Shriver, Jr., the superintendent of the Cumberland Road, reported the progress on December 30, 1815. He complained particularly about the contract system, which resulted in varying quality of work done by the different contractors, and he recommended substituting day labor. Shriver also noted that $1200 had to be expended to repair the road already completed, and he complained of the frequent abuses, "such as throwing down the walls, digging down the banks, falling trees, dragging along it, locking up wagon wheels, placing fences within 66 feet, and many other improper acts."[9]

Secretary of the Treasury Dallas reported to Congress on March 1, 1816, that of the $387,000 appropriated for the road, there remained a balance to February 27, 1816, of about $101,000. He estimated an additional $300,000 would be needed to complete the project.[10] On March 23, based on the Dallas report, John G. Jackson of Virginia reported for his committee on internal improvements calling for additional appropriations of $300,000 to complete the Cumberland Road. Jackson was expansive in his justification, "If Congress persevere with becoming spirit in this great public work, we shall soon see one of the best roads in the world over the chains of mountains which separate the western from the Atlantic waters, and which, but a few years since, were supposed to present insurmountable obstacles to a safe and easy intercourse." He refuted the charge that it was not politic to encourage western migration, arguing that the people would go regardless of the condition of the roads. The advantages were many. It would bind the country together, raise land values, and lessen the necessity of keeping up a large military force.[11] During the debate on the Jackson proposal, Henry Clay declared that he had traveled on turnpikes in Europe, "but had never traveled on so fine a road as the thirty miles of the Cumberland turnpike which were finished."[12]

Construction continued rapidly after 1816. The road was pushed through Pennsylvania from Uniontown to Brownsville, on to Washington and West Alexandria, and then into Virginia, reaching Wheeling in 1818. Although no new technology or innovations in road engineering were introduced on the road, which ran for 130 miles, it was indeed a superhighway for the time. Measuring sixty-six feet across, with a crowned surface, and good drainage on each side, it had a stone base about a foot high, with successive layers of rock adding an additional twelve inches, making it essentially a good gravel road. The cost averaged more than $13,000 per mile, easily exceeding the original estimate of the commissioners of $6,000.[13] In time, other turnpikes were built as feeders to the National Road. There were, for example, several roads that connected with Pittsburgh and southern Pennsylvania and with Maryland turnpikes to Baltimore.[14]

Throughout its long life, the National Road never paid for itself. Tolls collected failed to finance the constant repairs necessitated by the deterioration of the road. Frequent appropriations from

Congress were required to keep the road in a passable state of repair. Nevertheless, the road met the objective of connecting the Atlantic seaboard with the Ohio River and beyond. Millions of people streamed into the West, and it provided a valuable trade connection between two sections of the union. Although perhaps unintended, the National Road had powerful ramifications for the future of the United States. As one historian wrote, "The National Road, in effect . . . divided North from South literally and figuratively, even as it connected East and West literally and figuratively."[15]

Even as the Cumberland Road was reaching towards the Ohio River, steamboats began to make their appearance on western waters. The first steamboat to operate on the Ohio and Mississippi Rivers was a Pittsburgh-built steamboat, *New Orleans*, which successfully descended to New Orleans in 1811 (surviving along the way the great earthquake while anchored near New Madrid, Missouri). Not until 1816, however, was a steamboat, *Enterprise*, able to make the return trip upstream to Pittsburgh. By 1817, seventeen steamboats were operating on western rivers. The first steamboat also began to operate on Lake Ontario in 1816, and shortly thereafter they were introduced on Lake Erie.[16] Steamboats also facilitated travel in the East, particularly between New York and Philadelphia and Baltimore, as well as from New York to Albany and to Boston. Fares were high due to the novelty of steamboats, although travel was, of course, easier and more rapid.[17]

The rapid expansion of transportation hastened the opening of the West, as well as providing connectors to facilitate commerce. Several projects were under consideration in 1816 in various states, not only to reach towards the West, but also to improve trade north and south. In addition, plans were being made to improve rivers and harbors. In some cases, these proposals were made in order to be competitive with other sections or cities along the east coast. For some states, the improvements in turnpikes, canals, and steamboats were viewed as a mixed blessing. Workers were being drained from the East and some regions east of the Appalachians were becoming depopulated.

Internal improvements were also seen as an antidote for this problem. For example, Archibald D. Murphey, on December 6, 1815, reported to the North Carolina Senate that an estimated 200,000 inhabitants had moved West from his state. The state's economy was "at a stand," and although the state had rich agricultural soil, it had done little to improve conditions. Internal improvements, he argued, were essential to prosperity, and it was the state government's duty "to aid the enterprise of its citizens," such as opening rivers, cutting canals, and building turnpike roads. Such improvements would eventually double the state's population and bring in increased revenue to enable the state to promote education and cultivate the arts and sciences. Moreover, internal improvements would foster the growth of commercial towns on the Roanoke, Neuse, and Cape Fear Rivers that might rival Philadelphia, Baltimore, or Charleston. Murphey's report, in fact, generated acts from the legislature to improve navigation on the Roanoke, as well as authorization for cutting a Cape Fear River canal.[18]

An even more impressive report by the Committee of Roads and Internal Navigation was presented to the Virginia House of Delegates on December 23, 1815. This committee report was generated in response to Governor Wilson Cary Nicholas's message to the legislature citing many needed internal improvements. Despite an abundance of natural resources, the report stated, Virginia allowed "the principle part of her commerce and almost the whole of her navigation [to] pass out of her hands to enrich the coffers of her neighbors." While other states were advancing in wealth and population, Virginia "remained stationary." In fact, the eastern region of the state had declined. "How many sad spectacles do her low lands present, of wasted and deserted fields! of dwellings abandoned by their proprietors! of Churches in ruins!" It was argued that Virginia, because of her geographical location, could play an important role in establishing commercial ties to the western country, thus serving not only its own interests but that of the union as well.

The crux of the report was the proposal to establish a Fund for Internal Improvements to foster private initiatives to make the principal rivers navigable and connect the market towns of the state, as well as the Eastern and Western waters, by public highways. Rather than public projects, the state would subscribe to forty percent of the company's stock. The rationale was that such projects would be more economically made by investors seeking private gain than by public officers or agents. Thus the incentive of profits would stimulate public improvements, while the government investment would check abuses to the public interest that might result. A Board of Public Works was proposed to supervise the fund.[19]

Although concerns were expressed in the Senate about the "just and equitable distribution and application of the fund," the bill was passed essentially as proposed by the committee, 11–10. Governor Nicholas signed the bill on February 5, 1816. Over the years, the fund provided for numerous projects that lasted down to the Civil War.[20] Numerous other bills were passed in this same session providing for the incorporation of turnpike companies, as well as measures for improving navigation on several of its rivers, and authorizing further support for the Dismal Swamp Canal Company.[21]

In other states, governors called upon their legislatures to look at internal improvements to benefit their states. For example, Governor David B. Mitchell's message to the Georgia legislature not only called for various projects but also the appointment of state officials to supervise such projects. Governor Simon Snyder of Pennsylvania likewise noted to his legislature in March 1816 the need for Pennsylvania, Maryland, Ohio, North Carolina, and Virginia to support inland navigation for the defense of the nation. He asserted that they should particularly support the Chesapeake and Delaware Canal. In his annual message on December 5, 1816, he also urged the legislature to consider subscribing to the stock of a canal company that would connect the Susquehanna River to Seneca Lake in New York.[22]

Governor Isaac Shelby opened another issue when he asked the Kentucky legislature to consider whether the state should lend its aid to the development of steam navigation or to leave it to private enterprise. The Ohio legislature further raised the pertinent question of who was authorized to use steam navigation on Western waters. A resolution was proposed to instruct their senators and representatives in Congress to inquire about this subject. It contended that citizens of Ohio and the Western country generally were being hurt due to conflicting claims as to the exclusive use of the invention. "Sundry individuals and companies threaten to prosecute those who construct or navigate steamboats without permits." Louisiana, they noted, had granted the Livingston and Fulton Company the exclusive privilege of navigating the waters in that state, and individuals procuring rights from other patentees were not only exposed to suits but were actually excluded from the important port of New Orleans. Ohio's representatives were asked to obtain a legal or judicial opinion on the conflicting claims to an exclusive use of the steamboats and whether recent improvements made by others entitled the discoverer to the benefit of a patent. They were also to enquire whether the Louisiana legislature had exceeded its constitutional power by enacting their law.[23] The Ohio Resolution foreshadowed the debate over exclusive rights on Western waterways that was not resolved until the Supreme Court decision against the Livingston-Fulton monopoly in Gibbons v. Ogden in 1824.

The general support for internal improvements found additional advocates in the national legislature. Senator Jeremiah Morrow of Ohio presented a report on February 6, 1816, for the Committee on Roads and Canals during the first session of the Fourteenth Congress setting forth a bold plan similar to Gallatin's earlier proposal. At this time there were not more than 100 miles of canals throughout the United States. Morrow's premise was that roads and canals would increase the wealth of the nation by stimulating industry and agriculture. Reduction in transportation charges would increase land values and benefit manufacturers by lowering the cost of raw materials. Moreover, it would "bind together the whole, with the strong bond of interest and affection, giving stability and perpetuity to the Union." He also mentioned the advantages for national defense, and that only the national government had the resources to execute major projects, while states could develop local works. Morrow neglected to mention that such projects would also benefit his section, the West, but his plan also offered benefits to other sections.

Morrow proposed five major projects: canals to open inland navigation on the Atlantic coast; a north-south turnpike; turnpikes connecting the Atlantic and Western waters; military roads communicating with the frontier posts; and a canal around the Falls of the Ohio at Louisville. First attention, he contended, should be given to the Chesapeake and Delaware Canal, "the central link in that great chain of inland navigation along the seacoast." Twice before this project had been brought before Congress, first in 1806, when a Senate committee report suggested a federal subscription to the stock of 2000 shares at $200 per share. The Senate bill was, however, postponed in the House. The second time was in June 1813, but again the project was postponed due to the war. The advantages of a canal were obvious. From the head of Chesapeake Bay by sea to Philadelphia was 500 miles versus a canal of twenty-one miles. Likewise, New York to Philadelphia via a canal would take twenty-four hours instead of about a week coastwise. From Trenton, New Jersey, to New York City, nearly 300 miles would be saved by a canal of twenty-seven miles. Following the inland canals from New York to Baltimore would shorten a trip usually taking a week to ten days to a little over two days. The committee recommended two bills: one to appropriate $600,000 annually to support various internal improvements projects and a second bill to subscribe to the Chesapeake and Delaware stock.[24]

Both bills, however, were eventually postponed indefinitely by a two to one margin. The debate was not recorded, but it appears the Senate could not agree on how the money would be expended. During the debate, Armistead T. Mason of Virginia dropped in an extraneous motion to instruct the Committee on Roads and Canals to inquire into the expediency of subscribing $50,000 to the Great Coastwise Canal and River Navigation Company to cut a canal from Norfolk through the eastern branch of the Elizabeth River to the channel of Currituck Sound. A week after the two bills were defeated, an understandably annoyed Morrow asked that the committee be discharged from further study of Mason's motion. Mason then introduced a resolution to require the secretaries of war and navy to report to the next session their opinion on subscribing to the stock of the Great Coastwise Canal, which was accepted.[25]

Despite the lack of interest by Congress, the views of the Senate committee were eventually carried out by others. For example, a committee was appointed in 1816 by the New Jersey legislature to survey a route for the Delaware and Raritan canal from New Brunswick to Trenton. A charter was granted in 1820, but work on the canal did not begin in earnest until 1830, and it was not opened until the summer of 1834 at a cost of about $3 million.[26] The Chesapeake and Delaware canal connecting the Delaware and Chesapeake Bays eventually received federal support ($450,000 in stock subscriptions), as well as smaller amounts from Pennsylvania, Maryland, and Delaware, and that project was completed in 1829.[27]

The greatest canal project of the era, to connect the Hudson

River and Lake Erie, also failed to gain federal support. Gouverneur Morris has been credited for first suggesting such a canal, but the idea got a particular boost from Jesse Hawley, writing under the name of "Hercules" in the *Genesee Messenger* in 1807 and 1808. Hawley's fourteen essays stimulated public support, and Gallatin's Report in 1808 further encouraged the idea of a canal through New York. In 1808, the New York Assembly authorized James Geddes to conduct a survey of a possible route. His report in 1809 showed the feasibility of a canal, but a delegation that visited President Jefferson received no encouragement for federal support, despite the Gallatin Report.[28]

The turning point, perhaps, came in 1810 when De Witt Clinton was enlisted in support of the canal. Clinton's influence in the state was great. He had served in many positions, including a United States senator and mayor of New York, and he even ran as a candidate for president in 1812. Such was his enthusiasm for the canal that it was often referred to as "Clinton's Big Ditch." With his support, the legislature created a canal commission in March 1810, which included Clinton, who became not only the leader of this group but also the most eloquent advocate of the canal, as well as other leading New York politicians such as Gouverneur Morris, Stephen Van Rensselaer, Simeon De Witt (Clinton's first cousin), William North, Thomas Eddy, and Peter B. Porter.[29]

A proposal for federal assistance, introduced into the United States House of Representatives in 1810 by Porter, received little support, and a similar bill was postponed without action in the Senate in March 1811. Some of the objections raised included constitutional concerns, but there was also evidence of sectionalism where politicians saw little or no benefit to their area of the country. Discouraged, the commissioners began to explore financing by the state, but the War of 1812 interrupted efforts to obtain a loan that had been authorized by the legislature. After the war, however, Clinton and other canal supporters were determined to make another great push. Clinton, in particular, had an additional motivation: that of repairing his tattered political reputation after his loss to President Madison in the 1812 election. Because of the strong Federalist support he received, he was disavowed by Republicans and stood as a man without a party. Undoubtedly, he saw his support of the canal as a way to regain public favor in New York. Although Clinton

De Witt Clinton, by John Wesley Jarvis. National Portrait Galley, Smithsonian Institution, Washington, D.C.

collaborated with the Federalists in support of the canal, this did not mean he was shifting his party allegiance. Nevertheless, many Federalists were involved in advocacy for the canal. The first canal commission, for example, included four Federalists and three Clintonians. Many Federalists were also large landholders in western New York and saw an opportunity to raise their land values, as well as a way to increase their favor with the people. Supporters of the canal resorted to several tactics to gain approval. They memorialized the legislature, held public meetings, and they collected over one hundred thousand signatures to send to the legislature.[30]

A mass meeting in New York City on December 30, 1815, adopted a memorial to the state legislature. In addition, a circular letter drafted by Clinton appealed for public support and asserted the canal was supported by the "enlightened and public spirited men . . . of the state." Signed by Clinton, Cadwallader D. Colden, John Swartwout, Thomas Eddy, and William Bayard, it asked for public assistance to distribute a memorial and for any other effort "best calculated to make a just and favorable impression on the Legislature."[31]

The memorial, written by Clinton, and signed by over 1700 prominent individuals, argued that inland navigation was as important as exterior navigation. It discussed the benefits of uniting the Western country with the Atlantic and argued that connecting Buffalo with New York City by water would make the latter "the great depot and warehouse of the western world." Clinton also addressed the controversy over the route. While all agreed on the route from the Hudson River to Rome, opinions differed whether it should run to Lake Ontario or Lake Erie. Clinton opted for the latter, citing the expense of cutting around the cataract of Niagara, as well as the possibility that the Lake Ontario route might "enrich the territory of a foreign power." He estimated the canal would cost $6 million and take ten to fifteen years to complete. Donations of 106,632 acres had already been subscribed, and he anticipated receipts from canal tolls "may be so great as, in a short time, to extinguish the debt." Other arguments included the benefits of the canal for national defense, stimulating the growth of the frontier, raising the value of land throughout the national domain, and cementing a common interest between the Eastern and Western sections of the country. In completing this project, he asserted, the

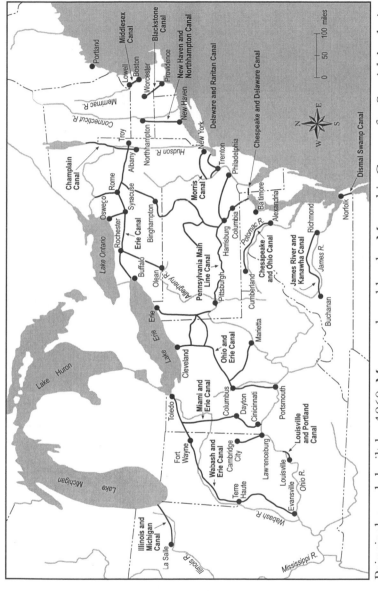

Principal canals built by 1860. Map produced by the Memphis Center for Spatial Analysis (MCASA), University of Memphis, Department of Earth Sciences (Geography).

legislature would "erect a work more stupendous, more magnificent, and more beneficial, than has hitherto been achieved by the human race."[32]

Clinton also wrote three letters as "Atticus" in support of the canal. In the first, he argued that no state in the union would be helped as much by a canal. He cited statistics to show the canal would reduce current shipping costs by nine-tenths as well as raising land values threefold. In the second, he asserted that New York City would become "one of the most splendid commercial cities on the face of the earth." The third letter argued the canal would capture most of the commerce of the West; otherwise, "it will infallibly pass to the city of Montreal."[33] Another pamphlet in 1816 by "A Friend to His Country," made the same point as Clinton. Completion of the canal, he wrote, would "secure the devotion of the western section of our state to the union, and its neglect may attach it to Canada."[34]

Governor Daniel D. Tompkins's message to the New York legislature at the end of January 1816, reflected his suspicions of the motivations of Clinton and the Federalists. He gave a tepid recommendation that they should consider a water communication between the Hudson River and the western lakes and Lake Champlain.[35] While memorials continued to pour into the legislature in favor of a canal, they also received a report on March 8 from the Canal Commissioners, written by the old Patroon, Stephen Van Rensselaer, the richest man in New York and the largest landlord in the country. He recommended engaging an engineer, preferably an American, to examine the ground and decide on the most expedient route. The report assured the legislature that a loan of one million dollars, and more later, could be obtained by the state at a rate at or under six percent, and it proposed that the middle section of the canal from Rome to the Seneca River be opened first to divert trade from passing down the Oswego River to Lake Ontario and on to Montreal. Also, no doubt for political reasons as well as economic, a canal was urged from Lake Champlain to the Hudson.[36]

On March 21, 1816, Solomon Van Rensselaer, cousin of Stephen Van Rensselaer, delivered a report from the joint committee of the Senate and Assembly. After considering "several thousand" petitions and memorials from around the state favoring the grand canal, reviewing plans and surveys of the route, the report of the canal commissioners, as well as advice from professionals, they believed canals from the Hudson River to Lake Erie and from the Hudson to Lake Champlain could be built at a moderate expense, at not more than $6 million for both. Building these canals, they argued, was entirely practicable and the means were at the disposal of the government to begin and continue these projects for several years. They also believed "the wisdom and patriotism of future legislatures, will foster and cherish the undertaking, and furnish such additional sources of revenue as may be sufficient to complete the said works."[37]

The report also proposed that a Board of Canal Commissioners supervise building the two canals, as well as a controversial recommendation to raise tax revenues from those areas which would most likely benefit from the canal. Revenue for the canal would be raised from taxes on salt produced in the western district of the state; on property along the canal; on bank stock; a portion of the auction fees of New York City; a moderate tax on official seals and on steamboat passengers; proceeds from land sales in the western part of the state; and certain sums to be raised by lotteries; all of which, combined with the proceeds from tolls on the canal, would be pledged to redeem the principle and interest on the money borrowed to build the canal.[38]

A bill was introduced on March 2 that laid out the proposed duties of the canal commission in some detail, such as hiring agents, surveyors, and engineers, with salaries the board thought proper. Also, the board would secure the rights to land (including using the process of imminent domain), and seek voluntary contributions from persons, as well as from states and the federal government. Further, $140,000 was authorized to compensate the Inland Navigation Company for their rights and property, and the board was empowered to borrow up to $250,000 per year for the first two years and $500,000 per year in the subsequent five years at six percent.[39]

The Assembly debated the bill during the first two weeks of April. There was strong opposition, and several efforts were made to delay the beginning of the canal. One opponent, Thomas J. Oakley of Dutchess County, successfully introduced a motion to levy taxes upon the lands and real estate adjacent to the canals extending out for twenty-five miles on each side of the canal.[40] No doubt the selectivity of the tax made it less popular among those who most favored the canal, but ironically the amendment made the canal less objectionable to those areas that did not expect to benefit from the canal. Their complaint had been that they would be paying taxes that would give an advantage to others.[41]

The Assembly also set the number of commissioners at thirteen, with eight year terms. The top two listed were De Witt Clinton and Stephen Van Rensselaer.[42] The bill was treated harshly in the Senate, however. It was brought out that the precise route had not been staked out by the Canal Commission. Following the lead of Martin Van Buren, who may have been as much influenced by his rivalry with Clinton as he was by the haste of the Assembly to build the canal, the Senate struck all of the sections authorizing a canal and left only the enabling provisions allowing surveying to establish a precise line. The number of canal commissioners was reduced to five. Clinton and Van Rensselaer were retained, while Joseph Ellicott, agent for the Holland Land Company, which had donated a little over 100,000 acres for the benefit of the canal, Myron Holley, a representative from Ontario County, and Samuel Young made up the remainder of the commission.[43] The Assembly rejected the Senate amendments and adhered to its position, but no doubt aware that the Senate passed their measure by a 19–6 margin, finally recognized the futility of their situation and accepted the Senate amendments. The bill became law on April 17, 1816.[44]

One individual not included in the list of commissioners was one of the canal's earliest advocates, Gouverneur Morris, presumably because his views on the construction and course of the canal (he favored a route to Lake Ontario) did not coincide with the prevailing consensus. Morris wrote his friend Rufus King in the spring of 1816, somewhat bemused, "I was laughed at, a few years ago, for my wild notions (so they were called) ... Now that the plan has grown popular it finds fathers by the dozen."[45]

Essentially, the law only enabled a survey and planning for the Lake Erie and Lake Champlain canals. The legislature's action was a disappointment to canal advocates, but the commission used the time before the next session of the legislature productively to produce a detailed and valuable study which benefitted the future canal builders immensely. Every inch of the canal route was surveyed, and the report provided answers to many technical questions that might arise. The commissioners even sent a delegation to examine the Middlesex Canal, which tapped the Merrimac River in New Hampshire to Boston, and was considered to be the best built canal in the country. They also began negotiations to obtain a loan in Europe.[46]

The canal commissioners further prepared a memorial to Congress in December 1816, seeking financial aid in the form of cessions, grants of land, or money. The benefits derived from the canals, they argued, would contribute "to the safety and opulence of the people, and the reputation and resources of the government." They also asserted that the money saved in transportation costs by the region northwest of the Ohio River would raise the value of public lands, lessen the influence of foreign governments, and bind the country closer politically. An easier communication would enhance the fur trade of the northwest, which would be directed eastward and not to Canada. The project, they noted, had been well studied and the canals would not exceed $10 million to complete.[47]

The commissioners also wrote the New York delegation in Congress in January 1817 urging them to support the proposed Bonus Bill, which would set up a federal fund for internal improvements ($1.5 million plus the net annual dividends paid by the Bank of the U.S.). New York's share would be $85,000 annually. Presuming Ohio's interest was identical with New York in relation to the Erie Canal and Vermont's in relation to the Champlain canal, they calculated that New York could raise about $140,000 annually for construction of the canals. By spreading the expenses over several years, the great works could be completed without imposing new taxes upon the people of the state. The federal government, they argued, should confide the expenditure of the money to the states, providing that it be applied to the building of the canals. The commissioners frankly addressed the political question, "that some of you may not be friendly to the contemplated canals," but they hoped none would be hostile to an appropriation of revenue which would "promote the object without any inconvenience to your constituents."[48]

The support of the federal government failed to materialize due to President Madison's veto of the Bonus Bill in March 1817. Undaunted, canal supporters again took their case to the state legislature, and this time they prevailed, largely because Martin Van Buren, sensing the strong public support for the canals, threw his followers behind the bill. It received the approval of the Council of Revision on April 15, 1817. This law, like the one proposed in 1816, provided only for building the middle section of the canal between Rome and the Seneca River. Work began on the canal on July 4, 1817, on the outskirts of Rome, and the first section was completed by April 1820. The legislature passed another law on April 7, 1819, authorizing the completion of the canal. The Champlain canal was completed in the fall of 1823, and the Erie Canal, over 363 miles long, in October 1825.[49]

Beyond a doubt, the Erie Canal's success far exceeded even the most sanguine hopes of its supporters. The canal essentially finished the trend started by the completion of the national road of reorienting the flow of Northwest trade to an east-west direction and eventually bound the Northeast and Northwest into a single section economically and politically. Economically, the Erie Canal was spectacularly successful. In its first full year of operation it took in tolls of over three quarters of a million. Numerous branch canals were added later, and New York City, tapping the riches of the northwest region of the country, became the dominant port of the United States. The Erie Canal also begot numerous imitators. A canal craze followed in which states invested heavily, hoping to have the same success. Between 1816 and 1840, $125 million was invested in canals, but none were as successful as the Erie Canal.[50]

The failure of the federal government to support the building of the Erie Canal reflected in part the fact that Congress was confronted with a vast number of proposals for assistance in building local road and canal projects which, if enacted, would have depleted the treasury and necessitated raising taxes—neither being palatable alternatives. Sectional jealousies no doubt also entered into political considerations. Rather than act on a few proposals, Congress generally preferred to act on none. This tendency also demonstrated the ongoing disagreement over the constitutional division of federal and state responsibilities and power, which was clearly illustrated by the controversy over the Bonus Bill.

The first session of the Fourteenth Congress did not undertake any internal improvements, and President Madison's annual message on December 3, 1816, reminded them that they should exercise their "existing powers" by developing "a comprehensive system of roads and canals" to draw the country together and promote prosperity.[51] John C. Calhoun, acting on the president's invitation, moved on December 16 to appoint a committee to inquire into using the $1.5 million bonus paid by the Bank of the United States as an internal improvements fund. He was appointed to chair the committee, and on December 23, he reported a bill to use the bonus and dividends from the government stock, with the fund to be administered by the secretary of the treasury.[52] Not until February 4, 1817, however, did the House take up the bill. Calhoun, well aware of the pitfalls confronting the measure, admitted that he feared the bill would be praised but not adopted. He argued that internal improvements would add strength and prosperity to the nation. Many of the projects proposed were on too great a scale for the finances of states or individuals and required the resources and general superintendence of the general government. He stressed also the military advantages of good roads and canals, and he argued that they would allow the republic to exist in a large area, a matter of concern for some who believed that republics were intended to exist in small areas and only a despotism could hold together a large area. A lack of roads and canals made it difficult for the extremes to communicate with the center of the Republic and weakened the Union. In an oft-quoted phrase, he said, "We are great, and rapidly—he was about to say fearfully—growing. This . . . is our pride and danger—our weakness and our strength." He added in a rhetorical flourish, "Let us then . . . bind the Republic together with a perfect system of roads and canals. Let us conquer space." He warned against a "sordid, selfish, and sectional spirit," and he called for "enlarged views" in interpreting the Constitution. As to the argument that a plan should be presented before any money was appropriated, he countered that a bill filled with details would have little chance of passing, but he did offer his views on possible projects. He estimated the fund would set apart about $650,000 per year, sufficient to initiate new projects and complete the great works already begun. "The money," Calhoun closed, "cannot be appropriated to a more exalted use."[53]

Opponents worried about intrigue and bargaining to gain a share of the fund. Some worried about too much meddling in state affairs by the federal government. There were concerns that allowing the federal government a role in internal improvements would not only consolidate the country but also lead to consolidation of power in the federal government. Still others questioned Calhoun's loose interpretation of the Constitution.[54] Thomas B. Robertson introduced an amendment to apportion the fund among the states according to their representation in Congress. Clay opposed the motion, arguing the first step should be to establish the fund and settle the details later. Leaving internal improvements to the states might result in great projects that required the cooperation of many states being ignored and never accomplished. He pointed out that the Cumberland Road would cut travel time from Baltimore to Wheeling from eight to three days.[55] Proponents argued that the amendment would remove the objectionable feature of pitting states against each other to gain more than their proportion. Robertson's amendment passed, and another motion to strike the first section (to defeat the bill) was rejected 70–61, suggesting a close vote on the final bill.[56]

Several other amendments were offered to the House. John W. Taylor successfully modified Robertson's amendment to read "according to the House of Representatives in Congress." An amendment to broaden the measure to include improving navigation of rivers, was unsuccessful.[57] Cyrus King, suggesting the House should first reduce direct taxes and import duties before they became prodigal with the people's money, moved to postpone the bill indefinitely, which launched a prolonged debate on the expediency and constitutionality of the measure.[58] Thomas R. Gold of New York noted the constitutional question had been argued for twenty-five years, and it was time to put the question to rest. Great national enterprises, such as New York's canal had been resisted by prejudice, narrow calculation, and short-sighted views. One-third of the commercial revenue of the nation came from the port of New York, more than enough to build the canal.[59]

Samuel Smith observed that Maryland's portion under the bill would only be $32,000, not enough to build four miles of turnpike. He supported projects of national importance, but not "small and insignificant sums, to be applied to objects within the power and means of States individually."[60] While several members objected to the measure as unconstitutional, Thomas Wilson of Pennsylvania took the expansive view that the national government had the power to do whatever was necessary to provide for the common defense and general welfare. The measure was expedient, he asserted, because it would open up the products of the West to foreign trade. At present "articles of indefinite amount remain as useless as the waters of the wilderness."[61]

John Ross from Pennsylvania suggested that this bill was as important as any that ever came before the national legislature. It raised the question of where states' rights ended and those of the national government began. He cited powers of the national government to compel states to allow goods of other states to pass through versus the right of a state (e.g. New York) to bar vessels of other states to navigate her waters. He also noted the Constitution forbade states to enter into compacts without the consent of the federal government. Great national projects needed the aid of the general government.[62]

There is little doubt that constitutional arguments masked baser motives, particularly sectional feelings. Among them were the local jealousies that could not see any benefit from supporting other regions. John Randolph, as always, captured these views in relation to internal improvements in the Western country. His region of Virginia, he noted, had received little of "the sunshine of Government," because they were "in the habit of living on their own means, not of quartering themselves on the nation." He could not see why all the benefits of an expense, borne equally by all, should go entirely to the Western States and Territories.[63] Cyrus King also reflected the sectional views expressed by some other members. He stated bluntly that he had heard much talk about the grand canal "to build up the already overgrown State of New York," and what was said of the Cumberland Road was "a mere tub to the whale." The post roads in New England were now good. "If they are not so elsewhere, let those concerned make them so." If good military roads were built, he said somewhat absurdly, cries for war would be heard in Congress. Many forgot, he added, that good military roads would be equally convenient for invaders.[64]

Robert Wright, who supported indefinite postponement, accused the House of arrogance. The people had given them "a *broad hint* that they had lost their confidence." Now they were "laboring under a paroxysm of the disease that brought them to their end." He asserted the Chesapeake and Delaware Canal had been defeated by the votes of the South and West, and he asked why the older states, who had expended millions on their public improvements, "should now be taxed to cut roads in the new States." Only the new states, he argued, would benefit from the fund provided by the bill.[65]

King's motion to postpone indefinitely was defeated, 86–74. A substitute motion by Timothy Pickering, opposed by Calhoun, who objected to the phrasing "with the assent of the State," was adopted without division.[66] Further efforts to amend were defeated. The engrossed bill was read a third time on February 8, 1817. John Randolph rose and spoke for three hours in opposition. Others also added final words for and against the bill. Finally, the bill was passed by the close vote of 86–84, and was sent to the Senate.[67] The division indicated that seventy-five of the opposition votes came from New England and the slave states.

The Committee on Roads and Canals in the Senate, chaired by Abner Lacock of Pennsylvania, reported the bill on February 14, 1817, without amendment and with strong support.[68] Debate did not begin until February 26, 1817. A motion by Connecticut's David Daggett to postpone until March 4, 1817 (to defeat the measure) was vigorously debated, essentially along the lines of constitutionality and expediency, and it was rejected by only one vote, 19–18.[69] Further efforts by opponents to amend the bill were all rejected. However, Robert H. Goldsborough from Maryland, a supporter of the measure, successfully added an amendment to divide the fund annually according to each state's ratio in Congress. The bill was finally passed by the Senate (20–15) on February 28, 1817.[70] The distribution of the vote, as in the House, showed the minority was from New England and the South, while the majority came from the Middle States and West.

The House took up the Senate amendments on March 1, 1817. Two motions to postpone, one indefinitely and one to March 3, 1817, were both defeated by two-vote margins. The House then concurred with the Senate amendments and passed the bill.[71] In its final form, the Bonus Bill was a weak measure, and no doubt Calhoun and Clay, the primary advocates, saw it as merely a foot in the door, upon which a national program might be built later. It is doubtful whether this bill would have achieved their dreams of a national system of internal improvements. Far from providing for a national plan, it merely distributed funds to each state for internal improvements, and the requirement for state consent to connect such improvements weakened federal control and influence over such projects even more. Perhaps for this reason, President Madison, who supported the Gallatin plan and favored national control over an internal improvements program, decided to veto this bill. Henry Clay, who learned of Madison's intention, tried to dissuade him from doing so, even suggesting that as Madison surely agreed with the object of the bill and differed only on its constitutionality, he leave the bill to his successor, Monroe. Clay contended that if Monroe signed it within the ten day period it would be a valid law.[72]

Nevertheless, on March 3, 1817, Madison vetoed the Bonus Bill on constitutional grounds. He cited the lack of an enumerated power and denied that it could be implied under the "necessary and proper" clause, the power to regulate commerce, or the "provide for the common defence and general welfare" clause. Further, "the assent of the States in the mode provided in the bill cannot confer the power." He was aware of the value of internal improvements, but the way to achieve these objects were provided for by the Constitution, namely by amendment.[73] The House vote to override passed only by a 60–56 margin, far short of the two-thirds requirement. On this question, Speaker Clay exercised his right to vote, but it was a futile gesture.[74]

Ironically, Madison's veto has been interpreted as a reversion to his states' rights roots. After straying by signing such bills as a protective tariff, a national bank bill, and other measures whose constitutionality had been questioned, his veto has been seen as a belated atonement for his past indiscretions and an attempt to burnish his reputation as a states' rights advocate.[75] In fact, it is far more likely that he vetoed the bill not only because it was a bad bill and would have failed to provide for a planned development, but also because he feared an element of corruption would evolve between interested groups in the states and the national government. Madison understood that his party was deeply divided over federal involvement in internal improvements. While many feared the dangers of consolidation inherent in a national system of roads and canals and that a too-powerful central government would strip the people of their liberties, others, like Calhoun and Clay, feared quite the opposite, that all power would be drained away from the central government to the state governments. Internal improvements were a way of binding the country together. The Bonus Bill, as they saw it, would at least make the federal government a player in the game and give it influence over internal improvements. They fully understood the competing interests and the petty politics that operated within and between the states and hoped to broker these interests for the public good. While Madison feared the Bonus Bill portended corruption and consolidation of national power, Calhoun and Clay saw it as a fulfillment of the new dynamic of democratization, restoring a balance or partnership between state and federal governments.[76]

A national system of internal improvements never was adopted. Internal improvements were essentially local, and interests any distance from a road, canal, or river navigation improvement rarely saw any benefit to themselves. Any program proposed by a distant government aroused fears of consolidation, and mixed with a complex of local and state jealousies, prevented any such development. Roads and canals were built in the years ahead, some with federal support such as land grants and purchases of stock, but that development was a result of local initiative and state enterprise. Regardless of this obvious display of regional interest, however, the growing sense of nationalism and the importance of the democratic "common man" in national policy was plain. Nowhere was this more evident than in the Fourth of July celebrations that took place nationwide in 1816.

Chapter 7

Fourth of July Celebrations

The Fourth of July was by far the most important American national holiday in 1816. Celebrated by all Americans, no other holiday, not even Christmas, was as widely or wholeheartedly honored. Many newspapers each year printed excerpts from John Adams's letter to his wife, Abigail, that the anniversary of independence "ought to be commemorated, as the day of deliverance, by solemn acts of devotion to God Almighty. It ought to be solemnized with pomp and parade, with shows, games, sports, guns, bells, bonfires, and illuminations, from one end of this continent to the other."[1] Each year, Americans followed Adams's advice. Whether it was celebrated on a grand scale in the larger Eastern seaboard cities or on a lesser scale in the outlying areas, there was a clear sense of the moment being celebrated. The "Day" called up memory, reinforced a sense of community, and developed a growing national consciousness. In terms of contemporary holidays, the Fourth of July in 1816 was a combination of Independence Day, Washington's Birthday, Memorial Day, Veteran's Day, Armed Forces Day, and Labor Day all in one. This Fourth of July in 1816 was the fortieth anniversary of the Declaration of Independence. While this was not a magical number, it was an indication of the endurance of the nation and prospects for its longer duration.

While there was a certain sameness to the rituals of the celebration, there were endless varieties in the way the day was honored. Typically, all businesses were closed for the day, which would begin with the firing of cannon or the ringing of bells. Most towns, large and small, usually had a parade, which had been announced and the procession clearly planned so that everyone knew their place in the line. Local officials commonly marched at the head of the parade; then came the militia; followed by clergymen and the orator of the day; members of schools and organizations, such as the Society of Cincinnati, mechanics and manufacturing societies, firemen, and the like. Each member of the community marched with the group he belonged to or with whom he identified. Most towns had a generic place for "citizens," who followed in the rear.

It is not clear whether women and children were included in the term "citizen." Very likely, they were expected to be the observers and, as the parade passed by, they joined at the end and followed the parade to its terminus, usually a church or the town commons. More striking than the hierarchy assigned to the procession was the egalitarianism with which it imbued the community. The town commons or park, for example, was a place where everyone could assemble on common ground and act out his or her role in the community symbolically within his assigned group. Wealth and station, were, in the context of the holiday, deemed of lesser importance than civic identities. On this day, a farmer or common man might be raised to an esteemed place in the community as a militiaman or a veteran.

The parade also brought the community together for a more important object lesson. They usually gathered in a large public hall or a church. If they met in the latter, the meeting was often rotated to different churches from year to year to allay sectarian jealousies. Once assembled, the entire Declaration of Independence was read to the crowd, and then an oration was delivered by the speaker for that year. Thus the sacred text and the "sermon" on patriotic themes amounted to an exercise in a kind of civic religion. Following an oration intended primarily to bring the audience to a shared value system and a common set of beliefs, a prayer was given and the crowd, now free to celebrate the remainder of the day in their own way, dispersed to various large picnics or other small gatherings. In many small towns, an afternoon picnic with most of the town in attendance was a centerpiece of the day's activities. In larger urban centers, groups like the Society of Cincinnati, Washington Benevolent Society, American Revolution Society, Tammany Society, and others enjoyed banquets and had their own orations and toasts. Many places also noisily fired off booming cannons and organized fireworks demonstrations for the public.[2]

In Charleston, South Carolina, on July 4, 1816, artillery was fired at dawn. At noon cannons boomed from the forts in the harbor, as well from the vessels in the port, and the artillery in the town. The militia was reviewed that morning in preparation for the parade. They then marched down to the battery where they fired volleys of rifle fire before being dismissed. Later that morning, they reassembled for the parade. Various associations, such as the Cincinnati and Revolution societies joined in the procession to St. Michael's Church, where the customary reading of the Declaration of Independence was heard, and then an oration was delivered. Afterwards, the people went to prearranged dinners and heard more orations. That evening, when the people assembled for a fireworks exhibition, the seats prepared for the audience unfortunately collapsed, injuring several people, including three children. The seats had been inspected prior to the day and were deemed safe, but apparently they could not bear the load of people who showed up for the display. Although this incident somewhat marred the celebration, the *Charleston Courier* reported a "Grand and Brilliant Display of Fire-Works," put together by the Charleston Rifle Corps and dedicated "Joyfully to commemorate the Day when America separated herself from Great Britain, and freemen threw off the yoke of tyranny and oppression."[3]

In urban seaboard centers like New York City, Boston, and Charleston, while they shared some rituals in common with smaller towns, such as parades, public oration, and the like, they also offered their citizens greater spectacles and multiple venues as part of the holiday. A single community festival was impractical in urban centers, so more exclusive entertainments were organized for a particular group, or required admission fees. One particularly extravagant leisure activity was an afternoon or evening steamboat cruise. Steamboats (still a novelty in 1816) in both New York and Washington sold pleasure cruises. The steamboat *Fulton* cruising the Hudson River on the Fourth promised its passengers a more impressive view of the evening fireworks set off from the battery and Governor's Island.[4]

In the nation's capital, Washington, D.C., although much smaller relative to other more established cities, Independence Day ceremonies were no less grand. Washington's steamboat conveniently embarked at a location near the McKeowin Hotel, where a well-attended banquet was held every year. They also held a parade that terminated at the Capitol. The reader of the Declaration of Independence in 1816 was William S. Radcliff, who, one observer noted, did "well enough to satisfy us that he could read it a great deal better." Afterwards the oration was delivered to the assembled crowd, including most members of Congress.[5] One theater, decorated with a litany of banners honoring national heroes, an impressive design called the Temple of Concord and an altar of peace dedicated to the "Genius of America," ran a complete patriotic revue, including a melodrama, and a comic opera.[6] Completing the day, the Ordinance Department produced a public fireworks display at the president's residence. Undoubtedly, these vivid spectacles were well-attended by city dwellers.

Fireworks were extremely popular, but they were not limited to organized display. Anyone on the street could obtain some kind of fireworks, or, as the Newark, New Jersey *Centinel of Freedom* put it, a "squib" was in the hand of "every boy and negro that can raise a penny." Many, according to the editor of the *Centinel*, felt these "squibs" were too dangerous in the hands of irresponsible youth for the good of the public. In fact, four fires on housetops were reported during Newark's Fourth of July in 1816. Authorities blamed all four on firecrackers. For sport, some malicious boys even threw firecrackers at people on the streets. There was even a report that a black woman was fatally burned after her clothes caught on fire from a firecracker. The outrage caused by this incident and the antics of locals on the Fourth led to a call for an outright ban on the sale or purchase of firecrackers.[7] Some cities like New York had already limited fireworks to prearranged public displays.

One of the spectacles provided in New York City was a large transparent painting to commemorate the Declaration of Independence. A female figure of liberty was depicted dressed in yellow robes. Beneath her was the globe. In one hand she held the standards of the United States and was planting it upon America. In her other hand was an olive branch, and beneath it was a white lily (symbolizing purity and serenity). The painting further displayed three boys, one holding and pointing to a book which had on it the

Declaration of Independence and July 4, 1776. Also portrayed was the American eagle hovering over and covering a globe.[8]

Boston, more prosaically, provided a circus to entertain the public. In addition, there was a parade headed by Governor John Brooks, complete with a troop of Boston Light Dragoons. The day was highlighted by the presence of two of General George Washington's aides-de-camp, Generals David Cobb and David Humphrey. Also present was former President John Adams, aged eighty-one, who still retained "the appearance of health and cheerfulness."[9]

The symbolic spectacle of the Fourth of July celebrations around the country revealed much about how the Americans saw themselves and their country as well as displaying their growing sense of community and nationalism. Just as much can be learned from the words of the holiday. Newspapers faithfully reprinted the toasts, and in some cases the orations delivered. These words give another dimension to the thoughts and feelings behind the celebration. In addition to the toasts given at local dinners, newspapers often published toasts delivered in other communities. In this way the newspapers played a crucial role in leaving a broader historical record, as well as circulating ideas from one place to another. The result was an emerging consensus of common themes, which made the holiday sentiments expressed seem universal. Because so many of the dinners continued to be political gatherings, they retained a partisan flavor.

The banquet toasts also had a ritual. There were eighteen prepared toasts (matching the number of states in the Union). Following the prepared (and printed) toasts, individual toasts were offered Many of the latter were quite clever, reflecting no doubt that they were not spur-of-the-moment offerings but perhaps the product of a year of meditation. Typically, the printed toasts of the day began by recognizing the Declaration of Independence, the memory of George Washington, the American people, the Constitution, the Army, Navy, and Militia, heroes of both the Revolutionary War and the War of 1812, freedom and liberty, and usually concluded with a tribute to the ladies, the "American Fair," or the "Daughters of Columbia." Sometimes political figures, such as retired President Thomas Jefferson or the current President James Madison, a governor or congressman, or venerated figures, such as Alexander Hamilton or Benjamin Franklin, were also toasted. The volunteer toasts usually touched on the political issues of the day, often from a partisan point of view reflecting the political hue of the gathering. Many times they reflected a growing sense of nationalism; sentiments in support of the Union and its institutions.

In 1816 the memory of the War of 1812 was still fresh. Not surprisingly, many toasts of this year related to that war and not to the Revolutionary War. Among the heroes remembered in toasts were Oliver Hazard Perry and his great victory on Lake Erie. William Henry Harrison's victory over Tecumseh and his Indians was also celebrated. Andrew Jackson naturally was hailed for his victories over the Indians as well as over the British at New Orleans. For example, a toast in Charleston, South Carolina, declared, "Major General Jackson—He humbled at Talapoosa the savage and defeated at New Orleans the foreign foe."[10] Generals Jacob Brown and Winfield Scott were also toasted for their gallant conduct on the Niagara peninsula. Another toast was: "[Alexander] Macomb and [Thomas] Macdonough—Twin brothers in fame, Champlain and Plattsburg attest their valor. One subdued a numerous fleet, the other expels from our soil an insolent and superior foe."[11] Commodore Stephen Decatur and the memory of General Zebulon Pike were also saluted, as was General Nathanael Greene of the Revolutionary generation.[12]

Only in very rare cases did a gathering fail to acknowledge the prowess of the army, the navy, and the militia. Few Federalists, however, could bring themselves to offer unqualified praise to the army and militia. At best, they considered the army a potential tool of the Republicans or a threat to governmental authority in general, which was reflected in a Poughkeepsie, New York, toast: "The Army—may its leaders recollect that they are created for the people and not the people for them."[13] The navy, on the other hand, received praise from all segments of the political spectrum. Southern and Western gatherings were particularly given to references to the navy's recent actions against the Algerine pirates. Federalists took credit for the navy's origins, and there were many happy references to the Americans solving a problem which had confounded Europeans by forcing the Barbary pirates, the terror and scourge of Europe, into submission.[14]

The pride of Americans shone through their toasts. Kentuckians declared that the United States held "the highest rank among the nations of the globe." Salem, Massachusetts, citizens agreed the United States was "the last great Republic in the world." A Washington D.C. toast called the United States the "Land of the free, and the home of the brave," no doubt alluding to the words of Francis Scott Key, and another speaker assured his audience "our institutions confessedly present the most perfect model of government yet offered to the world."[15]

Nor did Americans shy away from allusions to the partisan and sectional rancor that had divided the country during the recent war. The anti-war Hartford Convention at the end of the War of 1812 was remembered. For example, at one gathering in Boston the convention was characterized as "An incendiary, who endeavored to fire the Temple of Liberty while its defenders were at its gates opposing a foreign enemy." A Virginia toast was to "Massachusetts—Our sister strayed from the path of duty; the Union family is ready to forgive her," which suggested that some Americans were ready to heal the wounds brought about by the war.[16] Another toast declared: "The Union of the States—The vital source of National Independence, glory and happiness—the first breach lets in the enemy." A theme of many banquets was a call for an end to party strife. For example, there was a plea for "The extinction of party feuds—The reign of good principles and the harmony of friends." Patriotism, a concept of the budding nationalism, was only then beginning to have currency and eroding state loyalties. A South Carolina toast specifically used the term: "Patriotism—planted in the luxuriant soil of freedom; may its growth never be destroyed by the rude storm of factions, or the chilling blast of ingratitude."[17]

There were many other interesting toasts on a variety of topics. A favorite at many gatherings this year were the revolutionaries of South America and Ireland. One example was: "The Patriots of South America—We cannot but sympathize with those who are struggling for the principles which we this day celebrate." Similarly, there was a toast to "Ireland—may her next attempt to gain her Independence be as successful as that of America."[18] Another topic was the Compensation Act which, as one editor observed, was "toasted until it is black."[19] Local issues were also subjects of salutes. For example, Kentuckians acknowledged that the Indiana Territory was in the process of forming a state constitution and a state government: "The state of Indiana—Destined to become a bright star in the West constellation."[20] In Augusta, Maine, there was an allusion to the push by citizens of Maine to gain separation from Massachusetts. One said: "Maine—A new star of the first magnitude gleams above the political horizon, among the constellations of the North." Another referred to the upcoming vote in September on separation, "The Electors of Maine—Enlightened, patriotic, and determined: push them to five ninths for a legal majority, and death alone will keep them from the polls."[21]

The centerpiece of every Fourth of July celebration was the oration. No greater honor could be conferred upon an individual than to be chosen as the orator for the Day. Stylistically, these speeches were firmly grounded in major themes and reflected their great sense of the historical significance of the revolution and the Declaration of Independence, as well as schooling the people in the lessons of its history. While each speaker gave these lessons their own peculiar twist, there was a certain uniformity in these speeches. In 1816, Americans were invariably given dire warnings that they must be worthy to maintain their freedoms. Just as invariably, the speakers engaged in boosterism, the wonderful conceit that Americans were a chosen people destined for greatness.

It was customary to review the events of the American Revolution. References to the Romans and the Greeks abounded, as many speakers saw a relationship between these ancient republics and the American experiment. The people were warned that what had happened to the ancients could happen to them. One orator, for example, informed his audience in Hartford, Connecticut, "The freedom of Rome was not subverted till Romans were unworthy of freedom."[22] It was almost obligatory to mention the role of George Washington. The character of Washington was a model of patriotism. Rather than his martial skill, it was his virtuous leadership that established national character. His conduct reflected dignity in both his public and private life, and citizens were exhorted to model their character on the spirit of Washington. Whether the words of the Declaration of Independence were cited, as well as its author Thomas Jefferson, depended upon the partisan makeup of the meeting. The Constitution was more frequently hailed, and all speakers agreed, whatever their party affiliation, that the people were blessed to live under the rule of that document.

Rarely did orators fail to put a positive spin on the War of 1812.

A Georgetown, South Carolina, audience was informed, "Our virtuous citizens, strangers to the murderous art of war, but jealous of their rights, and tenacious of their honor, hastened to the conflict, humbled the bravest troops in Europe, commanded by the most gallant and experienced officers in the world." Another speaker argued the war had saved the nation from a mercenary disposition, "this moral gangrene . . . this moral poison upon declining patriotism." "Nothing but a war," he said, "could have revived the dying principle of patriotism in our country . . . ten more years of peace and speculation would have ruined the nation past redemption."[23]

An address to citizens at Charlestown, Massachusetts, was positively rhapsodic in its evaluation of the War of 1812. "The holy flame of the revolution was again rekindled, and we are now reposing on the laurels, won by our gallant countrymen on ocean, and on land." Another speech in Boston was equally ebullient: "One dazzling exploit followed another with such rapidity, that an admiring people had scarcely time to celebrate the achievements of one hero before another put in his claim to equal honor." A speaker in Cincinnati, Ohio, hailed "our little bands of valiant, though untaught soldiers, midst showers of internal faction, securing to us victory and safety in every quarter," which suggested to him "some mysterious power who has designed us for a chosen and a happy people."[24]

Perhaps the most common theme in the orations of 1816, as well as the toasts, was the corrosive effects of party spirit upon the nation. The bitter partisan strife between Federalists and Republicans during the War of 1812 was fresh in the minds of the people. It had culminated in the Hartford Convention at the end of the war, which in the minds of many threatened the permanency of the republic. In New England, nearly all of the extant Fourth of July orations alluded to the danger of political parties. One attributed the Hartford Convention to "the folly and wickedness of factions, violence, and disappointed ambition." The convention, he argued, sought to embarrass the government, "The Union was to be severed, and the 'Nation of New England' to be formed." He added, "*Discord*, holding in her bosom a dagger, destined to give a *deadly thrust* at the Union, and the Constitution, *was cherished*; and melancholy to relate, Fanueil Hall was her cradle!"[25]

Orators also celebrated the failure of the Hartford Convention.

One speaker declared the convention, "that first-born of the Junto," that "threatened to prostrate our liberty . . . only shook its branches, and caused its roots to strike deeper and more firmly in the soil." He added, however, a note of forgiveness; the mass of Federalists were "doubtless as firm in their republican attachments as we are," but the character of the leaders gave "the tone and temper to the whole." Another agreed the convention "plotted the prostration of the colossal pillars of our republic," but he would also "cast the veil of charity" over their actions. For all true Americans, he said, "*Union* is the rallying word."[26]

Federalist orators, obviously, had a different view of the subject. One characterized the Hartford Convention as "notwithstanding all the cruel things which the hard-hearted newspapers have said of them, altogether *harmless*." Another declared that the Federalists were being proscribed as the enemies of the country, yet they had "foretold the disastrous result of that fatal policy [of war], and struggled to avert the impending ruin."[27]

Despite the continuing partisan references in orations and toasts, there was also a spirit of conciliation. Benjamin L. Lear, the orator in Washington, D.C., while he gloried in the victories of the late war, also focused on the practical evidence of national unity during the war. "The most powerful enemy and the most inveterate opposition have both been withstood without one trial for treason, or even one prosecution for libel."[28] Newspapers also recorded a growing congeniality between the two parties. In some communities the passions had abated enough that there were reports of "republican citizens" and "respectable federal gentlemen" cooperating in the arrangements and enjoying the festivities of the Fourth of July together "upon National principles." The *Camden* (SC) *Gazette*, related that in their community during the processions, orations, and banquets an attitude of "temperance and harmony reigned over all."[29]

The general consensus was that political passions had nearly brought down the republic. As one orator noted, "*Party spirit* is an evil of immense magnitude." Another warned, "Regard the man who would induce you to enlist under the banners of *any* party, as an enemy. Suffer no man to dictate your vote. Look at *principles*, not *names*." Yet another advised, "Sacrifice party feelings to the good of our common country. Party spirit paralyzes the noblest emotions of the human mind."[30]

Charles G. Ferris was one of the few orators who had anything good to say about political parties, perhaps because he spoke before a highly politicized organization, the Tammany Society in New York City. Founded in 1786, this society had adopted Indian rituals, whether as a caricature of the aristocratic Society of Cincinnati is unclear. Additional Tammany Societies were organized in other states, but the New York organization was the most influential. Politically, they were anti-Federalist, and they were nationalistic. They also marched in parades dressed as Indians and celebrated Washington's birthday as early as 1790. Further, they popularized the ritual of reading of the Declaration of Independence on the Fourth of July. The spirit of party, Ferris told the society, should be "strictly guarded, although not entirely suppressed . . . within due bounds, it is a check upon ambitions, excites a spirit of useful enquiry into the merits of the candidates that may be proposed for popular support, and makes us vigilant in examining the conduct of our rulers and their administration of public affairs." He did warn, however, that factions destroy the peace and happiness of the state. He advised the republicans to exercise power with justice and impartiality, beware foreign attachments, and follow the maxims of Washington.[31]

Some orators saw excess party spirit as subsiding. One informed his audience in Windsor, Vermont, "It is highly gratifying to observe the decline of that infatuation which lately rendered so many worthy men blind to their country's interest, and their own reputation. We now hear nothing of *conventions*; nor *dissolving the union*; nor of *commissioners* sent to take the President by the beard; and but very little of Washington Benevolent Societies." He added forgivingly, "We hail the delivery of our fellow citizens from political phrenzy, as we would their recovery from a fever, and its attendant delirium."[32] A Federalist speaker also saw a new era in politics, "The asperity of party is softening; the tone of recrimination is assuming a milder accent." He added that Federalists would "cheerfully extend the hand of fellowship, and make a united effort, while reason predominates in our councils, to redeem the nation from those calamities which a mistaken policy has precipitated upon us."[33]

The spirit of reconciliation was also manifested at this same gathering of Federalists by Francis Blake, the President of the Day, who also addressed the audience and whose comments were added to the published oration. Blake, alluding to the apparent decline in party spirit both in Congress and in the state legislature, observed that it "seems also most happily to be banished, in a great degree, from our social intercourse with each other." Interestingly, he credited the Republican Party for much of this change. Perhaps, he suggested, they had "magnanimously resolved to offer up their party feelings and passions, as a sacrifice of atonement, upon the altar of their country." Federalists were not exempt from the passions that governed the predominant party, he noted, but he hoped "the shades of difference which seem now to be rapidly melting away, may soon vanish altogether." His toast was, "A new Political Confederacy! Its exclusive object the good of the whole—and not the predominance of a party!"[34]

While George Sullivan, a former Federalist congressman from New Hampshire, agreed that party passions were subsiding, he took another view of political parties. He told his Boston audience, "Parties are the soul of free government." Parties, he contended, stamped the national character and shaped the public spirit. He asserted that the present political calm "doubtless presages a new eruption. Its lava may separate old friends, and bring together old enemies." He suggested that the source of this new eruption would come from the rapidly growing region of the West, and he worried that their warlike and adventurous habits indicated that they were not the best depositories of power. Sullivan's perception that the growth of the West might further diminish New England's role in the nation was no doubt on the minds of many in his audience. New England, he hinted, must repair its relations with the other states, "because she alone has wrongs to pardon and forget," and be prepared to cooperate with them.[35]

Not everyone saw the growth of the West with dread. There are also many examples of incipient expansionism found in these orations. Francis Gilmer predicted that in forty years the population of the United States would spread all the way to the Pacific, "one nation, speaking one language, governed by the same laws, born to inherit the same freedom, the same enterprize, the same valor, the same love of country." A Worcester, Massachusetts, audience was reminded, "Each day the forests of the West recede from the genius of cultivation." Another orator declared at Georgetown, South Carolina, "Let none presume to assert that our territory is too extensive, or our interest too dissimilar. A small territory is the seat of faction, when the malignant spirit of discord is prevalent, it pervades every section, infuses its poison into the bosom of families, and contaminates the whole." A government of an extensive country, he argued, promised "duration, permanency and stability."[36]

Of course, the orators developed many other themes. A favorite was the superiority of the American republic and its institutions. A gathering in Brookville, Indiana, was told, "If ever a people were truly favored, it was the people of the United States." Francis W. Gilmer, in Winchester, Virginia, called Americans "the freest people upon Earth," with the "freest institutions which any people, ancient or modern ever enjoyed." Charles G. Ferris, declared to the Tammany Society in New York City, that the United States was "the sanctuary of freedom—the only asylum of oppressed and persecuted man." Another speaker summarized the superiority of the government created by the Constitution by stating, "May it stand to passing ages the monument of wisdom and admiration like the great, wise and good men who formed it. The world talks of liberty," he added, "there is one free government in it; a republic, which is the world's last and best hope." Finally, one stated simply that the United States was "the best country the world ever saw."[37]

There were also numerous examples of exuberant nationalism in these orations. None, perhaps, matched Francis Gilmer, who exclaimed, "I thank God, that I am an American." Another declared, "Wherever a citizen of this land may sojourn, however conspicuous his virtues, his talents or his rank, his greatest distinction will be the appellation of an AMERICAN." Similarly, a speaker at Charlestown, Massachusetts, said, "To be known as an American citizen is *every where* a passport to fame." George Sullivan also asserted that our countrymen were once humiliated abroad, but now they were honored and respected. "None is so humble among us," he said, "but participates in the pride, which now swells through the nation." An orator in Cincinnati summed up the feeling of most speakers, "The prospects of America are great."[38]

Americans were also informed that our example inspired the patriots of South America, and would also infuse the abused people of Europe with the courage and strength to burst the bonds of tyrants, priests, and mercenary armies. Americans were obviously in the process of constructing a special mission to spread the tenets of freedom around the world. A speaker in Charleston, South Carolina, also saw us as a beacon of freedom. "We are on a lofty summit which commands a wide and extensive survey of all the political world," he declared. "Banished from the ancient world, freedom has fled for safety to our land."[39]

Thus the discourse in the Fourth of July celebrations was both reflective and prospective. While there is no doubt the rhetoric was overblown and exaggerated, there was also an element of sincerity in the speeches and toasts that reveal their hopes for the future or at least a sense of the peculiarity of the American "experiment." Americans were beginning to look forward to an era of United States leadership in a world where republican ideals were bringing revolution to the Western hemisphere, and they were looking forward to a greater destiny for America and every nation that embraced these republican ideals. In order to achieve this kind of international influence, however, the United States had to maintain the quality of a standing military such as had challenged Great Britain in the War of 1812.

Chapter 8

National Defense

American reliance upon citizen soldiers or militia for defense was given a stern test during the War of 1812. The fear of standing armies was deeply ingrained in Anglo-American thought, and in the Constitutional Convention it was agreed that while a national defense force would be maintained, the main reliance would be placed upon the militia. The result was a shared authority. The national government could call upon the state militia (Art. I, Sec. 8) "to execute the laws of the Union, suppress insurrections, and repel invasions," and "provide for organizing, arming, and disciplining the militia," but the states were to appoint the officers and train the militia according to the discipline prescribed by the federal government. The basic law, the Uniform Militia Act of 1792, however, failed to provide for a uniform militia. It merely prescribed that all able-bodied men between eighteen and forty-five must join a militia unit and provide their own arms and accouterments.

States responded indifferently to their responsibilities, and militia organization and discipline varied widely. Militia musters were widely regarded as farces, providing little or no training whatsoever. A lack of weapons held by militiamen forced Congress to respond in 1808 by providing an annual fund of $200,000 for arming the state militia. The Jeffersonian Republicans in particular advocated militia in lieu of standing armies, but despite calls from every president, Congress, for various political and ideological reasons, did nothing to improve the situation. Consequently, the nation was forced to fight the War of 1812 with largely raw, untrained, ill-disciplined, ill-equipped militia. The result was predictable, and there were many instances during the war where the militia broke and ran in the face of the enemy, such as at Bladensburg, or refused to cross international borders, such as at Queenstown and Detroit. Moreover, the state governors of Massachusetts, Connecticut, and Rhode Island refused to allow the national government the use of their militia on grounds that the conditions prescribed by the Constitution were not met.[1]

Of course, there were a few notable successes, especially the Battle of New Orleans, which gave militia advocates grounds for arguing for continued reliance upon militia after the War of 1812. Congress, however, responded by establishing a standing army of 10,000 men. The Act of March 3, 1815, was a positive step towards a professional army, as well as an indication of disenchantment with the idealized but inefficient and unreliable militia. Federal officials continued to place a verbal reliance upon the militia, but the growing professionalism of the post-war army was accompanied by an increasing neglect of the militia.

After the war, virtually all of the state governors recognized the need to improve their state militia in their annual messages to their legislatures. Governor Isaac Shelby of Kentucky declared in December 1815 that a time of peace was a time to strengthen defenses. He urged his legislature to reorganize the state militia to "prevent in future those evasions and delays, in complying with executive requisitions for militia, which were so severely felt during the last war."[2] Similarly, Governor Thomas Worthington of Ohio asserted that while the federal government should adopt one general plan and regulation for the discipline of the nation's militia, the state had its responsibility too. He urged particularly setting aside a place for arms, ammunition, and camp equipage.[3] Instead of amending the state's current militia law, however, the Ohio legislature chose to instruct its representatives and senators to urge Congress to provide more effectually for the organizing, arming, disciplining, and calling out all state militia. The resolution acknowledged, "on the *extent* of these *powers*, and whether they be *exclusive*, or only concurrent with the *state sovereignties*, a diversity of opinion still exists," but it added that "the want of uniformity in the organization of the corps of militia did during the late war, greatly retard the operations of the general government."[4]

In Pennsylvania, Governor Simon Snyder's message of December 8, 1815, stated simply: "Experience has shown the futility of the idea of converting every man into a soldier." In lieu of the mass militia he recommended creating a select corps that would always be organized and disciplined. Joel B. Sutherland from the House Militia Committee reported a proposal on January 16, 1816, to arm and equip a "select corps." He outlined the features of a bill his committee was considering, but he wanted to test the sense of the House first; otherwise it would be a waste of time to prepare and report a bill that would be rejected. They proposed a force of 15,000 men between the ages of eighteen and twenty-eight who would parade one week a month each year. Officers would be selected by the governor, and they would rate the same pay as the officers of the United States Army. Non-commissioned officers and privates would receive uniforms, "the foundations of all military ardor and enthusiasm," as well as $1 per diem for military duty. Sutherland justified a tax to cover the costs of this plan, noting that no individual in the commonwealth paid any state tax for the support of the government. Moreover, the tax would "operate principally upon the rich and the affluent, who have property to defend." Under the present law, rich and poor paid equally for militia delinquency, which was unjust and irrational.[5]

The committee proposal was discussed at length for four days, but the report was finally rejected by the House on January 23 primarily because it was thought the new organization "would be at variance with the long established habits of the people, and attended with unusual expense, or that might be novel in its principles and untried in its operations." The next day, however, a resolution was introduced to instruct the militia committee to bring in a bill that would be the most efficient, least oppressive "judicious combination of the militia and volunteer systems." The motion was, however, rejected.[6] Instead, the Pennsylvania Senate adopted an amendment to the current militia law that allowed individuals the option of enrolling in a militia company or becoming an exempt (but not from service if the militia was called out) upon payment of six dollars.[7] This amount was too high to benefit the average man, but it allowed the wealthy to escape militia training. Moreover, it did nothing to address the governor's charge to the legislature. In his next message on December 5, 1816, Snyder repeated his call for militia reform. He now proposed the regular militia would meet for training one day a year and use the commutation fee of exempts to support a select corps of young men.[8] The legislature, however, declined to take any action.

Virginia's governor, Wilson Cary Nicholas, declared to his legislature on December 4, 1815, that the state's militia system was "defective in all its parts." Until Congress changed the present organization, he added, no improvement was to be expected. However, the state should do what it could. He advised particularly arming the state militia, requiring them to pay a deposit to care for and return the weapon.[9] Other states where the governors requested their legislature to reform the state's militia included New Hampshire, Georgia, and Louisiana.[10]

Delaware presented a unique situation regarding its militia. When the House Militia Committee reported on January 17 that it was inexpedient to make any changes in the existing militia law, Nathan Vickers of Sussex County introduced a resolution to repeal all militia fines. Surprisingly, the bill gained significant support. An effort to refer it to a committee was defeated, 13–6, and then it was passed on January 20 by a vote of 12–6. The Senate passed it easily, and the bill became law on February 2. After the House action, Victor DuPont responded by moving a resolution that "repeal of all militia fines will effectually put an end to the present militia system of this state," and that as it was important to keep us a military spirit within the state, a volunteer corps should be encouraged. However, a bill to encourage volunteers was eventually rejected.[11] DuPont's assessment of the effect of abolishing militia fines proved to be accurate. In 1820 the Adjutant for the Delaware militia related to the War Department that the consequences of the February 2, 1816 law had been "a total neglect of every appearance of militia duty."[12]

On the national level, President Madison, in his annual message on December 5, 1815, also called to the attention of Congress the need for militia reform, particularly reorganizing and classifying the militia (grouping militia so that younger men received longer and more intense training). Experience had shown, he stated, "that skill in the use of arms and that familiarity with the essential rules of discipline . . . can not be expected from the regulations now in force." Madison further called for enlarging the West Point Military Academy, "and the establishment of others in other sections of the Union." He also noted the difficulties in executing the act of

March 3, 1815, fixing the military peace establishment, which would require legislative aid. Finally, Congress should consider "the expediency of continuing upon the peace establishment the staff officers who have hitherto been previously retained."[13]

Little was done in the first session of the Fourteenth Congress. A bill to organize, class, and arm the militia was postponed indefinitely in the House on April 19, 1816. It had not been seriously discussed, and that same day Richard M. Johnson, chair of the Military Committee, moved to request the secretary of war to report at the next session a system of organizing and disciplining the militia "best calculated, in his opinion, to promote the efficiency of that force when called into the public service."[14] In the Senate, a bill was introduced by the head of the Militia Committee, Joseph B. Varnum of Massachusetts, to address the issue that arose during the War of 1812 when three New England governors refused to allow the government to use their militia. Varnum's bill provided that when the governor or commander of the state militia refused a call out from the national government, the president was authorized to call upon officers of state militia to comply with the requisition. His bill was discussed at length in the Senate and repeated efforts to amend were beaten back, only to have discussion of the bill postponed, on motion by James Brown of Louisiana, to the fourth Monday of July, effectively killing the bill.[15]

Another issue considered in the first session was a proposal made on December 29, 1815, by Richard M. Johnson to establish three additional military academies: one at Mt. Dearborn, South Carolina; another at Newport, Kentucky, at the junction of the Ohio and Licking Rivers; and the third in the District of Columbia. In committee of the whole, congressmen immediately began offering alternative sites. George W. Campbell from Tennessee suggested Columbia, South Carolina as a better place for the Southern Academy. Israel Pickens of North Carolina offered the more upland site of Ashville, North Carolina. Both motions were defeated. Thomas Burnside from Pennsylvania moved to add a fourth academy at Carlisle, Pennsylvania, but it also failed. Richard Wilde of Georgia proposed only one new academy and would place it in the District of Columbia to give it a national character. Timothy Pickering also favored only one additional academy, but he preferred Harper's Ferry, Virginia. Alfred Cuthbert, like his Georgia colleague Wilde, believed there was an advantage to having an academy under the watchful eye of the national government. It would be "purely national," and it would attach the youth in the academy "to the dignity and splendor of the nation; where they should acquire, not State feelings, but patriotic sentiments."[16]

Johnson, who no doubt had an interest in seeing an academy established in his state, opposed Wilde's motion. If the object was to establish a great national military academy, then the bill should also abolish the West Point Military Academy, he said. It had not created local jealousies. Moreover, all three additional academies would not cost more than $400,000 annually. John W. Hulbert, a fellow member of the committee, supported Johnson. He noted that leading members of the administration supported only one academy in the District of Columbia, but the intent of the committee was to distribute a school to each section. The West, Hulbert said, was increasing with unexampled rapidity. He wished it was not increasing quite so fast, but the territory beyond the Allegheny, he believed, would soon contain a majority of the people of the United States.[17]

Henry Clay also supported his friend Johnson's proposal, which would additionally benefit Kentucky. Establishing several academies in different parts of the union would increase "the affection of the people for the Union." John Forsyth also favored three additional academies, but he doubted an academy in the District of Columbia would necessarily benefit the district, which had long suffered from neglect, and there was no evidence an academy would fare any better. He agreed with the theme that was heard often in this debate that state feelings and jealousies ought to be destroyed.[18]

Calhoun observed that the question appeared to be the best mode to produce a national spirit. One central school, he argued, would be filled with the sons of wealthy men. During the late war, he asserted, military talent was more likely to arise from the middle and lower ranks of men. They had a stronger stimulus to exertion. More than one academy would diffuse military science. Robertson of Louisiana, however, asked why the preservation of the union depended on military spirit. The best way to extinguish state jealousies and local feelings was to associate youth from various parts of the country in the District of Columbia, which would have the advantage of preventing the creation of a military spirit distinct from the general interest. John Sergeant from Pennsylvania, however, believed the District of Columbia was the worst place to put an academy, where political or party dissension burned with the most intense heat. The young would not escape its contagion. The amendment to strike out three academies and insert one passed with ninety-one yeas.[19] Pickering then moved to strike the District of Columbia and insert Harper's Ferry. Clay, however, suggested that Pickering vary his motion to leave the location blank. Clay then moved to fill the blank with Pittsburgh. At this point the committee rose.[20]

When the committee met again on January 3, Clay withdrew his motion and moved to establish the additional academy near the mouth of the Licking in deference to the committee. It was rejected, 68 to 58. Successive motions to fill the blank with Nashville, Harper's Ferry, and Carlisle were also rejected. Finally, Newton Cannon of Tennessee succeeded with a proposal to place the academy in Knoxville, 84–63.[21] The debate was hardly over. Efforts to limit admission to under twenty-one and to require military service after graduation were rejected. Another issue was the number of cadets to be admitted. Pickering and John W. Taylor argued for less than the proposed 800, while Calhoun and Forsyth supported the higher number. Calhoun argued that the cadets returning to the body of the people would diffuse that knowledge to the militia.[22] The question of filling the blank with 600 passed with seventy-seven yeas.[23] The details apparently having been worked out, the bill then faded away. Whether it was the additional cost of the new academy or whether it had been amended so much that no one had a real vested interest in it is not clear. When Pickering offered a substitute bill favoring continued support of the one academy at West Point on March 20, it was received without objection by the House.[24]

The academy question was instructive. While the votes were probably there to pass the legislation, a general consensus emerged that the measure did not have strong support and perhaps needed time for more reflection, so it was allowed to drop. Johnson did not give up. In the second session, he reported a bill to establish three additional military academies as originally proposed by his committee at Mt. Dearborn, Newport, and Washington, D.C. The House eventually postponed the bill indefinitely.[25]

It should be noted that Congress did give additional support to the West Point Academy. An act of April 29, 1816, appropriated $115,800 for new buildings and an additional $22,171 for maps, books, and instruments. A Board of Visitors composed of "gentlemen versed in military and other science" had been created in 1815 to render semi-annual reports on the status of the academy and examine orally the competency of the cadets. Perhaps most important of all, the academy was infused with new vigor by the appointment of Major Sylvanus Thayer as superintendent in 1817. Under his leadership the academy became the principal entry point into the officer corps and one of the finest military schools in the world.[26]

Madison's call for the retention of some staff officers in his annual message adverted to the interpretation put on the reduction act of March 3, 1815, that the 10,000 established by the law did not include officers and staff. Secretary of War William H. Crawford, in response to a request from Johnson's committee for recommendations, delivered a report on December 27, 1815, which became the basis for an Army Staff bill passed on April 24, 1816. Crawford argued essentially that the military staff "should be substantially the same in peace as in war, without reference to the number or distribution of the troops," and that full staffs should be established in each of the two divisions created by the general order of May 17, 1815.[27] In fact, the army had never had a general staff or a commanding general. Prior to the War of 1812, most of the staff officials were assigned to the principal army (such as the Quartermaster General), rather than being stationed in Washington. The coordination of staff activity was largely the responsibility of the secretary of war. During the War of 1812, a general staff bill was passed on March 3, 1813, but while it gathered more officials in Washington, they were deputies or assistants who assisted the secretary of war. As constituted, it was more a housekeeping staff than a general staff.[28] The debate in the House revolved more around the status of certain staff officers provisionally retained after the passage of the army reduction act of March 1815, but there was no substantial objection to Crawford's recommendations. The House, in fact, passed the bill easily, as did the Senate, and it became law on April 24, 1816.[29]

No attempt was made to centralize the command of the army under a single officer. Two separate divisions were created, the Northern commanded by Maj. Gen. Jacob Brown, and the Southern commanded by Maj. Gen. Andrew Jackson. One reason, perhaps, was that Brown was the senior officer, and the prickly personality of Andrew Jackson suggested he might not accept a secondary position or would not have worked well in a subordinate position.[30] Jackson was even allowed to use his home, the Hermitage, as his military headquarters. Jackson and Secretary of War Crawford immediately clashed over a treaty with the Cherokees in March 1816 that returned land the tribe claimed Jackson had mistakenly included in his Treaty of Fort Jackson with the Creeks in 1814. Jackson angrily appealed to Secretary of State James Monroe accusing Crawford of siding with the Indians against American citizens.[31]

In fact, Crawford and Jackson had widely varying views on treatment of Indians. In a report in April, Crawford urged the government to carefully supervise dealings between Indians and American traders to avoid exploitation. "The utter extinction of the Indian race," Crawford asserted, would be the result of unregulated trade and continual warfare, which he declared, "must be abhorrent to the feelings of an enlightened and benevolent nation." While this statement did credit to Crawford, his view was not only out of step with Jackson but the people of the West generally. He then compounded his error by suggesting that a way to preserve the Indian race was to "let intermarriage between them and the whites be encouraged by the government."[32]

Crawford was a rising power in the Republican Party. Born in Virginia, he practiced law in his adopted state of Georgia and rose in politics to become a United States Senator. His physical presence, affability, and undeniable talents attracted many supporters, particularly among those generally known as Old Republicans, or followers of Jeffersonian principles. A supporter of the War of 1812, Crawford served as Minister to France during the war and returned at its end to become secretary of war. The negative reaction in the West to his views on Indians was not confined to Jackson alone, and Crawford hastily retreated. He authorized Jackson to head a three-man commission to negotiate with the Cherokees, Choctaws, and Chickasaws. Negotiations began in September 1816. Jackson imperiously demanded the tribes turn over vast chunks of their territory. He concluded treaties with the Cherokees and the Chickasaws in September, facilitated by bribes of the tribal leaders, and in October 1816, commissioners headed by John Coffee concluded an agreement with the Choctaws. Not only did the United States gain huge tracts from the Indians, but these land grabs paved the way for the removal of the so-called civilized tribes from the Eastern United States.[33]

On another matter Crawford and Jackson agreed, and that was the problem of the so-called Negro fort. This fort, which was located on the Apalachicola River in Florida about sixty miles south of the United States border, was a haven for about 250 to 300 fugitive slaves, Indians, women, and children. The fort was not only a magnet for runaway slaves, it was also a base for marauding expeditions against slaveholders in the region.[34] On March 15, 1816, Crawford, describing the inhabitants as "well armed, clothed and disciplined," instructed Jackson to call this "evil" to the attention of the Spanish military commander. If the Spanish failed to act, the United States would destroy the fort. Jackson needed no persuasion, and on April 8, he gave Brig. Gen. Edmund P. Gaines the discretion to destroy the fort, but he cautioned him to notify the Commandant of Pensacola, Mauricio de Zuniga, of his intent. Then, two weeks later, Jackson addressed Zuniga himself that if the fort was not put down, the United States would be compelled in self-defense to destroy the fort. On June 4, Jackson received a message from Zuniga pleading an inability to carry out the task themselves, and granting the United States permission to destroy the fort. Zuniga even offered to assist Jackson in this effort. Gaines, however, took care of the task. In July, United States troops led by Col. Duncan Clinch laid siege to the fort. After ten days, a direct hit on a powder magazine caused a tremendous explosion, killing all but about forty of the inhabitants of the fort.[35]

Jackson's aggressive personality was also revealed in a dispute with the War Department that extended from 1816 into 1817. In the summer of 1816 the War Department instructed Maj. Stephen H. Long, a Topographical Engineer, to report to Washington. The department was only following an earlier *bad* precedent by not sending Jackson a copy of this order. He only learned indirectly that Long had been pulled from his command. Jackson informed Acting Secretary of War George Graham on January 14, 1817, that this order was "inconsistent with all military rule, and subversive of the first principles of that subordination which ought, & must be maintained." Graham's reply was unsatisfactory: "It is distinctly to be understood, that this department at all times exercises the right of assigning officers to the performance of Special duties, at its discretion." Jackson's response was to issue a division order on April 22, 1817, forbidding officers under his command from obeying any order from the War Department, unless it came through the commanding general of the division.[36]

Jackson, who placed such importance on subordination, thus countenanced Brig. Gen. Eleazer Ripley's refusal in the summer of 1817, in conformity to his division commander's order, to obey an order directly from the War Department. Jackson distinctly threatened retirement if his view was not upheld. Fortunately, the new Secretary of War John C. Calhoun, assuaged Jackson by promising not to issue any orders to his subordinates, except where the "public interest" might require a deviation from that rule, and even in that case a copy would be forwarded to Jackson.[37] It should be noted that Jackson did not contend for the right to contest War Department powers to transfer officers from one division to another, but he did gain his point that when such transfers were made that the orders come through him.

When the second session of the Fourteenth Congress convened, Acting Secretary of War George Graham's report, responding to the House resolution of April 16 for a plan for classing and arming the militia was awaiting them. His plan, dated December 13, 1816, would break the militia into three classes: a minor class, 18–21 years old; a junior class, ages 21–31; and the senior class, 31–45. The minor class would serve only within the state, the senior only in adjoining states and territories. Emphasis was placed on the junior class, which would be called to serve anywhere and would be trained in two encampments per year for one month. They would be given the same organization as the regular army, and while in encampments they would be placed under the orders of the president. Graham's estimate for training 100,000 men at regular army pay for one month was $173,850, and $1.5 million for one million militia.[38]

Graham's plan also included details about how the militia would be supplied, paid, the method of call-outs, punishments, and many other particulars that would have undoubtedly made the militia more efficient and possibly even effective. It was, however, far from being realistic politically. The War of 1812 hero, William Henry Harrison of the Committee on the Militia, reported favorably on Graham's plan. During the war, he argued, a great sacrifice of blood and treasure could be "traced to the want of discipline in the militia." A diffusion of military spirit would be a counterpoise "to that inordinate desire of wealth which seems to have pervaded the whole nation, bringing with it habits of luxury, manners, and principles highly unfavorable to our republican institutions."[39]

Timothy Pickering, a former secretary of war, opposed Graham's plan, declaring militia could never be disciplined without placing them on the footing of regular soldiers, an idea that had long been abandoned. The government, he said, should be satisfied with arming and regimenting, leaving discipline to the states. Harrison, however, persisted. On February 28, he proposed a constitutional amendment to enable the government to adopt a system of military instruction and discipline for the militia, concurrently with the states. He also recommended teaching military knowledge as part of the curriculum of every school. Congress, however, refused to take on the responsibility and cost of training the militia, and Harrison's proposal was laid on the table.[40]

The lack of interest in militia reform was in part due to the growing professionalism of the army as well as a developing conviction in Congress that the militia was not a reliable defense force. No doubt, the fear of a standing army was also declining. The *Albany Argus*, in fact, declared shortly after the Act of March 3, 1815, establishing a 10,000–man force, that it represented the "predominance of popular feeling."[41] The support for the army did not run deep, however. Almost as soon as the act passed there was an almost constant pressure to reduce the size of the army. During the first session of the Fourteenth Congress, the army came under attack particularly during the debate on retention of the direct tax. Benjamin Hardin of Kentucky was among those who asserted the taxes had to be maintained to support the army, and he denied any need to keep a large standing army. National glory, he maintained, was reducing the national debt and government expenses to allow people to enjoy the fruits of their labor.[42] John Randolph agreed that retention of the tax was to pay for an unnecessary military establishment.[43] Samuel S. Connor of Massachusetts, however, stated that he considered the army honorable and useful, and he lacked the confidence in the militia that Hardin expressed. Connor declared that he would never prostrate the defenses of the country.[44] Calhoun pointed out that the country was growing rapidly and was certain to be regarded by the British "with a jealous eye," requiring the maintenance of a strong army, navy, and fortifications.[45] Cyrus King, a Federalist, launched into a diatribe against the "oppressive taxes" to support an "overgrown, expensive" military establishment, and he declared he had never expected "to hear eulogies on this floor in favor of standing armies."[46]

Nothing came out of the anti-army rhetoric in the first session. When a bill was introduced during the second session on January 10, 1817, making a partial appropriation of $400,000 for subsistence of the army, opposition came from surprising quarters. Henry Clay declared that he thought the government paid more money and got less military service "than any other country in the world," and he wanted to know whether the extraordinary expenses of the War Department might not be retrenched. Randolph expressed his pleasure at hearing "the long exploded word economy" in the House. He reminded the House of his motion in the last session to reduce the army. Clay responded that he did not yet think the military establishment ought to be destroyed.[47] The issue of army reduction had at least been raised, and it was the subject of considerable debate during the discussion on the direct tax.[48] In the Senate a motion was made by Jeremiah Mason from New Hampshire on February 17, 1817, to reduce the army to 5000. He was opposed vigorously by James Barbour and James Brown, and Mason's motion was easily beaten back by a vote of 24–11.[49] Army reduction continued to be an issue in subsequent years, and the anti-army faction finally succeeded in reducing the army to 6000 men in 1821.[50]

During the Senate debate, it was argued that a 10,000–man navy was more efficient and cheaper than the 10,000–man army ($4 million versus $6 million). Jeremiah Mason contended it was also the "most congenial to the principles of our Government." Both Barbour and Brown acknowledged the value of the navy, but they insisted that both could be supported.[51] The navy was a particular favorite of both parties, and all shades of the political spectrum. As Cyrus King stated, "The Navy is the darling of the people. They will protect it."[52] Not only had the American navy won glory in several naval engagements during the War of 1812, it had recently chastised the Dey of Algeria. Consequently, there was little objection to President Madison's suggestion in his annual message of December 5, 1815, to enlarge and maintain a standing navy.[53]

Secretary of the Navy Benjamin Crowinshield, asserted in his message to Congress on December 11, 1815, that a permanent naval establishment was "sanctioned by the voice of the nation." He recommended adding annually one seventy-four-gun ship-of-the-line, two forty-four-gun frigates, and two sloops of war. The House Naval Affairs Committee recommended instead an annual appropriation of $1,000,000 for eight years, which would add nine seventy-four-gun ships, twelve forty-four-gun ships, and three steam batteries. Instead of sloops of war, the priority should be heavy ships. Each seventy-four-gun ship was estimated to cost about $385,000; each forty-four-gun ship about $268,000, and the three steam batteries about $1,000,000.[54]

Congressional attitudes about the navy had already been clearly revealed during the debate over revenue measures. Calhoun, in addition to calling the navy "the most safe, most effectual, and the cheapest mode of defence," also asserted its importance in maintaining American security in the new situation after the late war. His concern was that the United States was more vulnerable and endangered by the outcome of the War of 1812. The navies that had challenged Great Britain prior to the war, the French, Dutch, and Spanish, had been mostly destroyed and American commerce was more exposed to depredation. He noted that our American interests collided with only two nations, England and Spain. England was the most formidable power. America's growth had aroused her jealousy, and a future war with her was not only possible but probable.[55] Randolph, while he declared that he did not object to taxes for national defense, was a lone voice of skepticism against a large navy. Building up the navy, he said, "becomes in the end nothing better than a great job."[56]

There was little debate on the naval bill; as James Pleasants of Virginia, chair of the House Naval Affairs Committee said, "the public mind is made up on this subject." Instead, the House argued where the steam batteries should be located, and whether they were superior to ships for defense. The measure passed on April 15. The Senate made a minor amendment, which was agreed to by the House, and Madison signed the Naval Expansion Act of 1816 on April 29, 1816.[57] One historian declared this act "one of the most important in the legislative history of the Navy as it committed the United States, for the first time to a policy of building up a fleet in peacetime which was comparable to those of European powers." In the next few years nine ships-of-the-line and nine frigates were completed. The steam batteries proposed by the law were not undertaken until the 1830s.[58] While these ships were assigned duties primarily to defend American commerce, eliminate piracy, and interdict the slave trade, the larger navy was also a diplomatic weapon the United States did not hesitate to display particularly to the Spanish and the rebels in Latin America, which contributed to diplomatic successes such as the Adams-Onís treaty in 1819.[59]

Although appropriations fluctuated following the Act of 1816, the navy came out better than the army and the executive department. In the retrenchment in 1821, naval appropriation cuts were not as deep as those for the army, which was reduced to a 6000–man force. The navy suffered only a drop of twenty-one percent in 1821, while the army was cut by twice as much.[60] This setback was only temporary, and by the time John Quincy Adams was elected president in 1824 naval appropriations were on the rise once more.

Overall, Congress could take some pride in the military build-up after the War of 1812. It had established a 10,000–man force composed of veterans from that war, and the officer corps was very high quality. It had also provided funding for coastal fortifications, and it had improved the West Point Military Academy. Finally, it provided for the creation of a world-class navy. Some of this can be attributed to the lessons learned from the War of 1812. Another factor was a growing nationalism and pride in the outcome of the war. Perhaps the most important reason, however, was a genuine fear of a renewed war with the British and anticipation of a possible conflict with Spain in the borderlands or in Latin America.

Chapter 9

State Developments

Much was happening at the state level during 1816 that would have significant consequences in the future. In addition to important projects begun in the Middle Atlantic states to develop canals and roads in that region, in New England a dispute between the trustees and the president of Dartmouth College would eventually result in an momentous Supreme Court decision in 1819, and the people of Maine were struggling to gain statehood by separating from Massachusetts, which was finally achieved in 1820. There were statehood movements in the South and West, as well as other issues between the states, including border disputes that were resolved or were moving to resolution in 1816.

At Dartmouth, relations between the Board of Trustees and President John Wheelock, son of the founder, Eleazar Wheelock, deteriorated and finally erupted in 1816. John Wheelock had become the president of the college in 1779, and he was accustomed to running the school in his own way. In time, the trustees began to rebel against Wheelock's tyrannical rule. Sensing he was losing control, Wheelock attempted to put down the trustees and regain authority over the school. In the spring of 1815, he wrote a pamphlet, *Sketches of the History of Dartmouth College*, accusing the trustees, among other things, of misappropriating funds, and he followed this with a call to the legislature to investigate the affairs and management of the institution.[1]

The dispute thus became a political issue. The trustees became identified with the Federalists, and the Republican Party supported Wheelock. A hearing was held before a committee appointed by

Governor John T. Gilman, beginning on August 16, 1815. On August 26, the trustees, without waiting for the committee's report, stated their lack of confidence in Wheelock, accused him of numerous improprieties, dismissed him as president of the institution, and stripped him of all relationship to the college. Two days later the trustees appointed the Rev. Francis Brown as the new president of Dartmouth.[2]

The Republicans, with whom Wheelock had little in common, made him a martyr, and the whole affair became a big political issue in the spring 1816 election for governor. Many Federalist friends of Wheelock supported the Republican candidate for governor, William Plumer, a former Federalist Senator who had left the party prior to the War of 1812 and who had served a term as governor during the war.[3] Plumer won the March election over his Federalist opponent, James Sheafe, 20,338 to 17,994. Voters also elected a majority Republican legislature. In his inaugural address on June 6, 1816, Plumer immediately raised the Dartmouth College problem. The state, he contended, had contributed liberally to its funds. He characterized the 1769 charter that gave the trustees power to supply vacancies as "hostile to the spirit and genius of a free government," and he asserted, "The college was formed for the public good, not for the benefit or emolument of its trustees." He recommended changing the mode of their election and increasing the number of trustees. Further, the president of the college should report annually to the governor on the state of the college, which would act as a check upon the proceedings of the trustees and give the legislature information to enable them to act with greater propriety upon whatever related to that institution. He called for "material changes" in the charter, and he declared the legislature had the authority to act upon this subject.[4]

Plumer proudly communicated a copy of his message to former President Thomas Jefferson, who replied that it contained sound republican principles. "The idea that institutions established for the use of the nation cannot be touched or modified," Jefferson wrote, "because of rights gratuitously supposed in those employed to manage them in trust for the public ... is most absurd." The Sage of Monticello continued that the doctrine that preceding generations had the right to impose unalterable laws upon succeeding generations insinuated that "the earth belongs to the dead, and not to the living."[5]

The next day, June 7, Plumer sent to the legislature the investigating committee report, dated April 23, 1816. The committee reviewed Wheelock's charges against the board and cited numerous documents, but it refrained from drawing any conclusions from the disputed facts.[6] On June 21, based on this report, a Senate committee recommended an enlarged board of trustees which would give more regard to public opinion and would be "less likely to transmit to successors those prejudices and acrimony, from which beings possessed of human passions cannot be expected to prove exempt."[7]

The House of Representatives accepted the investigating committee report on June 20. A proposal was then made to change the name of the institution from Dartmouth College to Dartmouth University, raise the number of trustees from twelve to twenty-one, and create a board of overseers with a veto power over actions of the trustees. Motions to recommit and to postpone were defeated. An opposition motion on June 25 to request an opinion of the state supreme court whether the bill was consistent with the constitutions of the United States and New Hampshire and whether the bill would "endanger or affect the title of Dartmouth College to any of its present funds or donations, in this, or any other state," was defeated, 94–88, which gave an indication of the probable outcome.[8]

After the bill passed the House, one of the members, Edmund Topping, gave notice that he and others would enter a protest against the bill. Two days later, their protest was entered into the journal of the House, signed by Topping and seventy-four others. They asserted that among the rights and privileges bestowed upon the trustees by their charter was holding real and personal property, which had "every feature of a contract." In fact, various grants had been made to the trustees which would not have been made had it been believed the legislature could, "for political, or any other sinister purposes . . . enlarge, diminish and modify, at their arbitrary will and pleasure, the corporation of the college." Interference with the rights of the trustees "without judicial enquiry or proof of misconduct," they argued, was a violation of contract and a clear violation of the United States Constitution (Art. 1, Sec. 10) which declared that no state shall make "any law impairing the obligation of contracts." The protest also contended the trustees were virtually declared guilty of the charges of Wheelock by the law, without being heard in their own defense. It also asserted that the college was prospering and that legislative interference was not only unnecessary but might endanger the future prospects of the institution, which would become "subject to every change and revolution of party."[9]

In the Senate, all efforts to amend and postpone were easily defeated, and the bill became law on June 27.[10] The legislature thus transformed a private college into a public institution. The Board of Trustees, however, refused to go along with the new law. In fact, they declared they would not recognize or act under its authority. They also denounced it as dangerous to the best interests of society; that it violated their rights; subjected the college to the arbitrary will and pleasure of the Legislature; and was unconstitutional.[11] The governor and his council, however, in accordance with the law, duly appointed nine additional trustees (making twenty-one) and twenty-five members to the Board of Overseers. However, when Plumer called a meeting for August 26, in Hanover, there was no quorum due to the non-attendance of the original trustees, and no official action could be taken.[12]

When the legislature convened for its second session in November, Plumer called upon them to ponder "whether a law, passed and approved by all the constitutional authorities of the State, shall be carried into effect; or whether . . . *a minority* of the trustees . . . shall be encouraged to inculcate the doctrine of resistance to the law, and their example tolerated, in disseminating principles of insubordination and rebellion against government." The legislature responded promptly by reducing the number necessary for a quorum and gave the governor authority to fill vacancies occurring on the board of trustees.[13]

Armed with this new authority, Governor Plumer convened another meeting of trustees in February 1817, and this time the original trustees could not prevent a quorum by staying away. President Brown, two professors, and three members of the original board were removed from office. Wheelock was restored as president, and the buildings were taken over by the state. The original trustees, however, still refused to accept the new situation. They retained the vast majority of the students, and they arranged for classes to meet in borrowed rooms off campus. Thus there was a college and a university operating simultaneously, a fact confirmed by the award of honorary degrees by both the college and the university to President James Monroe when he visited New Hampshire in the summer of 1817. The trustees also instituted a suit against William H. Woodward, the college treasurer, to return the charter and other college records and insignia. Unfortunately for the college trustees, they lost their case in the New Hampshire Superior Court in November 1817. They appealed to the United States Supreme Court, where they were represented by one of their most distinguished graduates, Daniel Webster, class of 1801.[14]

Webster argued the case before the Supreme Court in March 1818, essentially that the act of the legislature was a taking of private property. The issue was whether the college was a public institution and whether the charter was a contract protected by the Constitution. Chief Justice John Marshall announced the decision of the court on February 2, 1819. He ruled that the college was a private institution and that the charter was a "continuing contract with a continuing obligation," and was protected from invasion of its rights by the state legislature.[15] The case's lasting significance was summed up by historian John Garraty: "It confirmed the charter rights not only of Dartmouth College but of all private colleges. It protected and encouraged business corporations as well as non-profit corporations."[16]

Although they may not have liked the Supreme Court decision, there is no indication that New Hampshire considered rejecting the Marshall court's action. Virginia, however, did attempt to nullify a Supreme Court case, which led to another landmark decision in 1816. The issue was the legal status of the Fairfax estate in the Northern Neck of Virginia that had lingered in the courts for a quarter of a century. In simplified terms, the state had seized the lands during the Revolution, and had disposed of a portion of the lands to David Hunter. The heir of the estate, claiming rights under the Treaty of Paris of 1783, maintained his possession and disposed of many of the same lands to others. Chief Justice Marshall was closely associated with his brothers in a number of lawsuits to establish clear legal title to lands they had purchased from an heir to the estate. While they won some cases, a Virginia Court of Appeals case in 1810 affirmed the Hunter claim. The Marshalls appealed to the United States Supreme Court. In 1813, the Court, with Marshall not participating, reversed the state court's ruling in *Fairfax's Devisee v. Hunter's Lessee*. The Virginia Court of Appeals, dominated by Judge Spencer Roane, refused to comply, and announced in December 1815 their defiance of the decision. The basis of their argument was that the Supreme Court's appellate jurisdiction did not extend to the Virginia court and that Section 25 of the Judiciary Act of 1789 was unconstitutional. On a writ of error, the nature of the Supreme Court's appellate jurisdiction became the basis of the nationalistic decision, *Martin v. Hunter's Lessee*, delivered by Justice Joseph Story on March 20, 1816. He reaffirmed the earlier decision and asserted unequivocally that the Constitution gave the Supreme Court the power to rule on decisions of state courts.[17]

Although Story's opinion was powerfully argued, it was not conclusive as far as the Virginia judges and Spencer Roane were concerned. The issue of the Supreme Court's jurisdiction was raised again in 1821 on another appeal from a Virginia court, based on Section 25 of the Judiciary Act of 1789. The case was *Cohens v. Virginia*, a simple appeal of a conviction for selling lottery tickets from the District of Columbia in Virginia. Marshall, for the Court, ruled for the state, but not before he again affirmed the principle of the jurisdiction of the federal courts over state courts; otherwise the federal government would be prostrated "at the feet of every state in the Union."[18]

Citizens of Maine in 1816 were trying to gain separation from Massachusetts in order to gain statehood status. Maine entered the union as part of Massachusetts, but it was physically separated, and citizens of Maine believed their problems were neglected or poorly understood in Massachusetts. They complained that trade regulations enriched Boston and hurt Maine, that they were denied appropriate representation in the legislature, and that the taxes and fees levied by Massachusetts were inequitable and worked a hardship on Maine. A movement for independence from Massachusetts began as early as 1785.[19]

While the agitation never ceased, the War of 1812 gave an impetus to the movement. Maine's citizens believed their defense during the war suffered from neglect. A Maine historian noted, "No event in all the previous history of the union of Massachusetts and Maine so blatantly revealed the extent to which the interests of Maine could be sacrificed to those of Massachusetts proper."[20] In the post-war period, several new young, vigorous leaders joined with the acknowledged leader of the separation movement, William King, the brother of New York Senator Rufus King. Among the new leaders were Albion K. Parris, a United States Representative; William Pitt Preble, the United States District Attorney for Maine; and John Holmes, who was elected to Congress from Maine in 1816.[21]

Their efforts culminated in approval by the Federalist-dominated Massachusetts legislature to allow the people of Maine to vote on separation on May 20, 1816. An apparent motive of the Massachusetts Federalists was that a separation of the mostly Republican Maine would strengthen their control over Massachusetts. Conversely, Federalists in Maine feared becoming a perpetual minority, and many (but not all) now opposed separation. The voter turnout in the May election was very light, reflecting perhaps voter indecision rather than any firm conviction for or against separation. While the pro-separation forces prevailed by a margin of 10,391 to 6,501, less than half of the nearly 38,000 eligible voted. The voting pattern generally reflected the Republican interior against the Federalist coastal region. Some Republican seaport towns, however, defected to the anti-separation side, probably because of how separation would affect their shipping business. Under the 1789 Coasting Law, ships were required to enter and clear customs houses (and pay a fee) in every state not contiguous to their state. Thus vessels from Maine could travel as far as New Jersey without stopping. Separation would remove that advantage, because only New Hampshire was contiguous.[22]

When the Massachusetts legislature met in late May 1816, the Maine vote result was one of the issues considered. Opponents of separation contended that the large number of non-voters should be considered an expression of opposition, while supporters suggested the opposite conclusion. A joint committee of both houses, chaired by Harrison Gray Otis, simply concluded "that the great majority of the people are in a state of indifference in relation to the question," and that some other means of determining the sense of the people was necessary. If the people of Maine desired separation, for whatever reasons, Otis continued, it was better for mutual harmony to allow them to do so, but only on sound principles. The committee submitted a bill that was passed by both houses and received the approval of Governor John Brooks on June 20, 1816. The law provided another vote by the citizens of Maine would be taken on September 2 whether to separate. They would also elect delegates equal to the number of representatives Maine sent to the Massachusetts legislature for a convention to be held on the last Monday in September. If the people by a five to four margin voted for separation, then the convention delegates were authorized to draw up a constitution and petition Congress for admission into the union. Conditions or terms for separation, such as division of public lands and the state debt, and other such details were included.[23]

Opponents of separation seized upon the conditions placed upon Maine as an additional reason for defeating the question. A convention held at Brunswick on August 1, composed of delegates from Cumberland, Oxford, Lincoln, and Kennebeck counties, submitted an address to the people of Maine raising questions about the expediency of separation. They contended that Maine presently received many benefits from their connection with Massachusetts, but with separation it would not only lose these benefits, but Massachusetts would make as good a bargain for herself as she could. They asserted that setting up a government in Maine would cost $30,000, and running the government would force a raise in annual taxes of approximately $40,000. The expense of erecting a statehouse, a new prison, and other public buildings would force the state to borrow perhaps $150,000. Expenses would double the present taxes, and they asked, "Is this not paying too dear for the mere name of Independence?"[24]

The result of the vote on September 2 seemed to support the argument that those who did not vote previously were opposed to separation. While the separation vote increased about 1600 to 12,007, the anti-separation vote rose dramatically by nearly 3900 to 10,382.[25] More importantly, the margin of difference did not reach the five-ninths required by the law. When the Brunswick Convention convened on September 30, it was found that the separationists held a slight majority of twelve out of the 188 that eventually attended. William King was elected president of the convention by that margin. He appointed a committee to examine the returns, with John Holmes as the chair. Their report was, however, largely the work of William Preble. It argued disingenuously that there were two ways of interpreting five-ninths. It was not clear to the committee that it meant simply the excess of one number over another. In fact, they concluded that the term majority applied to the votes of the towns. By applying that standard, they found that the aggregate majority of yeas in towns in favor was 6,031 and the aggregate majority of nays in the towns opposed was 4,409, which of course exceeded the five-ninths required by the law.[26]

The committee tried to gloss over the problem, stating that they believed any interpretation of the law should "comport with the public will," which they asserted "has often been decidedly and unequivocally expressed." They also argued that the Massachusetts legislature would undoubtedly "confirm this construction, or otherwise, explain or modify the law, so as to give effect to the voice of the majority of the people."[27] The report also recommended the formation of a committee of five to apply to the Massachusetts legislature to confirm Maine as a separate state; a committee of twenty-five to report a constitution; and a committee of three to apply to Congress for statehood and, in case of separation, "to procure a law relieving coastal trade of additional embarrassment."[28]

The opposition was livid at this brazen attempt to by-pass the law and ram statehood through the convention. Nevertheless, despite their vigorous attacks upon the report, it was adopted on October 8 by a vote of 103–84. King, the presiding officer, then appointed the designated committees, and the convention adjourned on October 9. The anti-separation forces, however, appended a protest to the proceedings of the convention. Signed by seventy-two members, the dissenters asserted that since the result of the election plainly did not meet the requirement of a majority of five to four, nothing remained to be done by the convention. Any further action taken by the convention should be considered as "a usurpation . . . mistaken in principle, and dangerous in their tendency, and if effectuated, will be subversive of the liberties of the citizens."[29]

Anti-separation newspapers heaped scorn on the Brunswick Convention report. The Massachusetts legislature formed another joint committee, again chaired by Harrison Gray Otis, which reported on November 16 that "the Convention have misconstrued the act by which their powers were defined." They rejected the specious reasoning of the report, declaring that it was self-evident the terms of the law were not met and, consequently, that the powers of the convention were at an end. While the majority vote in favor of separation appeared to reflect a disposition for separation, it was by no means conclusive. They noted the committee had not recommended the five-ninths majority and that it had been added in the legislature "with the full approbation and consent of the advocates of separation." Moreover, from the results of the two votes in May and September, it did not appear that the tide in favor of separation had been greatly augmented. No prejudice could arise from delay, they asserted, and they declared it was inexpedient "to adopt any further measures in regard to the separation of the District of Maine."[30]

The Massachusetts legislature approved on December 4, 1816, and the separation movement was temporarily thwarted. For a time the movement languished. Not until December 1818 did the advocates again muster enough interest to renew their call for separation. Their effort was aided by the support of Rufus King in Congress, who got a revision of the coasting law permitting coasting vessels to pass from Maine to Georgia without entering or clearing. This law, and William King's promise to the Federalists that he would share one third of the appointments in the new government, removed the last obstacles to separation. In June 1819, the Massachusetts legislature passed another law authorizing a vote on separation that followed closely the terms of the 1816 law. The vote on July 26, 1819, gave an overwhelming victory to the separationists, 17,091 to 7,132. The state constitution was drawn up in October. Maine's petition for statehood got entangled in the Missouri controversy, but it was finally admitted as the twenty-third state on March 15, 1820.[31]

Both the Dartmouth College case and the Maine statehood movement reflected the growing maturity of the nation. New Hampshire's attempt to "republicanize" an educational institution in their state may have been well intentioned, but it was misguided, and the United States Supreme Court had the courage to challenge state authority and establish an important precedent regarding the sanctity of contracts. The Maine statehood movement culminated successfully because the legislature of Massachusetts was willing to accept gracefully the loss of a considerable portion of the state's territory, but only after the people of the District of Maine were able to show clearly their disposition to separate.

Despite the apprehension of many Americans, the rapid growth of the West in the post–War of 1812 era led to two statehood movements in the western territories by 1816. The petition for Indiana statehood was acted upon affirmatively, while the request of the

Mississippi Territory, which was also asking for statehood, was put off. In fact, the Indiana petition was more advanced. They had conducted a census and sent a certified statement to Congress showing their population exceeded the required 60,000. The Mississippi Territory had not done so. A House committee reported on December 29, 1815, that they had no clear idea of the population of the Mississippi Territory. William Lattimore, the territorial delegate, confirmed that four years earlier "a small minority" of the lower house of the territorial legislature had opposed the statehood movement and that about a year later, "a considerable number of the people themselves petitioned that all proceedings in Congress on the subject might be postponed." He now believed there was strong support for statehood, and he asked that a census be conducted to confirm the population requirement had been met by the territory.[32]

The Indiana enabling bill passed the House overwhelmingly, 108 to 3, on March 30, while the Mississippi petition was recommitted by a 70 to 53 vote.[33] Concerns were raised about the size of the Mississippi Territory (which included present-day states of Alabama and Mississippi), and many believed it should be divided into two parts. Slavery does not appear to have been an issue at this time, although undoubtedly Southern supporters understood that division of the territory into two states would enhance the Southern position in the United States Senate. In the Senate the two petitions followed a similar path. A census was called for in the Mississippi Territory to distinguish the numbers of inhabitants on the east and west sides of the Tombigbee River. The Senate postponed the Mississippi statehood bill on April 25.[34]

The Indiana statehood bill from the House was approved by the Senate on April 13, with amendments, which were accepted by the House two days later. President Madison signed the enabling bill on April 19. A constitutional convention met at Corydon on June 10 and the state constitution was proclaimed to the people on June 29.[35] When the second session of the Fourteenth Congress met, the Senate immediately took up Indiana statehood on December 2. The House received a resolution from the Senate on December 6 on admitting Indiana. In committee of the whole on December 9, some members criticized the unseemly haste, but the state constitution was read, approved, and passed unanimously. Formal admission of Indiana as the nineteenth state was approved by Congress on December 11, 1816. William Hendricks took his seat in the House that same day, and the following day the credentials of James Noble and Waller Taylor were read, an oath was administered, and they took their seats in the Senate.[36]

The Mississippi statehood movement was also taken up in the second session. William Lattimore reported an enabling bill on December 23, 1816, to form a state constitution and seek admission into statehood. His report included a breakdown of the territory's population: 45,085 whites, 356 free blacks, and 30,061 slaves, a total of 75,512. His bill would divide the territory and admit the western half. On December 30, a legislative petition from the territory was presented to the House accepting a division of the territory and praying admission.[37] One complication arose, however. Israel Pickens of North Carolina submitted a petition on January 9, 1817, from a convention of fifteen counties in the Mississippi Territory praying that the territory not be divided but admitted as a state with its present limits. Eight days later he delivered a report to the House sustaining this position.[38]

In fact, there was sentiment in the territory against division, but there was also support for division of the territory into two states. An anonymous address to the people of the territory on December 4, 1815, by "Tempus Nunc," argued that with nearly 100,000 square miles, the territory was much larger than even the largest state, Virginia, which had about 71,000 square miles. The time was now, he asserted, to achieve statehood for the western section of the territory. Although he denied any sectional feeling, he noted that the North was about to increase its influence, with Indiana, Maine, and Illinois soon to become states. By dividing the territory into two states, the people would have an equal number of representatives in Congress but double the number of senators and electors for president.[39]

In the meantime, the Senate had been working on its own bill. Charles Tait of Georgia introduced a bill on January 17, 1817, to enable the western part of the Mississippi Territory to form a constitution and seek statehood. At the same time he presented another bill to organize the eastern part into a separate territorial government. The statehood bill was amended slightly in the committee of the whole and then was passed by the Senate on January 31, 1817, by a two to one margin.[40] The Senate bill was received by the House that same day, but it did not act on the bill until February 24, 1817. A motion by Pickens to strike and insert admission of the whole territory was rejected, as was an attempt by John W. Taylor to postpone the whole bill indefinitely. The House approved the statehood bill on February 26, 1817, and the Senate approved the bill the next day. Mississippi was officially admitted on March 1, 1817.[41]

State boundaries during this period were in many cases still in dispute. One example was the line between North and South Carolina. On December 9, 1815, Governor William Miller of North Carolina informed his legislature that a line had been run and accepted by representatives of the two states, which if approved, would "put an end to this long subsisting difference." The enclosed report detailed the work of three representatives from North Carolina, Thomas Love, Montfort Stokes, and John Patton, with South Carolina representatives, Joseph Blythe, John Blasingame, and George W. Earle, who met and approved the new line drawn by surveyors Ross Alexander for North Carolina and George Salmon for South Carolina. Adjustments were made "in the spirit of reciprocal accommodation" to the 1772 line and the Cherokee line run in 1797 which left all the waters of the Saluda River within the state of South Carolina and the Greene River in North Carolina.[42] The new boundary line was approved by both houses by December 20, 1815.[43]

A similar boundary dispute existed between Kentucky and Tennessee. A communication from Kentucky Governor Isaac Shelby informed his legislature on December 22, 1815, that Tennessee had passed a law to establish and settle the boundary between the two states, and they wanted Kentucky to pass a similar law. The Tennessee law stated that the so-called Walker line should be established as the official line. On January 4, 1816, a report from Secretary of State Martin D. Hardin detailed the history of the boundary dispute. The legislature of Virginia had, on December 7, 1791, while Kentucky was still part of that state, established the Walker line as the boundary between Virginia and North Carolina. However, North Carolina had, prior to the Virginia Act, ceded sovereignty of the area to the United States. Kentucky and Tennessee both took the position that the Virginia law was not conclusive nor binding on either state. Moreover, the boundary between Virginia and Tennessee had been adjusted since the latter had become a state. The Kentucky legislature authorized commissioners to run a line with Tennessee in 1801, but nothing was done. In 1803, Tennessee passed a similar law, but this time Kentucky did not follow up. In February 1812, the Kentucky legislature again authorized the appointment of commissioners to determine where the line should run, and they declared that if Tennessee failed to cooperate, they would run the line themselves. No response came from Tennessee, but no commissioners were appointed by Kentucky, and again nothing was done. In late 1812, however, a letter from Tennessee Governor Willie Blount declared the Walker line was to be the boundary line of the state, and the state had authorized commissioners to adjust and establish parts of the line that had not been run and marked. At the next session of the Kentucky legislature, they passed a law that directed the governor to communicate to Tennessee that Kentucky was determined to adhere to the principles of their law of February 1812, and they asked Tennessee to recognize these principles and adopt measures to carry them into effect. The letter was forwarded on March 30, 1813, but no answer was received from Tennessee, and that was the situation at the beginning of 1816.[44]

Hardin explained that a fire in the Capitol in 1813 had destroyed many of the documents relating to this matter, but he was able to include some. One document, forwarded to the governor of Kentucky by Col. Arthur Campbell of Virginia, dated December 1806, was a certificate or statement from Capt. Meriwether Lewis after his return from the Pacific, giving his observations and calculations on Walker's line at Walling's, about two miles from the Cumberland Gap on November 23, 1806, taken by instruments he had used on that exploration. By Lewis's observations, Walker's line was nine miles and one thousand and seventy-seven yards north of the 36° 30' line. Another document related another survey taken as a result of a lawsuit over a tract of land about two miles south of Walker's line. That report stated that the land in dispute lay north of the 36°30' line, but it did not give a distance.[45]

A select committee of the Kentucky House reported on January 13, 1816, that it was their opinion that a law should be passed to establish Walker's line as the boundary between the two states. Also, commissioners should be appointed to run and remark the line, on condition that Tennessee "will guarantee the title to the claimants to all the land which may be included within the chartered limits of the state of Kentucky, and south of Walker's line; granted, either by the state of Virginia or Kentucky." Further, Kentucky would guarantee all claims granted by North Carolina or Virginia, lying within the charter limits of Tennessee and north of Walker's line. The House amended the report to read, "on condition that Tennessee will compensate Kentucky for the land within the chartered limits of Kentucky and South of the Walker's line." Commissioners would fix the quantity and value of the land.[46]

On January 22, the boundary resolution was further amended to reflect more precision. A statement was attached to the end of the resolution that the true chartered line should be ascertained and from that point where the Walker line struck the Tennessee River, "a line at right angles to the said reputed line shall be ascertained and marked to the chartered line between the two states, and with the said true chartered line to the Mississippi River."[47] The Senate made some minor amendments, which the House concurred in and passed the bill on February 9. Governor Shelby signed it into law the next day.[48]

The boundary issue was far from being resolved. Tennessee passed a law the following year accepting the Walker Line as far as it had been run and called upon Kentucky to agree to a commissioner appointed by the president to draw the line to the Tennessee River. They tried again in 1819 calling upon Kentucky to appoint two commissioners to join with two from Tennessee to ascertain the boundary. Consequently, John J. Crittenden and Robert Trimble were appointed by Kentucky, and Tennessee designated Felix Grundy and William L. Brown. They agreed to the Walker Line to the Tennessee River, thence up the river to the Alexander and Munsell line laid out by Kentucky in 1819, and from there to the Mississippi River. This was approved by a convention of the two states on February 2, 1820. Congress gave their approval to this compact by a resolution approved on May 12, 1820.[49] The boundary line, however, continued to elude the two states. There was another attempt to more clearly delineate the line in the 1840s, and again in 1858 a joint commission of the two states attempted to run and re-mark the state line, which was certified in 1860. Further adjustments were made in the 1870s.[50]

Settlement of state boundaries reflected general good will and reciprocal concession on the part of state authorities. Potentially divisive, these issues were handled by the states without the intervention of the federal government. It was also an acknowledgment that the matter of boundaries was essentially who was to administer certain real estate rather than a question of sovereignty over the soil. It reflected the sense that each state and the people of that state were a part of a larger whole, and it did not make a whole lot of difference whether certain people were administered by one unit or another.

Other matters that gained increasing attention in the post-war years were the issues of franchise reform and democratic representation. As population stretched westward, the newly-settled regions lagged behind in gaining representation in the state legislatures. While Americans saw this growth in the West with pride, there was some apprehension in the East as well by those who feared the increasing power of the West politically. One such case was in Virginia. Beyond the Blue Ridge Mountains in the Shenandoah Valley, most of the settlers had small land holdings and few slaves. The eastern, slave-holding region maintained its dominance in the legislature, despite a growing population base in the western part of the state. There was also a divergence in interests as well, and the westerners believed their needs were being sacrificed to the concerns of the eastern portion of the state. Increasingly, they demanded their proportionate share of representation in the legislature. Also tied in with this movement was a demand for the extension of suffrage to all adult white males. While there was a general consensus that increasing representation was necessary, some of these reformers were more ambivalent about the suffrage.

When the Virginia House refused to call a convention to consider these matters in the spring of 1816, a movement began, led by Chapman Johnson and Henry St. George Tucker, to call a convention to meet in August 1816 in Staunton. Sixty-nine delegates attended from thirty-six counties, including a dozen from the eastern part. Federalists dominated the convention, which met on August 19, but some Republicans also attended. Gen. James Breckinridge, a Federalist congressman, was elected president of the convention, which also included several prominent members, such as congressmen William A. Burwell, Henry St. George Tucker, and Daniel Sheffey. The focus of the convention was to protest the inequality of representation in both houses of the Virginia Assembly. The meeting adopted a memorial, approved 61–7, which cited the fact that a little over one-third of the white population lived on the east side of the mountains, but they retained a majority in the House. The inequity in the Senate was even worse; the western region had only four senators to thirteen for the eastern region. The memorial asked the General Assembly to call a constitutional convention to amend the Virginia constitution. Interestingly, the convention report also included a protest by the minority, signed by six members, including Gen. Breckinridge. They believed the inequality of representation was "a political wrong, and a practical evil which ought to be corrected," but they did not desire an open-ended constitutional convention that would "commit the whole constitution, with all its consecrated principles, to untried hands."[51]

This fear that the convention might also approve universal manhood suffrage was best reflected by Archibald Stuart, a prominent state politician who supported equality of representation, but who worried that it might enfranchise all adult white males. "Experience has taught us," he wrote, "how even free holders who are in a state of dependence may be influenced to commit foolish acts; what then might be expected if the idle and vicious & worthless are to have an agency in carrying on our government?"[52]

The Virginia House responded partially to the Staunton Convention by increasing the number of Senators from the Western region from five to nine, but the East also gained two (to fifteen). The House also approved, in January 1817, a popular referendum on whether to call a constitutional convention not only to redistrict the state, but also to extend the franchise. It was, however, defeated in the Senate. The reform movement languished for a time. In 1825 the Senate again blocked a House-passed convention bill, which led to another meeting being held in Staunton in July 1825. It was not until 1829 that the Virginia Constitution was thoroughly revised to reflect the demands of western Virginia.[53] The meeting in Staunton in 1816 thus initiated a train of events that eventually brought about a reform of both representation and the franchise in Virginia.

The developments in Virginia were part of a broader movement taking place elsewhere. While most of the disputes reflected a back-country versus seaboard split, Maryland had an urban versus rural controversy. Representation in the House of Delegates was based on county vote, and each county elected four members, regardless of population. Baltimore city and county, with a population of over 65,000, and so staunchly Republican that Federalists seldom bothered even to propose candidates there, elected only six members to the House of Delegates, while six small Federalist counties whose total population was slightly less than 43,000, elected twenty-four. Hezekiah Niles calculated that while Baltimore city and county had one-third of the population of the state, it had only one-thirteenth of the legislative representation.[54] Federalists, by virtue of their dominance in the rural areas, were able to capture control of both houses of the legislature in 1816 and elect a Federalist governor, and they blocked the Republican attempt to alter the mode of representation. Obviously, the Federalists feared that increasing the state's representation for more populous areas would give Baltimore greater control over the government.[55] Their newspapers frequently reminded Marylanders that Baltimore was composed of "every sort of foreigner."[56] The latter statement was, no doubt, an oblique reference to another Republican measure introduced in this same session, the so-called "Jew Bill," that was an attempt to alter the sections of the state constitution which established a religious test as a qualification for civil office. Maryland was the last state to have such a law, and the failure to pass the law generated considerable adverse publicity. The issue surfaced again and again until its passage in 1826.[57]

Similar efforts were being made by politicians to liberalize the franchise in other Atlantic seaboard states, which resulted in several new state constitutions being written in the 1820s, such as Massachusetts (1820–1821) and New York (1821), which democratized the franchise.[58] The new constitutions of the recently admitted states in the West all provided for universal manhood suffrage. The consequences of these reforms helped to launch the so-called "Age of the Common Man." Another result of this increasing responsibility for their own governance was an growing public interest not only in crime, but in the psychology of the criminal and the appropriateness of his or her punishment, particularly the death penalty. The nationalistic "Era of Good Feelings" reinforced the importance of compliance with community standards of conduct, moral as well as legal, but it also reflected a growing humanitarian concern with the governmental moral stance implied in criminal sentencing.

Chapter 10

Crime and Punishment

The year 1816 had its share of crime, murder, depravity, and all forms of vile manifestations of man's inhumanity to his fellow man. Most such acts perhaps rose to public attention briefly and in a transitory way. A few events, however, not necessarily the worst, attracted and held public attention for prolonged periods. American responses to crime and its punishment led to a consideration of its causes and began tenuous movements towards correcting those causes as well as reconsidering the treatment of criminals.

Perhaps the most sensational trial of the year was the case of Richard Smith for the murder of Captain John Carson. The public was, no doubt, fascinated by the circumstances of this event. Central to this story is Ann Carson, the wife of John Carson, who was also the wife of Richard Smith. Deserted by her husband in February 1812, Ann met Richard Smith on October 14, 1815. Believing she was a widow after receiving a report from a sailor that John Carson was dead, Ann accepted Smith's proposal and they were married the next day. Ann and Richard apparently lived happily until John Carson arrived in Philadelphia in January 1816 to learn that his wife was living with another man.

The intersection of the lives of these two men eventually resulted in a tragedy. John Carson, the victim, was born on July 10, 1778, in Edinburgh, Scotland, the eldest son of an American physician then visiting Scotland. As a young man, Carson studied medicine, but he gave up that study for the sea and entered the United States naval service. He served under Commodore Stephen Decatur and later under Thomas Baker on the *Delaware*. Carson afterwards married Baker's daughter Ann in 1801, and he soon left the navy for the merchant service. Eventually, he commanded ships such as the brig *Ohio* and another ship, the *Pennsylvania Packet*, engaged in the East India and China trade. Unfortunately, Carson became an alcoholic, which ruined his naval career, wrecked his marriage, and led him to desert his family and go to Edinburgh, where his mother then lived.[1]

Ann struggled without the support of her husband. She rented a house in her own name and legally gained the status to hold property independent of her husband, to be sued, and to be imprisoned for debt. For a time she was actually confined in a debtor's apartment. At the time of these events she was renting a house at the corner of Dock and Second Streets for $500 per year. On the first floor she ran a shop selling china and other items. Living quarters were on the upper floors.[2]

Richard Smith was born in Sligo, Ireland, in 1793. Shortly thereafter his father died. His mother remarried and emigrated to the United States when Richard was three. At the age of seven he was placed under the care of his uncle, the prominent New Orleans businessman, Daniel Clark. Despite Clark's efforts to fit him out for a mercantile career, Smith rebelled, and by his own account "gave loose to dissipation." The declaration of war in 1812 found Smith "anxious to be released from the golden prison in which I considered myself confined," and he broke the "golden chains which bound me to the mansions of my adopted parent."[3]

Smith headed for Washington, D.C., and there, through the auspices of Louisiana Senator James Brown, Smith applied for and was granted an appointment as a lieutenant in the United States Army in May 1813. He served creditably during the War of 1812, first under Gen. Jacob Brown and then under Col. James Miller. During the trial, Col. James R. Mullany testified that Smith was "an active, intelligent, and useful officer."[4]

When the war ended, Smith had few prospects. His uncle had died, leaving nothing to Smith, who had no profession or close friends. He gravitated to Philadelphia where he met Ann Carson. Her independent means was obviously an attraction, but there is no doubt that Smith fell deeply in love with her. Ann's relatives visited them frequently and Smith believed they accepted the marriage. Ann's mother, Jane Baker, was at first friendly to the couple, but a dispute over a "pecuniary matter" caused a rift between her and Smith, and according to him she became his bitter enemy.[5]

The validity of the Smith marriage was raised during the trial. The defense cited a Pennsylvania law (March 13, 1785), which stated that when a man left his family for more than two years, his wife might remarry based upon reports "apparently well grounded" of her husband's death. If the husband subsequently returned, she was not guilty of adultery. The law provided the first husband might insist on having his wife back or divorce her within six months of his return.[6] In fact, Carson's first action upon his return to Philadelphia after learning of his wife's marriage to Smith, was to file for divorce on January 15, even before he ever called upon Ann. The defense contended that by this action Carson lost all legal right to Mrs. Carson and to any property she had acquired.[7]

Carson, however, soon changed his mind. The next day, January 16, 1816, he came to the Smith house. He appeared to be friendly and ate and drank with them. Carson became outraged, however, when he saw Smith giving directions to his children; he seized a knife and attempted to stab Smith, cutting his coat. Smith held him off while Ann tried to intervene and calm Carson. This only angered Carson more, and he grabbed a second knife, forcing Smith to flee from the house. As a consequence, Smith procured a pair of pistols from an acquaintance, and he also took out a warrant. At the hearing on the eighteenth, Carson was bound over to keep the peace and was required to post a bond of $500.[8]

On the fateful evening of January 20, however, John Carson appeared at the Smith house stating he intended to take possession. Smith went a friend's house, and Ann, learning that Carson would insist upon his connubial rights, also departed. Captain and Mrs. Baker were called to the house by Carson to witness his assertion of his rights to the property.[9]

About 10 p.m., Ann and Richard went to J.B. Smith's house. He was a friend and an attorney who had advised Smith earlier and had, in fact, loaned him the two pistols for his self-defense. Ann brought one of these pistols with her and laid it on the table. Smith took it, unloaded it, and put it away, perhaps fearing some trouble might arise. Eventually, Ann and Richard decided to return to their home. She went upstairs to the parlor where Carson and Captain and Mrs. Baker were waiting. Smith went to the bedroom to retrieve the second pistol. When he entered the parlor, Mrs. Baker, who had denounced Ann, turned on him. Carson ordered Smith out of the house. Witnesses generally agreed Carson approached him, showing open palms suggesting that he had no weapon.[10] Carson forced him into a corner. Smith had entered the room with his right hand concealed on his breast under his surtout coat. At this point he withdrew it, revealing a pistol, which he now aimed at Carson's face and shot him.[11] The ball passed through Carson's mouth, breaking off two teeth. The ball did not hit his tongue, but "the powder, from the proximity of the pistol, burnt and slit it in so shocking a manner, as to render his words for sometime almost unintelligible."[12] Richard threw down the pistol, which Baker described as a "horse pistol," about fifteen inches long, and ran out of the room. Captain Baker pursued and caught him as he stumbled and fell out the front door and into the street. A watchman assisted in restraining him.[13]

A physician was called who wished to sew up Carson's tongue, but he refused. Carson also suffered gun powder burns. Particles of charcoal were driven into his face. The wounds did not at first seem alarming but, after a week, he grew progressively worse. Throughout, Carson steadfastly denounced Smith. The dying victim declared that Smith "had come like an *assassin*, and shot him like a *coward*." Carson died on February 4, 1816, at about 11 a.m. of an "inflammation of the brain."[14]

Carson's death created a sensation in Philadelphia. Public opinion was quickly inflamed against Smith. During the trial, defense attorneys stated that the "public mind has been irritated to an unexampled extent," which had infected them "with an unheard malignity." The prisoner, they asserted, "should not be tried in the pulpits or the beer-houses."[15] Smith was arraigned for murder, and the trial began at 10 a.m. on Thursday, May 23, before a hostile audience. Judge Jacob Rush presided. Jared Ingersoll, the attorney general, presented the prosecution case. A distinguished battery of defense lawyers represented Smith, headed by William Rawle. Smith and Ann were tried separately; Smith first.[16]

The prosecution argued that this was a wilful murder; a deliberate and malicious act. These charges carried the implication of capital punishment, for in Pennsylvania only first-degree murder was punishable by death.[17] Richard's lawyers stressed self-defense and cited repeatedly his forbearance in the face of provocation by Carson, even attempted assassination.[18] Carson's actions, they asserted, "drew upon himself the fatal wound."[19] It was suggested that had Smith not acted, "in all probability, Carson would now be on trial."[20]

Attorney General Ingersoll reiterated that Smith's actions were intentional. In no way could the killing be considered, "*justified, excused,* or even *extenuated*." It was "*deliberate,* and *premeditated*."[21] He asked, "If he did not intend murder, why did he come into the room?" "No person in the room heard him *cock the pistol*." Showing his pistol only at the last moment to prevent Carson's retreating showed the more malice.[22]

If there had been any doubt in the jury's minds, they were undoubtedly erased by Judge Rush's charge to the jury on the afternoon of Tuesday, May 28. Ann, he said, was guilty of adultery and Smith had no rights. Carson had an undoubted right to take possession of the house and goods, and Smith was the intruder. Also, killing Carson in the act of making a peaceable demand was "in every principle of law, murder in the first degree."[23] He denied that self-defense was applicable and characterized Smith's act as "premeditated violence," and an "assassination."[24] The jury retired at five p.m. and returned at nine to deliver the verdict: "wilful murder."[25]

On Saturday, June 1, at 7 a.m., Judge Rush asked why the sentence of death should not be passed. Defense objections of public prejudice, Rush's conduct of the trial, and his charge to the jury, particularly not informing the jury that they could find Smith guilty of murder in the second degree, were quickly dismissed by Rush.[26] Judge Rush then addressed Smith and told him "to prepare for the *change* in your mode of existence," and he sentenced Smith to be hanged.[27]

In the interim period, Ann was brought to trial as an accessory to murder on Wednesday, May 29, at 10 a.m. After jury selection, testimony was heard. Much of the evidence was exculpatory, and Attorney General Ingersoll, after remarking that he believed she had committed crimes, declared, "I do not think the evidence on the part of the prosecution, is such as will justify me in urging her conviction."[28] Judge Rush then charged the jury that although Ann was certainly "a bad woman," the proper verdict was for acquittal. The jury, without retiring, returned a verdict of not guilty.[29]

During his confinement, Smith accepted his fate. How he felt about Ann is unclear. A "Confession," penned in prison, laid much of the blame on her, "the cause of my present misery." He called Ann an "evil woman . . . versed in all the wiles and machinations of that diabolical spirit which possessed the heart of the first of her race, and caused the fall of mankind."[30] His "Confession" was, however, likely designed to please the public. He asked for "a little charity . . . which they have hitherto denied me," and he hoped his unhappy fate might influence youth to "avoid those temptations which have beset me, and the commission of vices which inevitably lead to the blackest crimes."[31]

It is more likely his true feelings were expressed in a letter published in the Philadelphia *True American*, on August 4, 1816. "It is true, my Dear Ann, I did refuse to see you. I could not; indeed I could not. Dear as you are to me the sight would have opened anew the flood gates of sorrow to have drowned my soul. I have firmness enough to die—but not to meet you, and oh Heavens, to part with you! no-no-no-let me learn to forget the world and its joys, for they are mine no longer." He added, "I loved you—loved you to distraction . . . but another came and claimed you. He would have torn our hearts asunder. He would have rent the dove from its mate. . . . Furious passions raged in my breast. I saw you and happiness torn from me by the hand of a stranger, and O in my delirium, I slew him." He asserted again that his act was not premeditated, "in a moment of phrenzy—madness and despair, I did the rash—the dreadful deed."[32]

When the time came, Smith thanked his keepers at the prison for their kindness. A little after 10 a.m. on August 10, 1816, he ascended out of the west gate of the prison. He was accompanied by a clergyman, the Rev. Mr. Hurley, the Sheriff and Coroner and their several officers, constables and watchmen of the City and County of Philadelphia. His cart was driven by the executioner, a black man. Smith was accompanied in the wagon by Rev. Hurley and, due to the excessive heat of the day, a gentleman rode in the cart with them and held an umbrella to shield them from the rays of the sun. An immense crowd, reportedly "surpassing anything ever exhibited before in the city of Philadelphia upon the like occasion," witnessed the mile and a half procession. Despite the prejudices formerly expressed against Richard Smith, the crowd was solemn and "no occurrence of indecorum towards him took place."[33]

The entourage proceeded to the place of execution at North West Public Square. Smith and Rev. Hurley spent another fifteen minutes in prayer. Some of Smith's friends gathered around him and "grasped him by the hand for the last time."[34] The length of confinement had left him weak and debilitated, and he had to be assisted to the gallows. Smith "appeared cool, calm, collected, and resigned," but there is no report that he addressed the assembled crowd, as was the usual custom. Between the hours of eleven and twelve, Richard Smith "was launched into eternity . . . amidst the tears and sighs of thousands."[35]

The hanging of Richard Smith was not the only such event to attract widespread public attention in 1816. The case of Peter Lung, a common laborer, was another. Lung was born in Middletown, Connecticut, on July 9, 1768, and he had lived there most of his life. His wife, Lucy Kelley, had borne him nine children. Unfortunately, in his later years, Lung became an alcoholic, had a hard time keeping a job, and became abusive towards his wife. His wife was also frequently intemperate. On July 30, 1815, a quarrel between Lucy and Peter resulted in her being beaten and kicked in the side. This blow apparently led to her death on the next day.[36]

Lung admitted he "was in the most violent rage, and did not govern my passions as I ought to have done."[37] He also said that in his drunken rages he used threats against his wife, but "in my cool moments I never harboured any ill-will towards my wife."[38] The next morning, on July 31, Lucy was bruised, her eyes were swollen, and she complained about the pain in her side. Peter apologized and tried to make it up to her, but Lucy wanted more to drink, so Peter procured some for her. That evening, she refused to go to bed with him, and by his account he slept through the night. When he awoke, he found her slumped in a rocking chair, dead. Peter went to the eldest son, Joseph, who recounted finding his mother during the night on the floor "beating her head against the hearth as hard as she could." He tried to lay her on the bed, but she got up and flung herself on the hearth again. The second time, Lucy struck Joseph very hard on the face, and he left her alone. Joseph stated that he had tried to awake his father, but he was unable to do so.[39]

A jury inquest cited Peter for murder. A special court was convened on Tuesday, August 29. The trial concluded on Friday, September 1, and Lung was found guilty. He was sentenced to be hanged on November 23. Lung, however, appealed to the legislature on grounds that the Chief Judge of the Superior Court, Zephaniah Swift, had no power to call a special court or to direct the clerk to summon a grand jury. He complained of the suddenness of the trial, his lack of time to prepare his defense, and some irregularities. The legislature was sympathetic. They did not grant a pardon, but they annulled the judgment, stopped the execution, and directed that Lung be indicted and tried as if no judgment had been rendered against him.[40]

Judge Swift denounced the legislative action. He alleged the legislature was influenced by public passions on Lung's behalf. They could not justify a pardon; but bestowed "a special favour on a man convicted of murder on unquestionable evidence," and unjustly imputed a criminal act to him. He questioned the constitutionality of the legislature's action and asserted they showed more compassion for criminals than judges. "This was a petition for pardon, transformed by the Assembly into a petition for a new trial." The legislature was not the proper place to hear arguments over error. The power assumed by the Assembly, "will give them a discretionary right to interpose in all cases decided by courts of law. It will break down the judiciary, and destroy the system of jurisprudence . . . if they can annul and vacate one judgment, they can all."[41]

Nevertheless, the entire process was started all over again. Lung was again indicted on December 19, and the trial began that afternoon and continued for three days. On Saturday, December 23, the jury found Lung guilty of murder, and he was sentenced to be executed. The date set for the execution was June 20, 1816, between ten and four o'clock. Lung renewed his appeal to the legislature for mercy, but they refused to act.[42]

During the period of confinement before his execution, Lung was visited frequently by ministers and private Christians, but he gave no evidence of repentance, remorse, or emotion. He did, however, write a series of letters to his in-laws and his family, which were published. To his wife's mother, who testified against him at the trial, and who Lung characterized as "One of my most bitter enemies," he declared he forgave her and said that he would "go to death and judgment, with a firm persuasion that I have been most unjustly accused and condemned."[43]

In a letter to his mother, he exclaimed, "God has suffered my enemies to destroy me!" He reiterated that he did not intend to kill his wife. "Being a father, I could not imbrue my hands in the blood of the mother of my children!"[44] He declared that he forgave those witnesses who testified against him, although they were obviously blinded by prejudice and passion. He could not understand how accidentally abusing them in a state of intoxication should make them harbor ill will towards him.[45]

In the end, Lung reconciled himself to his fate and he conformed, much more so than Richard Smith had, to the ritual that had long since become accepted as the way of death. According to historian Louis P. Masur, public death for a variety of capital crimes had become a ritualized spectacle extending back for centuries. Execution day was "a spectacle of civil and religious order . . . a performance directed by magistrates and ministers and involving the condemned themselves." The event was both a warning to those who would commit wicked deeds against society as well as an affirmation of Christian values.[46] Lung understood that his role was to be penitent, and accordingly he confessed his wickedness and requested a sermon to be preached on his behalf on the day of his execution. On June 20, 1816, Lung was conducted from his prison to a church where the Rev. David Field preached a sermon, "Warning Against Drunkenness." At the religious exercise, Lung appeared to be resigned and composed. He was then conducted to the place of execution by a militia unit and a crowd estimated at between 11,000 and 12,000. At the gallows, Lung was "dressed for the grave," and the rope was fastened about his neck. After a solemn prayer was offered at his request, Lung, in conformity to the penitence expected from him, addressed the crowd that "they would take warning from him, prepare for eternity, and he bid them all farewell." An observer noted, "No trembling appeared in his voice or limbs, and when the platform was struck from under him, he expired without a struggle." He stated the spectators were silent and attentive and expressed the hope that "some lasting good resulted from the public and affecting execution."[47]

Whether any lasting good came out of public hangings was a lively topic of debate even in 1816. A citizen of Winyaw, South Carolina, condemned the use of capital punishment in his state. "Humanity shudders at the cold-blooded murders of public justice," he declared. He denied that it prevented the commission of crimes and suggested "substituting solitary confinement and hard labor."[48] In fact, opposition to public executions had been growing for some time, influenced particularly by the ideas of the Enlightenment, which saw capital punishment as barbaric and excessive. The influence of the republican and liberal ideology of the American Revolution also led to condemnation of the death penalty as unnecessary, and led to calls for punishment more fitting a new nation seeking a new order in society. As noted earlier, Pennsylvania had abolished capital punishment except in the case of first degree murder, but there were those who disapproved even that exception. Jonathan Walker, a judge of the Fourth District of Pennsylvania, strongly disapproved, and asserted that it was the "exercise of a power given to no human tribunal . . . society is under no moral obligation to punish this crime with death."[49] Like Walker, a Philadelphian, "Philo Humanitas," added his voice against capital punishment. His solution was basically to substitute life imprisonment in lieu of capital punishment.[50]

Another Connecticut case attracted attention in 1816. Miner Babcock was a young man, born on February 4, 1796, accused of murdering a black man named London, who was a servant in his mother's house in Norwich, Connecticut. On June 21, 1815, London and Babcock's mother quarreled. Babcock intervened and London went after him. As Babcock later related, "unfortunately I had a knife in my hand, which proved to be a mortal weapon to London, for I unguardedly let out his bowels in the affray."[51] A Grand Jury indicted Babcock for murder on October 3. The trial began on October 11, and he was convicted the next day. The execution was stayed on a technicality, and a new trial was ordered. The new trial began on January 4, 1816, and he was again convicted.[52]

On June 6, 1816, the ritual of death was played out for Babcock. A company of grenadiers came to the prison and escorted him to a meeting house where a sermon was delivered on his behalf. Then at 2 p.m., accompanied by his coffin, upon which he sat, Babcock rode to the place of execution about a half mile away. An observer stated that Babcock was "surrounded by a multitude of spectators as far as my poor eyes could discern."[53] The Sheriff, two deputies, the jailer, and Babcock ascended to the gallows. Babcock was visibly trembling and in a feeble condition and was apparently unable to address the crowd. After a prayer, Babcock was "launched into eternity."[54]

Not all murder trials ended this way, however. Perley Cutler and Ayers White were indicted on July 17, 1816, for the murder of Henry Holton and tried in Boston. The trial began on July 20, presided over by Chief Justice Isaac Parker, with Perez Morton, the attorney general, the prosecutor. Cutler and White were tried separately, Cutler first. They were accused of beating Holton so badly that the wounds eventually caused his death a week later.[55] The defense stressed Holton was an alcoholic, and that a fall was the cause of death. It was brought out that Holton continued to work after the beating, and was intoxicated on the second day afterwards. He even took out a casement and sash in a window the day before his death. Cutler's attorneys argued he was at worst guilty only of "excusable homicide in self-defense."[56]

Judge Parker's charge to the jury stated that if they doubted the blows caused Holton's death, they should acquit; if the event was a result of a sudden quarrel, then it was manslaughter. The jury retired and an hour later returned with the verdict of "not guilty of murder; but guilty of manslaughter."[57] Ayers White, after the prosecution dropped the murder charges, was tried before the same jury on the charge of manslaughter and convicted. Cutler and White were each sentenced to ten days solitary confinement and confinement afterwards to hard labor in the state prison for two years.[58]

A unique murder case was also heard by Judge Parker on September 19, 1816. George Bowen, convicted of petit larceny, disrespect for the Sheriff, and "occasional turbulence," was indicted for murder for encouraging a prisoner, Jonathan Jewett, a black man under sentence of death for the murder of his father, to commit suicide.[59] Despite a lack of evidence that Bowen actually abetted the suicide and testimony that the rope used by Jewett was provided to him by someone else, the jury pondered their decision for two hours before returning a verdict of "not guilty."[60]

Judge Parker was quite busy in 1816. He presided over yet another murder trial in December 1816. George Coombs, a sailor, was accused of kicking and beating Maria Coombs to death. Attorney General Morton asserted for the prosecution that killing someone in a heat of passion was more than just the crime of manslaughter.[61] A physician who attended to Maria on the evening of June 15, 1816, stated she was "weak and feeble." She appeared to have a bruise on the left side, between the spleen and kidneys. He was told she had fallen out of the door, being very intoxicated. He prescribed medication, but she refused. He was informed a couple of hours later that she was dead.[62]

Several witnesses from next door related that George and Maria had a fight, and heard Maria exclaim, "George Coombs, you have given me my death wound—you have killed me."[63] Another neighbor stated that she heard the disturbance, looked out, and saw Maria on the ground. She said she saw Coombs stomp on Maria twice with his right foot.[64]

The defense, however, attacked the credibility of these witnesses and questioned, "from their appearance and behaviour, whether they are entitled to credit." In other words, should the jury believe the testimony of prostitutes? They also asserted that Maria was an "abandoned woman" herself with a "turbulent and furious temper." She was frequently intoxicated and often uttered profane language. In any event, the affray was "mutual," in that Maria also inflicted blows upon George Coombs. It was further suggested that Maria's death occurred as a result of a fall. The defense produced a physician who testified that due to an injury to Coombs's left knee, if he attempted to kick with his right foot he would have fallen. They denied there was any evidence of malicious intent and cautioned the jury that when the act produced "an effect beyond his intention, your greatest care is necessary to make the distinction which the law allows," namely, "homicide by misadventure."[65]

In conclusion, the defense reiterated the contradictions and inconsistencies in the prosecution case. They also reminded the jury of the lack of credibility of the principal witnesses, asserted the good character of George Coombs and the bad character of Maria, and declared there was no evidence of malice on the part of George Coombs.[66] Morton, the prosecutor, cited the weight of evidence against Coombs and noted that a lack of justification for assault should not preclude a guilty verdict.[67] Chief Justice Parker's charge to the jury stated that Maria's death was certainly caused by violence, but the jury had to determine whether it was caused by the prisoner or was an accident. If it was in consequence of intoxication, then Coombs must be acquitted. If caused by Coombs, even if he had no intention to kill her when the fight began, pursuing the act constituted malice and murder. Parker addressed the credibility of the prostitutes, and he desired the jury to set aside their prejudices. "No juryman should say," he concluded, "a man is not guilty, merely because he thinks the punishment too severe."[68] Yet that is exactly what the jury did; after only an hour deliberation, they pronounced Coombs not guilty, and the prisoner was discharged.

It is hard not to conclude that Coombs was declared not guilty because of the jury's prejudice against the prostitutes. Nor is this the only case this year that reflected male chauvinism. In New York City, Thomas Burke, on October 16, 1815, beat his wife Hannah on the head with a broom handle. She lingered until October 26, when she died from "inflammation of the brain." Burke was convicted on November 30, 1815, for the murder of his wife. He was sentenced to hang on January 19, 1816, but New York Governor Daniel D. Tompkins stayed the execution and forwarded to the state legislature on February 13 several petitions to save Burke's life.[69] Among the documents forwarded to the legislature was a petition from the jury that had convicted Burke; eleven of the twelve asked Tompkins to postpone the execution and refer the matter to the legislature. Additional affidavits on behalf of Burke were included. Mrs. Burke, all agreed, was a drunken and lewd woman who had frequently beaten her husband, "an honest, and industrious man," in public without him responding. She was also a prostitute, with connections with black as well as white men. She was generally known as "the bully of Bedlow and George streets," who had been frequently taken into custody for fighting. As one appeal stated, "she was regarded as the worst among the bad in George street."[70]

Several petitions were also enclosed to the legislature, signed by many respectable inhabitants of New York City. One, signed by 295 citizens, declared that Burke's "reasoning faculties were suspended . . . the death of Mrs. Burke ensued from sudden transport and heat of blood . . . it is evident that he intended to have beaten her only, and never meditated her death."[71] Two other petitions, one signed by forty-one and another signed by twenty-five, also pleaded with the legislature to spare Burke's life. In the New York Assembly, the documents were referred to a select committee of three: Thomas J. Oakley, Henry B. Lee, and Peter A. Jay, the latter from New York City.[72]

On February 23, Oakley, for the committee, reported that while the facts presented "justified a conviction," yet they believed the circumstances of justice could "be answered by the confinement of the criminal in the State Prison for life at hard labor." Accordingly, he presented a bill to that effect, which was approved on March 5. The Senate attempted to limit Burke's confinement to hard labor for fourteen years, but the House refused to concur. The bill was officially signed into law on April 5.[73] Throughout the entire process, the attitude appeared to have been that Burke's wife probably got what she deserved, that he had only meant to beat her, and unfortunately she died from the beating. While the legislature spared Burke's life, imprisonment for life at hard labor was probably not much better.

Another murder trial in 1816 reached the United States Supreme Court. William Bevans, an eighteen-year-old sailor who was performing guard duty on board the United States ship, *Independence*, while it was in the harbor at Boston, killed a fellow sailor, Peter Lunstrum, on November 6, 1816. Lunstrum was apparently trying to steal ship stores that Bevans was guarding. Lunstrum tried to bully Bevans and paid no attention to the latter's warnings that he would kill him if necessary. After a heated altercation, Bevans plunged his bayonet into Lunstrum, who died from his wound. Although he had been provoked, Bevans was tried for murder before the Circuit Court of the United States in Boston in December 1816, with Justice Joseph Story presiding. Story rejected the defense counsel's question of the jurisdiction of the federal court, rather than having the case heard in a state court.[74]

The prosecution, led by Attorney General George Blake, noted the offense constituted murder and fell under federal authority because it was committed off the coast of Boston. Regarding the defense contentions of provocation, Blake asserted the only weapon used by Lunstrum was his tongue.[75] Judge Story's charge to the jury hinted at the unpopularity of the prosecution of Bevans. "It is a great mistake," Story stated, "that Jurors are at liberty in matters of law to disregard the opinion of the Court, upon fanciful distinctions, or opinions of their own; and they may, by such conduct, bring their consciences into peril, and their fellow citizens into jeopardy." Story also informed the jury that they should not betray "a false tenderness for human life." Words of reproach, he said, were not sufficient cause to free a person guilty of murder.[76]

The jury dutifully returned a verdict of guilty. The defense immediately filed an appeal, but the judges divided on whether Bevans's offense was within the jurisdiction of Massachusetts or the federal district courts. The case was then certified to the United States Supreme Court. Arguments were heard by the Court on February 14 and 16, 1818. Daniel Webster argued for Bevans and Henry Wheaton and Attorney General William Wirt represented the United States. The opinion of the Court was delivered by Chief Justice John Marshall on February 21, 1818.[77]

Marshall reviewed the applicable laws, noting they gave courts of the union "cognizance of certain offences committed on the high seas, or in any river, haven, basin, or bay, out of the jurisdiction of any particular state."[78] It was conceded that no jurisdiction was given even to courts of the United States when a murder was committed on a public ship outside the jurisdiction of a state. Such offenses were handled by courts martial. This case, however, having occurred within the territorial waters of Massachusetts, was not covered by a court martial. Wheaton and Wirt had argued that nevertheless it was a case of admiralty and maritime jurisdiction under the federal courts. Webster argued that Congress had not extended federal admiralty jurisdiction to cases in which state courts had concurrent common law jurisdiction such as murders committed in bays, and thus the offense was within the jurisdiction of Massachusetts courts.[79]

Marshall noted, however, that Congress exercised exclusive jurisdiction over places purchased by the consent of the state legislature, such as forts, magazines, dock yards, etc., and the ship of war where the murder was committed was "a *place* within the sole and exclusive jurisdiction of the United States," and thus federal courts "may consequently take cognizance of the offence."[80] That the federal government under its war powers "has power to punish an offence committed by a marine on board a ship of war, wherever that ship may lie, is a proposition never to be questioned in this court," he declared.[81]

Thus the Supreme Court in a somewhat convoluted way rejected Bevans's appeal, and the federal government had won one more small victory in Marshall's court over state authority. The fate of Bevans, still under conviction for murder, is unknown, but it is to be hoped that, given the lapse of years, his life was spared.

A common thread through nearly all of these cases was alcoholism. Americans in 1816 were not unaware of the evil effects of alcohol. Not only was intemperance a factor in murders and wife abuse, it also contributed to poverty. A society in Portland, Maine, founded to suppress immorality and intemperance, noted in their meeting in April 1816 that of eighty-five persons at the work-house, seventy-one were paupers because of intemperance. In addition, they believed that many other paupers provided for by the public were also intemperate. They estimated that alcoholism raised poor costs from $2000 to $6000 per annum.[82]

There is little doubt that public consumption of alcohol was increasing, although the amount was variously estimated. The Rev. David Thurston, in a sermon to the Maine Missionary Society, cited information from the New England Tract Society that Americans consumed about thirty-four million gallons of ardent spirits, or seven and a half gallons per person in 1815. Another tract, however, cited the same consumption and arrived at a per capita average at five and a half gallons per year. The former figure more nearly matches modern estimates of consumption by the drinking age population (15 and older) and the latter figure the per capita consumption.[83]

Several temperance societies were being formed during this period, such as the Massachusetts Society for the Suppression of Intemperance in 1812. Although not all ministers were involved, clergymen obviously played a leading role in this movement. In fact, the Methodist General Conference adopted a resolution in 1816 declaring that "no stationed or local preacher shall retail spiritous or malt liquors without forfeiting his ministerial character among us."[84]

Tract Societies also focused on the consequences of alcoholism. Dr. Benjamin Rush's famous 1784 essay, *Inquiry into the Effect of Ardent Spirits upon the Human Mind,* was reprinted in 1816 and widely distributed. His warning was frequently cited: "poverty and misery, crimes and infamy, disease and death, are all the natural and usual consequences of the intemperate use of ardent spirits." Another important temperance work, Mason Locke Weems's treatise, *Drunkard's Looking Glass,* originally published in 1812, was reprinted in 1816.[85]

The agitation against alcohol in 1816 was only a beginning and anticipated a much larger movement in the next few decades. Reformers understood that only through public education would they eventually achieve their goals, whether temperance or prohibition.

Inevitably, moral suasion took on a political aspect. Governor William Jones of Rhode Island in a message to his legislature in October 1816, condemned the use of ardent spirits, which "poisons the sources of domestic happiness, and even threatens the public prosperity." He added, "I know not whether an evil of this kind can be removed or mitigated by legislative regulation, but it is well worthy of your consideration." Governor Simon Snyder of Pennsylvania also called upon his legislature to place the property of habitual drunkards in the hands of trustees.[86]

As for public agitation, Dr. Jesse Torrey, Jr. published a series of essays in "an attempt to prove that the prevailing consumption of ardent spirits is a greater national calamity than war." For support, Torrey cited a speech by the Indian leader, Little Turtle, expressing the "shocking ravages of distilled spirits, on his aboriginal brethren." In one of his essays, Torrey urged a tax on alcoholic beverages to raise money to fund free public libraries. The matter deserved the consideration not only of Congress but of every state. "The safety of the nation is at stake!" he declared. The question was "whether Whiskey or Reason shall predominate?" Melodramatically, he characterized stills as "Satan's Steam Engines, whose serpentine throats disgorge oceans of the malignant *leaven* of human depravity." He quoted a letter from the *Richmond Enquirer* that about twelve thousand died each year from the use of ardent spirits.[87]

In fact, during the discussion on taxes in the first session of the Fourteenth Congress, it was proposed to levy a tax upon stills, not with the intent to use the revenues to aid libraries, as Torrey wanted, nor for the purpose of discouraging the use of spirits, but rather simply to raise a revenue. Lewis Williams of North Carolina objected that the proposed tax on stills was unfair because it was to be levied on capacity and not on quantity distilled. He argued it would put many distillers in his district out of business and would, in fact, reduce the anticipated revenue. A distiller who made ten times as much per day should pay ten times as much tax, Williams insisted. He was supported by several congressmen who feared their constituents would also suffer from the tax. Micah Taul from Kentucky asserted that the tax would inflict serious injury on the Western country and "prostrate nine out of ten of the distillers in the district which I represent."[88]

A motion was made to reduce the tax from 100% to 50% on

the capacity of the still. Enos T. Throop of New York stated that he wished it was 25%, because a high tax would benefit large distillers and drive the small ones out of business. "If, sir, it is intended seriously to suppress the vice, we set about it in the wrong way. It can be done only by prohibiting, under some penalties, the manufacture or importation of liquors."[89] Eventually the House reduced the rate to 50% by a close vote of 74–70. The final bill passed overwhelmingly.[90] The tax was dropped entirely in 1817. Limiting alcoholic consumption had never been the object of the tax, and reformers would have to wait for a later period to successfully pursue legal means of limiting access to alcoholic beverages.

Despite the numerous hangings of murderers in 1816, the vengeful mood of the people towards criminals was definitely waning after the War of 1812. Reformers and humanitarians were increasingly urging long term confinement in lieu of execution. The peace movement that developed after the war also contributed to the more compassionate attitude. Adna Heaton, in an anti-war tract published this year, argued there were "very few crimes that are thought worthy of death, and it is doubted by many, and *some in the most eminent stations too*, whether society has the right to take the life of man in any case whatever."[91]

Some were even suggesting the possibilities of rehabilitation of criminals. Governor William Jones of Rhode Island, for example, stated to his legislature in October 1816 his regret there should be "such frequent crimes, and a consequent necessity for the infliction of severe punishments." He asked the legislature to reconsider the penal code. "It may be a question," he added, "whether under our existing laws, the reformation of the offender, and the practicability of compelling him to make amends by his labour, have been sufficiently considered."[92]

Two prominent New Yorkers, John Murray, Jr. and Thomas Eddy, who wrote on behalf of Thomas Burke and two others sentenced to death, declared, "We are not warranted in depriving a fellow creature of life for any crime."[93] The implications of such a policy would require increasing the number of prisons and improving those currently existing. In fact, Governor Tompkins, called upon the legislature in 1816 to enlarge the prison system. They responded by approving a new prison in the western district of the state, at Auburn, which became a model for other states.[94] The new prison was built with small individual cells, with common dining quarters, chapel, and workshops. This is not to say that the prisoners were treated more humanely. Discipline was severe, punishment was harsh, and every convict was required to work long, hard hours to pay for their upkeep. The Auburn system, as it was called, was widely adopted in other states. One report noted the Auburn prison had expenses of $34,000 in 1829, but receipts from prison labor amounted to $40,000. By 1840, at least twelve new prisons had been built in other states modeled after the Auburn prison, and several other states had copied parts of the system.[95]

Thus Americans in 1816 were groping for a more humane and enlightened concept of justice. Punishment of criminals was swift and harsh, and the spectacle of public hangings was still a part of American life. Nevertheless, questions were being raised about capital punishment, and some Americans were even beginning to entertain the idea of rehabilitation of criminals. Efforts were also being made to reform a source of criminality, alcoholism. The humanitarian impulse that inspired action on these two issues was widespread in 1816, as the exponential growth of benevolent societies attests. Joined by these organizations, Americans worked to promote cures for a variety of social ills. Despite the ambition of these groups, however, many of the problems Americans confronted in 1816, including capital punishment and alcoholism, are problems that exist even to this day.

Chapter 11

The Humanitarian Impulse

In the years following the War of 1812 there was a great increase in benevolent societies devoted to many various causes. No doubt the general good will that was an outgrowth of the post-war period contributed to this mood of benevolence towards their fellow man, but the evangelical zeal that came out of the Second Great Awakening was probably the primary factor. The great religious revivals that began around 1800 in the West eventually spread all over the country. Concern for the public good and the general welfare of the people was a natural outgrowth of this religious movement, and it undoubtedly influenced the formation of many organizations after the war. There was also an element of social control present, an attempt to impose some larger sense of order and direction to the nation after its "Second War for Independence." Two major benevolent associations formed in 1816, the American Bible Society and the American Colonization Society, both played important roles in the years ahead. A variety of other important issues for the future were also addressed by Americans in 1816, such as the peace movement, education, and Sabbath reform.

Many Americans were deeply disturbed by the growing laxity in observance of the Sunday Sabbath. As the Rev. Richard Storrs said to a Sabbatarian convention at Dedham, Connecticut, on June 5, 1816, rulers should "provide effectually for the maintenance of the Sabbath," and the people's duty was to obey these laws.[1] New England most strictly observed the Sunday laws, yet even here they were not being enforced. As one observer noted, "On all our large roads, every Sabbath witnesses numerous and rapidly increasing violations of the laws, with hardly an endeavour to repress them. Droves of cattle and loads of produce for market, carts and waggons returning with goods to the country, and pleasure carriages, throng the roads."[2]

The Rev. David D. Field, speaking to the Connecticut Society for the Promotion of Good Morals in Hartford, agreed that "Gross breaches of the Sabbath must be suppressed. All who trespass on the day, by unnecessary labour, traveling or pleasure, are the proper subjects of punishment." He was particularly critical of the delivery of Sunday mail, which disturbed the day "by the noise of the whip, and the noise of the rattling of wheels, and the prancing of horses." Worst of all, by opening the mail and reading the letters and papers, "the minds of multitudes were taken off from the appropriate services of the Sabbath, to that endless variety of news, business, friendship and pleasure communicated or suggested by them." Fields concluded that there was no good reason why the mail should be transported on the Sabbath.[3]

A movement to stop the delivery of Sunday mail had begun before the War of 1812. The catalyst was a federal law of April 1810 that required postmasters to open their offices every day of the week. This law especially affronted local communities where the only vehicle allowed on the road on the Sabbath was the mail coach. Moreover, the local post office logically became, other than churches, the only gathering place on the Sabbath. Consequently, a petition campaign began to force Congress to rescind its law and to stop Sunday delivery of mail.[4]

Numerous petitions were introduced in the first session of the Fourteenth Congress, and at least one effort was made to carry out their intent. Benjamin Tallmadge of Connecticut offered an amendment to a postal bill that no mail would be transported nor any post office opened on the Sabbath. Delivery on the Sabbath, Tallmadge remarked, "had too long been a reproach to our legislative code, and exposed our country to the judgments of Heaven." His amendment was debated at considerable length and rejected by the substantial margin of 100–35.[5]

Undaunted, Sabbatarians flooded the second session of the Fourteenth Congress with more petitions. In the House, these petitions were assigned to a committee chaired by Elijah H. Mills of Massachusetts. The committee report included a letter from Postmaster General Return J. Meigs, Jr., who argued, among other things, that stopping Sabbath delivery would confuse the whole system of transportation on more than seven hundred routes. Mills's committee proposed two seemingly contradictory resolutions: that it was inexpedient to pass any law respecting the transportation of mail, but provision should be made to prohibit the delivery of letters at the respective post offices on the Sabbath. The resolutions were tabled. This defeat seemed to take the momentum out of the movement; it was not renewed for more than a decade.[6]

Another area attracting the humanitarian impulse was the crusade for peace. Obviously, the War of 1812 was a primary impetus. Noah Worcester, a Congregational clergyman from New England and outspoken critic of the War of 1812, for example, published his extremely influential anti-war thoughts in December 1814. *The Solemn Review of the Custom of War, showing that war is the effect of popular delusion, and Proposing a Remedy* went through five editions in the next two years. Worcester strongly advocated the formation of peace societies to educate the public. David Low Dodge also created a stir with his book in 1815, *War Inconsistent with the Religion of Jesus Christ*, which stressed the deleterious economic and political effects of war. Dodge and thirty other men, in August 1815, formed possibly the first peace society in the world in New York City. Literature against war appeared with greater frequency in 1816, in addition to the formation of peace societies.[7]

Perhaps the most active group was the Massachusetts Peace Society, formed at the end of December 1815. Among the list of subscribers were the governor, lieutenant governor, two judges, the president and several professors at Harvard. Officers were elected in January 1816, and the society issued a circular letter in March expressing its views, written primarily by Worcester, the society's Corresponding Secretary.[8] The circular addressed the diversity of opinion on whether war was a right of self-defense. Ministers of every denomination were invited to make clear in their sermons "that the *spirit of war*, and the *spirit of the gospel*, are at variance." As to why the society was forming at that time when the prospect of war was slight, he answered, "The time of peace is believed to be more favorable to the proposed design, than a time of war."[9] The Massachusetts Peace Society grew from the twenty-two charter members to two hundred by the end of 1816. It also sponsored a periodical, *Friend of Peace*, edited by Worcester. At his urging many more peace societies were organized. By 1819 there were at least seventeen such societies scattered over the United States, with many more branch societies.[10]

Despite the laudable goals of the peace societies, there were skeptics. When the Massachusetts Peace Society sought the endorsement of former Presidents Thomas Jefferson and John Adams, Jefferson expressed mild interest and accepted an honorary membership, but Adams replied that he had abandoned the principles of pacifism that he had once admired. "Universal peace," he wrote, "appears to me no more nor less than everlasting passive obedience and non-resistance. The human flock would soon be fleeced and butchered by one or a few."[11]

The most troubling issue confronting peace advocates was the problem of defensive wars. All agreed offensive wars were wrong, but some asked, as one author did, "is a reliance on *right*, a sufficient guard for men in a *wrong* world?" He concluded that "a *defensive* war seems not only justifiable but imperious; for the nation that does not contend for its own *right*, contends for the *wrong* of the encroaching nation." Admitting that many good people condemned war of every description, he still asserted, "*defensive war*, is the only war that can be justified upon the principle of *eternal right*."[12]

The Rev. William Ellery Channing, one of the founders of the Massachusetts Peace Society, also addressed this difficult question in a sermon to a convention of Congregational ministers of Massachusetts in May 1816. He noted that the time was coming "when it will be accounted no small honour to have been among the earliest laborers in the work of mitigating and abolishing war." Channing added that "War, as it is commonly waged, is indeed a tremendous evil, but national subjugation is a greater evil than a war of defence; and a community seems to me to possess an indisputable right to resort to such a war, when all other means have failed for the security of its existence or freedom."[13]

Another author, however, characterized a defensive war as contrary to Christian precepts and "a want of confidence in Divine protection." War involved the very evil it was designed to guard against.[14] "Philo Pacificus," agreed and entered a strong critique of the English author, Lord Kames, who argued that war elevated the virtues of courage, generosity, and disinterestedness. War was instead, he said, an unjust and wicked "custom which murders men by the thousands for the sake of military glory." "Philo" condemned particularly Kames's absurd argument that it was better men be active in destroying one another than to fall into debilitating luxury. If, as Kames's argued, wars got rid of idlers and criminals, "Philo" noted it also drained the country of many industrious and useful men. "I would by no means recommend this summary mode of freeing a state from idlers." Offensive or defensive wars were an enormous evil. He was convinced God was preparing the way for abolition of war, and he cited as evidence sermons, writings, and the formation of peace societies.[15]

An obvious object of charity and humanitarian concern were the poor. Almshouses were established in New York City as early as 1795. Also, schools for indigent children were established, widows and small children were cared for by charities which provided food and clothing, provident societies provided sustenance to imprisoned debtors and other needy persons, and New York even had an asylum for orphans. The city also had a large hospital for distressed and poor sick persons. The governors of the New-York Hospital reported to the legislature in February 1816, that 1500 persons had been admitted in the past year. They had added a building in the last year to care for lunatics, but it accommodated only seventy-five persons. Unfortunately, it was already filled, and they had been forced to refuse admittance to any new patients. As a result, they had purchased thirty-eight acres about six miles from the city for a new facility, but they needed state aid to complete the project. Their report showed 1595 persons admitted to the hospital in 1815, an increase of 654, attributed to poor men discharged from the army and navy. They had 151 lunatics under their care that year. Expenditures for 1815 were approximately $35,000, which nearly matched receipts (including annuities from the state).[16]

Philadelphians also confronted the effects of poverty in their city. The Philadelphia Orphan Society was organized in December 1814. The first orphans were admitted on March 3, 1815, and when the legislature incorporated the society on January 29, 1816, it held twenty-five children. The society began raising funds in 1816 to build a larger building. The list of officers showed all female managers, headed by Sarah Ralston. An asylum for mentally deranged individuals was also in the process of being built near Philadelphia. The land was purchased in the spring of 1814, and a large three-story building was opened in the fall of 1816. The funds for the land and building (approximately $12,000) were raised through private donations.[17]

Morality tales also circulated widely in the literature of this year.[18] For example, the Philadelphia Female Tract Society, which held its first meeting on January 1, 1816, published and distributed over 60,000 religious tracts in 1816 on fourteen different subjects to Sunday schools around Philadelphia and other tract societies, churches, and female seminaries throughout Pennsylvania, Delaware, New Jersey, New York, Rhode Island, Connecticut, Vermont, Virginia, and Kentucky, as well as to Scotland, England, Jamaica, and India. The society also helped form twelve Juvenile Societies and two other female tract societies in Philadelphia during the year.[19]

The New York Religious Tract Society's fourth annual report of February 12, 1816, stated it had printed 70,000 tracts in the last year to add to the 46,345 on hand, including 10,000 copies of the popular, "The Dairyman's Daughter." During the year, 85,576 tracts were distributed all over the United States, as well as to China, the West Indies, Europe, and the Cape of Good Hope. The report lamented, however, a shortage of funds. New York City, they calculated, had about twenty religious congregations, averaging 100 members, yet "not one in ten . . . in these Congregations . . . contributed even *the widow's mite* to the promotion of *His* Glory, and the interests of his Kingdom."[20]

No doubt the best selling morality tract, if it may be so labeled, was the story of Lucy Brewer, published in three parts, which went through at least ten editions in 1816 and eventually nineteen printings by 1818. The story was of a young woman, seduced and deserted, who fell into a life of prostitution in Boston but escaped and, in male disguise, served for three years on the *U.S.S. Constitution.* While her description of the brothels might have been titillating to some of the people of that time, the purpose, according to Lucy, was "to promote temporal and spiritual good" in young persons of both sexes. In her farewell address, Lucy, who had now married a respectable gentleman, warned of the perils facing young women: "one false step forever blasts the fame of a woman."[21]

Lucy's memoirs, which were clearly fabrication, sparked a fictional rebuttal and even a "copy cat" version. According to Rachel Sperry, who ran a boarding house where Lucy worked, and who was supposedly responsible for Lucy's turn to an immoral life, the real story was that she had taken Lucy in out of pity to work as a chamber maid. On her own, Rachel declared, Lucy turned to prostitution. "Never had I a boarder that made such rapid progress in all the deceptive arts of harlotry." Lucy eventually left to follow a young man who served on the *U.S.S. Constitution.* He procured her the clothes of a sailor and introduced her to the recruiting officer as a cousin from New York, and he helped her pull off the duties of a sailor without suspicion. Rachel confirmed that Lucy had now turned to a life of respectability.[22]

Another work, suspiciously similar in plot, told the story of Almira Paul, who also served on board English and American armed vessels disguised as a man. She was severely wounded, lashed, and reportedly fell, fractured her skull, and underwent trepanning without her sex being discovered. Returning to her female role, she "took board at a house of ill-fame" for six weeks in Baltimore. She moved on to New York City and again entered into prostitution for five weeks. She moved to Boston, where she did house work, but she soon fell into prostitution and, at the time of the writing, July 1816, she was languishing in jail, committed by her landlord for non-payment of board.[23]

Whether the tales of Lucy Brewer and Almira Paul were just morality tracts is disputed by historian Daniel A. Cohen. He claims they were much more than that. He suggested these works could belong to several literary genres, including female warrior narratives, sentimental seduction novels, and even to early muckraking literature exposing urban problems. Moreover, the story of a plucky, independent woman challenged gender roles which, Cohen suggested, also represented a cross-dressing narrative and even a radical gender point of view. Indeed, these works may be cross-genre narratives, but there is little doubt that the popularity of these stories, intended or not, had much the same effect as hundreds of other morality tracts disseminated in 1816 by various religious tract societies. In fact, the descriptions of prostitution in these books may have spurred the anti-brothel riots occurring in the mid-1810s to mid-1820s in Boston, as well as the establishment of a refuge for the reform of prostitutes at this same time, culminating in Mayor Josiah Quincy's police crackdown on prostitution in 1823.[24]

Tract societies were by no means the leading distributors of religious literature. A major post-war development was a proliferation of Bible societies, whose main objective was to distribute copies of the Bible throughout the United States and the world. The first Bible society in America was established in Philadelphia in December 1808, modeled after the British and Foreign Bible Society, formed in 1804, which had reportedly distributed by 1816 approximately 1.3 million copies of the Bible to various parts of the globe, including the United States. Additional Bible societies were established in Massachusetts, Connecticut, and New York prior to the War of 1812. There were forty by 1814, sixty-eight by 1815, and 108 by 1816, and greater growth occurred during 1816. New York led the way, matching the total number in all of New England (25 to 24). There were as yet only fifteen such societies west of the Appalachians.[25]

One western society in Louisiana reported in 1816 that it had received and distributed 1350 English Bibles, 2248 French Bibles, 1000 Spanish New Testaments, and 300 French New Testaments, in Louisiana and along the Gulf coast. The Bibles of the British and Foreign Bible Society were in greatest demand because of the superior beauty of their type and paper. Surprisingly, the Louisiana society reported, "a much larger proportion of the inhabitants of this state than was at first supposed, can both read and write; but, notwithstanding this, they were deplorably destitute of books of all kinds." Free people of color were particularly desirous to have their children taught to read and made numerous requests for Bibles. Many stated they had waited for years to acquire a copy of the Bible in French. Even Catholics were willing to receive copies of the Protestant Bible. A few priests had opposed distribution, but the people had largely ignored their warnings. Spanish inhabitants, they added, had received copies "with greater demonstrations of joy" than the French. Copies were also distributed to American soldiers and sailors, and even to some slaves who could read.[26]

In January 1816, Elias Boudinot, President of the New Jersey Bible Society, called for the establishment of a general Bible society to unite the effort of the various Bible societies, again to emulate the British and Foreign Bible Society. He noted there was no unified distribution system, just independent societies distributing Bibles in every way possible. Often these societies were sending Bibles into each other's district. There was little communication, and their printed reports were not reciprocally exchanged. Boudinot suggested not a confederation of existing societies but the formation of a new national society. Existing societies could associate as auxiliaries and be coordinated by a central organization. He recommended laymen run the society to allay sectarian jealousy and that the headquarters be established in New York City which was "fast becoming the London of America."[27]

Accordingly, a meeting was held in the City Hall in New York City on May 13, 1816, to organize a national Bible society. The meeting was attended by such luminaries as Peter Jay, the son of John Jay, Smith Thompson, chief justice of the New York Supreme Court, and two other judges of the court, William Van Ness and Jonas Platt, as well as James Fenimore Cooper, the novelist, several ministers, and members of Bible societies in the region. Peter Jay, one of the speakers, stated, "if the predictions which foretell a millennial period of happiness on earth, are ever to be literally fulfilled, it can only be by the accomplishment of another prophecy, that 'The knowledge of the Lord shall cover the earth, as the waters of the sea.'"[28]

The fledgling society was generously endowed with a gift of $10,000 from its President, Elias Boudinot, and it was generally accepted around the country. Many local Bible societies quickly signed on as auxiliaries of the national society, such as the New Jersey Bible Society, the Otsego County Bible Society of New York, the New York Bible Society, (which turned over its plates to the national society), and the Vermont Bible Society, which declared in its annual report, "the union will operate to the mutual advantage of the societies."[29] In Boston, a meeting in December 1816, chaired by Governor Brooks, with members of the legislature and local clergymen (including the Rev. William Ellery Channing), endorsed the American Bible Society and urged local societies to join the national organization.[30] By December 1816, there were 172 Bible societies, of which sixty-five had become auxiliaries of the national society. By 1830, the American Bible Society claimed 645 auxiliaries.[31]

To some, the formation of these Bible societies heralded a new

era. One observer noted, "The asperities of Christian sects have
been moderated. . . . Christians seem now more inclined to regard
each other as brethren."[32] There were, however, critics of the American Bible Society. "A Clergyman" attempted to answer some of the
questions raised about the society. "*Is there not a great want of Bibles?*"
he asked, citing shortages in the country, particularly in the West.
Only about 150,000 Bibles had been distributed by the Bible societies, merely enough to supply the needs of Kentucky alone. He
argued that small, distinct societies acting with a national institution
would be more effective. As to fears of New York influence, he
simply stated it had "greater conveniences, and greater advantages,
than can be found in any other city." He denied that Presbyterians
had undue influence just because many had been active in its formation. In fact, the president of the American Bible Society was
Episcopalian, as were several vice-presidents. The society would not
promote the establishment of a national religion, encouraging rather
a diffusion of the Scriptures that might allay "the fury of party spirit
. . . making us a holy nation."[33]

One interesting consequence of the growth of Bible societies
was the participation of women, particularly in the formation of
tract and Bible societies. The Rev. John C. Rudd, Rector of St.
John's Church in Elizabethtown, New Jersey, commended the organization of a Female Bible Society in June 1816. "You will, in the
first place, do it best by yourselves," he advised, "The fact need not
be conceded, that you have more zeal than the other sex." While it
would be proper "to solicit pecuniary aid from the other sex, it will
be a becoming employment to manage your funds independently
of them; and they, by consenting that you should, will evince their
desire to promote your importance in the estimation of the world."[34]
Rudd's open-minded attitude was perhaps influenced by the fact
that the president of the new society was Mrs. John C. Rudd.

Female tract societies also supported other works of Christian
charity. The Providence (Rhode Island) Female Tract Society, for
example, supported pious schoolmasters in the more destitute parts
of the state, particularly in the vicinity of manufacturing establish-
ments. They also supported schooling for the children of their town,
both in the eight public schools and the nearly twenty private schools.
The annual report of the society noted, "from the spirited and liberal support of free schools, during the sixteen years last past, almost

every child of ten years old, is qualified to read the scriptures with fluency." The society tapped the pool of college students at Brown University to teach children the Bible in Sunday schools. By the end of 1816, the society was supporting teachers in five schools, including a school for African-American children. An appendix included reports from these teachers. One related teaching about 130 children, and another, Abner Morse, had about 120. Morse declared the children now used less profane language and that violations of the Sabbath were less common.[35]

There is little doubt that the Sunday school movement was given a significant boost by Bible and tract societies, which was acknowledged by the Rev. John C. Rudd in an address to a Free-school Association in Elizabethtown, New Jersey. The objective of social control was laid out clearly by Rudd: "It is not only the dictate of Christian benevolence, but of sound policy, to instruct in the rudiments of useful knowledge, and the principles of religion, the lower orders of society." Noting that some objected that Sunday Schools occupied the Sabbath "unprofitably to the duties of private devotion and retirement," Rudd insisted the teachers were "engaged in the highest religious duty, that of promoting the honor of God in the instruction of his creatures." Moreover, under the eyes of their teachers, the children were prevented from abusing the Sabbath, committing crimes, or scandalizing society.[36]

Education in any form was increasingly becoming a value of citizenship. As one observer noted in 1816, "a government like ours, cannot be in full health and vigor, unless the body politic be sound throughout. And surely there is no remedy for political disease but education." Education, he asserted, was "a *national duty: all must be educated*, and if *parents will not* do it, the *public are bound* to do it."[37] Indeed, in some places, efforts were already underway to provide educational opportunities. For example, the Free School Society in New York City, founded in 1805 with De Witt Clinton as the first president, opened its first school in 1809 and was operating three schools by 1816. The Chatham Street school had 587 students, and two schools on Henry Street had 403 and 587. In addition, there was a school for indigent females (about 400), which the Board asserted gave them arguably "advantages superior in their kind to those for the most part enjoyed by the children of the more affluent." The status of supplies was indicated in the Board's report which enumerated, among other things, those students who could "form letters in the sand." The method of instruction was the Lancasterian plan (whereby the older students taught the younger students), which enabled a single teacher at each of the schools to handle such large numbers. The board of the society proudly noted the "pleasing prospect that the benefits to be derived from the Lancasterian method of instruction, will very soon be more generally known and enjoyed, in the United States."[38]

Public education in the form of literary and scientific societies was not necessarily thriving in 1816. New England set the standard, but their institutions were suffering from neglect, as a report of a Massachusetts legislative committee showed. The American Academy of Arts and Sciences, established in 1780, had occupied a room in the State House until 1812, but its library and collection was now housed in a rented room ($100 annually), "subject, at every moment, to be ejected, at the will of the landlord." Its income for 1815 was only $134 from private sources, with nothing from the legislature. The Massachusetts Historical Society, established in 1791, likewise had received no patronage from the legislature, except the copyright of a map, producing $300 for the society. The library's 3000 volumes, as well as the newspapers, manuscripts, and other collections were deposited on the third floor over the arch in Franklin Place, "in danger of being wiped out by fire." The society had raised and expended nearly $7000 in publishing and distributing thirteen volumes of historical collections, and its cash balance in 1816 stood at $14.28. The Boston Athenaeum, established in 1807, also received no public financial assistance. Its 10,000–volume library, "inferior to none on the continent, that of Harvard University only excepted," was housed in a wooden building in the central part of Boston. Its present income was inadequate to meet ordinary expenses, and it certainly had no funds for book procurement. The Linnean Society (a museum of natural history) had a collection valued at only $4000. The Agricultural Society of Massachusetts had received a small sum from the legislature, but it had no room to exhibit its machines, and its library was housed at the Athenaeum, exposed to the same danger of fire.[39]

The committee's solution was for the state to provide $50,000 so that the societies could concentrate their libraries and collections in a central, convenient public building. The committee contrasted the parsimony of Massachusetts with other states. New York, for example, purchased Dr. David Hosack's botanic garden for $80,000 in 1810. It had granted the medical society $50,000 and the New York Historical Society $12,000. Pennsylvania's support for Charles W. Peale's museum, they said, was "more than thirty times greater, in each year, than the legislature of Massachusetts have ever extended to all the literary societies . . . in the whole course of their existence."[40]

Peale had another view of his situation. In an address to the citizens of Philadelphia on July 18, 1816, he lamented how he and his museum were treated. When he learned the city had purchased the State House, he believed he would finally obtain a permanent site for his museum, but the annual rent "amounted to a total expulsion." He had acquired his collection at great expense to himself, but he believed his museum was a great public benefit to Philadelphia. Many came to see his collection, and their visit was a "means of bringing wealth into our city." Maintenance of the museum and a large family, he declared, had always kept him poor. He had repeatedly asked the legislature of Pennsylvania for support. In 1802, they had granted him the use of the upper rooms of the State House. In 1815, the legislature enacted a law authorizing the county commissioners to let the museum stay in the State House, provided he pay a rent of $400 per annum. He had paid it, but at the last legislature they sold the State House to the City of Philadelphia, and a committee had proposed the museum should pay an annual rent of $1600, which far exceeded his ability to pay. It was up to the people to decide whether the museum should remain "amongst the national ornaments or useful improvements which Philadelphia has given to the western world, or whether it shall be driven like an outcast . . . to some more liberal or opulent city."[41]

The reception of Peale's implicit threat to remove his museum to another city was mixed. The council remained unmoved by his plea, but many prominent citizens supported him and sought a compromise. Peale even visited New York City, where he was received well, but eventually a compromise was reached on the rent, and his museum remained in the Pennsylvania State House.[42]

Of all of the issues attracting the humanitarian impulse, the most sensitive and deserving of attention was slavery. Slavery had its critics during the colonial period, but the Revolutionary War gave an impetus to the anti-slavery movement. Many northern states either abolished slavery or adopted gradual emancipation. The issue was too sensitive to be addressed directly in the Constitution, which did not mention slavery, but it recognized the institution. The Founding Fathers have been criticized for not doing more to end slavery, but defenders have argued they narrowed the scope of slavery and made it a Southern or "peculiar institution," sowing the seed of its eventual destruction.[43]

The period between 1808, when Congress banned the further importation of slaves, and 1831, when William Lloyd Garrison began his crusade for abolitionism, has generally been considered a quiet period in the anti-slavery movement. Nevertheless, Americans in 1816 were very conscious of the evils of slavery, and there was more agitation against the institution than might be imagined. Many were also aware of a growing international condemnation of the slave trade. Calls for its suppression were included both in the declaration of the Europe nations in the Congress of Vienna and in the Treaty of Ghent which ended the War of 1812.

Americans were also aware of the potential danger of slavery. At least two slave conspiracies were uncovered in 1816 that could have had tragic consequences. In Virginia, a white man, George Boxley, apparently conceiving himself as a liberator, conspired with slaves to march on Fredericksburg and then on to Richmond. A slave informant, however, prevented the rebellion from happening. About half a dozen slaves were executed and a like number were banished. Another plot by slaves was also foiled by a slave informant near Camden, South Carolina, which was to have started on the Fourth of July. Six slaves were hanged and others were also banished.[44]

Evidence of a growing hostility against slavery was manifested even in the South. A convention held in Lick Creek Meeting House in Greene County, Tennessee, on November 21, 1815, organized the Manumission Society of Tennessee. The prime mover was Elihu Embree, a Quaker who later published an anti-slavery journal in Jonesboro, Tennessee. An address to the people of Tennessee by the society condemned slavery and expressed sympathy for "this much injured people . . . groaning under the iron hand of oppression— retained in involuntary subjection—doomed to wear the chains of perpetual slavery." They added, "we cannot exercise an unjust dominion over a fellow creature, but that by a wise ordering of providence we unavoidably injure ourselves." The tenth article of the Treaty of Ghent declaring the slave traffic "irreconcilable with the principles of humanity & justice" was cited favorably. They pledged to work to "avert the impending storm, designed to scourge those who persist in stubborn disobedience to the eternal rules of justice." Slavery was declared to be "repugnant to the principles of the Christian religion," and ministers of the Gospel were encouraged "to promote the glorious work of undoing the heavy burdens, and letting the oppressed go free." Article twelve of the society's constitution urged its members to help elect governors and representatives to the various legislatures that would work for gradual emancipation.[45]

At about the same time, an organization founded in Ohio under the influence of Benjamin Lundy called the Union Humane Society, called upon all who were "willing to aid and assist in devising means to release them from the chains which have so long held them in the most grievous bondage." Others were urged to form societies to work for emancipation.[46]

On January 9, 1816, the American Convention for the Abolition of Slavery met in Philadelphia. Representatives from Pennsylvania, New York, and Delaware condemned the slave trade and adopted resolutions to distribute literature against it and to draft a memorial to Congress regarding restriction of this traffic. The memorial they adopted noted, among other things, that the 1808 law barring the further importation of slaves into the United States was being evaded and that many Africans were being smuggled into the southern states. They called for strengthening the law and its penalties. They also complained of the kidnapping of free blacks in the northern states and selling them into slavery in the South.[47] It should be noted that slavery still existed in the North. Slaves were still being offered for sale in New York newspapers. New York City, in a census taken in April 1816, counted 617 slaves (228 males and 309 females) and 7774 free blacks in a total population of 100, 519.[48]

Representative John Sergeant from Pennsylvania presented the society's memorial regarding the slave trade to Congress on February 27. On March 1, John Randolph, himself a slave owner, stood up and denounced the slave trade that was at that very moment being carried on "under their very noses; proceedings that were a crying sin before God and man; a practice which . . . was not surpassed for abomination in any part of the earth." Nowhere, he added, "was there so great and so infamous a slave market as in the metropolis, in the very Seat of Government of this nation, which prided itself on freedom." Randolph made it clear he did not wish to interfere in the relationship between an owner and his slave; he had voted against a bill to ban the slave trade because it assumed the prerogative to interfere in that right of property, but he emphasized that he was no advocate of "the most infernal traffic that has ever stained the annals of the human race." He moved the Committee of the District of Columbia devise some speedy means to end it.[49]

When the chair of that committee, fellow Virginian Henry St. George Tucker, demurred, Randolph offered to take his share in the enterprise. He was aware, he said, that the demands of cotton, tobacco, and sugar created a demand for slaves. "The increase in the price," he noted, "was the temptation for which their base, hardhearted masters sold out of their families the negroes who had been raised among them." He related that he was lately mortified when a foreigner of high rank said to him, "You call this the land of liberty, and every day that passes there are done in it at which the despotisms of Europe would be horror struck and disgusted." Despite some opposition, a resolution passed and Randolph was designated to chair the committee. On April 30, he reported testimony collected by his committee, but no other facts or opinions were offered. The report was ordered to lie on the table.[50]

The Philadelphia convention also noted that many blacks remained in bondage because slaveholders who wished to emancipate their slaves saw no means of removing them from their midst. They suggested setting aside a part of the United States territory "for the colonization of legally emancipated blacks." The convention was not the first to suggest a scheme for colonizing freed slaves. The idea of setting aside an area in the territory of the United States was proposed, in fact, by the Kentucky Colonization Society at its annual meeting in Frankfort in October 1815. Their proposal was addressed in the House of Representatives by Thomas Robertson of Louisiana on January 18, 1816. His committee recommended the petition not be granted. Among the disadvantages of establishing a settlement of freed slaves on the frontier was the concern that they might combine as our enemies with Indian neighbors or with European nations who had settlements adjacent to the United States.

They might also encourage slaves to run away from their masters, as well as providing a haven for escapees.[51]

Perhaps the most spirited denunciation of slavery in this year was by the Rev. George Bourne, an English-born Presbyterian, who lived in Virginia. His work, *The Book and Slavery Irreconcilable*, denounced slavery so vigorously that disciplinary action was taken by his church, and he was forced to flee the South.[52] Bourne asserted that, "Every man who holds slaves and who pretends to be a Christian or a Republican, is either an incurable idiot who cannot distinguish good from evil, or an obdurate sinner who resolutely defies every social, moral, and divine requisition." He particularly attacked ministers who defended slavery, "perverting the word of God, into a sanction of their abominations." The laws supporting slavery, he declared, denied the doctrine of natural rights and were a lie, and he left no doubt that he was calling for the abolition of slavery. Throughout he used terms like "man-stealers" and "man-thief." He dismissed those who declared slavery an evil but opposed measures to eradicate it as inconsistent with the national interest. "What is this," he asked, "but to establish a competition between God and Mammon, and to adjudge the preference to the latter." His uncompromising attack upon slavery has often been cited as influencing the leading abolitionist, William Lloyd Garrison.[53]

In August 1816, the Columbian United Abolition Society was formed in Eaton, Ohio. The new society was moderate, calling upon its members to promote the gradual abolition of slavery. It addressed the people of Ohio and Indiana, contending that the arguments of those who asked, "what shall we do with them," were a dangerous maxim "to make necessity a plea for injustice."[54] The president of the new society was David Purviance, a senator in the Ohio legislature, and his attitude may have been shaped in part by a dispute in the Ohio Senate in January 1816 on a proposed bill regulating blacks and mulattoes. The bill would have required, among other things, blacks or mulattoes entering the state to post a $500 bond so that they would not become chargeable to any township or county for maintenance. Purviance's motion to reject this article was defeated, 14–13, as was his motion to strike the $50 fine for harboring a fugitive. Another article required blacks and mulattoes migrating into the state to file a certificate with the clerk of court of common pleas as evidence of their freedom, subject to presentation of evidence of a right to their service by a citizen of the United States, as provided by the federal fugitive slave law. A motion to prohibit blacks and mulattoes from being witnesses against any white person was, however, defeated, 16–12, and eventually the whole bill was defeated by a tie vote, 14–14. It should be noted, however, that the Ohio legislature in 1816 did include a thinly disguised anti-black section in an act for the relief of the poor. Any person who would likely become a township charge could be warned to depart and, failing to do so, they could be forcibly removed out of the county or state.[55]

Despite the Northwest Ordinance of 1787 which forbade slavery or involuntary servitude, various forms of bondage existed during this period in the areas north of the Ohio River (Ohio, Indiana, and Illinois), generally under the subterfuge of long-term indentured servants, but also including rental contracts, enforcement statutes, as well as recognizing slave status for those residing in the territory before 1787. An anti-slavery attitude was reflected, however, in the Indiana Constitution when it was admitted in 1816. The constitution explicitly banned slavery and involuntary servitude and, in a unique piece of constitution writing, allowed the constitution to be revised, but declared, "no alteration of this constitution shall ever take place so as to introduce slavery or involuntary servitude in this state."[56]

Elsewhere the humanitarian impulse also was reflected in efforts to establish schools for African-Americans. One example was by the Synod of New York and New Jersey of the Presbyterian Church of the United States. At a meeting in New York City in October 1816, the directors of the African School issued an address to the public stating the goals of the synod. The primary objective was to educate young men of "respectable talents, sound discretion, [and] undoubted piety" to become teachers and preachers to their race. The directors assured the public of the caution and prudence of their proceedings and that only the most faithful and discreet would be selected "to inculcate subordination according to the apostolic example."[57] The fact the directors went to such extremes to reassure the public that they had nothing to fear from educating African-Americans suggested that such efforts to integrate free blacks into American society, while it was a viable option, was expected to meet with resistance. An apparently preferable option was also being explored at this time and presented to the public—that of removing free blacks from their midst and colonizing them back to Africa.

The leading figure in the colonization movement was the Rev. Robert Finley, a Presbyterian minister in Basking Ridge, New Jersey. It may be that Finley derived his first interest in such a society indirectly from Charles Fenton Mercer, a member of the Virginia House of Delegates, who learned in the spring of 1816 about secret resolutions passed by the Virginia legislature in 1800 to colonize the slaves involved in the Gabriel plot. Mercer enthusiastically took up the idea himself, and in the summer of 1816, on his way north, he visited Washington, D.C., and there elaborated his ideas for a colonization society to Francis Scott Key, an influential Georgetown lawyer, and Elias Boudinot Caldwell, a clerk of the Supreme Court. The latter wrote to his brother-in-law, Finley, who took up the idea as his own. Mercer also visited friends in Baltimore, Philadelphia, and New York City, spreading his ideas about colonization as he went. No doubt, Mercer's activity elicited discussion about such an organization, which influenced Finley to initiate such a plan.[58]

Of course, colonization was an old idea, and it did not originate in 1816. Proposals for black emigration to Africa went back to the eighteenth century. Quakers were particularly associated with this idea, but there were British influences as well. A Quaker physician, William Thornton, came to the United States in 1786 and actively promoted colonization of blacks to Africa.[59] A Quaker convert, Paul Cuffe, a free black who had become a successful and wealthy merchant in Massachusetts, was involved for many years in advocating the return of free blacks in America to Sierra Leone, a British colony in Africa. Cuffe was a Pan-Africanist who believed that emigration of free blacks to Africa would not only benefit them but Africa as well. In December 1815, Cuffe paid the passage of and carried thirty-eight free blacks to Sierra Leone. While Cuffe communicated with other advocates of colonization, including Finley, his untimely death in September 1817 prevented him from having a direct involvement in the new society.[60]

In November 1816, Finley presented his plan for a colonization society at a meeting in Princeton, New Jersey. Unlike Mercer, Finley apparently conceived a society that would encourage voluntary emancipation, and he believed federal support was necessary to carry out such a scheme. Several resolutions were passed at this meeting urging their legislature to seek support from Congress.[61] In December, Finley journeyed to Washington, D.C. where he enlisted the support of numerous influential men, particularly Caldwell and Key. He also published his views in a pamphlet, *Thoughts on Colonization*, which attracted further notice. His eight-page pamphlet argued essentially that blacks would always be kept down by prejudices if they lived among white men. Whites also would be hurt by their presence and would tend to rely on black labor rather than developing habits of industry. His message was non-threatening to slaveholders. Laws could be passed, he argued, "permitting emancipation of slaves on condition that they shall be colonized." Such an undertaking needed "the patronage of the nation," which would also "repair the injuries done to humanity by our ancestors by restoring to independence those who were forced from their native land, and are now found among us."[62]

The support of prominent figures were enlisted, such as Supreme Court Justice Bushrod Washington, Speaker Henry Clay, and several congressmen and senators, including John Randolph, Samuel Smith, Daniel Webster, and Robert H. Goldsborough, and clergymen, as well as numerous other distinguished individuals from the District of Columbia and the surrounding region of Virginia and Maryland. Colonization publicity was also published in the *Daily National Intelligencer*, which culminated in a meeting presided by Clay in the Davis Hotel in Washington, D.C., on December 21, 1816.[63] In his opening remarks, Clay noted the "unconquerable prejudices" against free blacks. He revealed his own motives when he cited colonization as a noble cause, "to rid our country of a useless and pernicious, if not dangerous portion of its population." He warned those present to avoid the delicate question of emancipation, noting that was the condition on which the men of the South and West had attended this meeting.[64]

Whether Finley had intended it or not, his proposed society had been made respectable. He may have clung to his belief until his death in 1817 that colonization would eventually emancipate the slaves, but the distinguished gentlemen who participated in this meeting made it clear that slavery had nothing to fear from the colonization movement. Other speakers argued that free blacks could never become valuable citizens and that colonization was the only solution. John Randolph even argued that colonization would make slave property more secure by removing the free blacks who were a source of mischief and discontent among slaves, as well as hatching insurrection plots and serving as depositories of stolen goods.[65]

A second meeting was held on December 28 in the hall of the House of Representatives, where a constitution for the American Society for Colonizing the Free People of Color in the United States was adopted. On New Year's Day, 1817, the first annual meeting was held in the Davis Hotel, with Clay again presiding. Bushrod Washington was chosen president, and a distinguished group of thirteen vice-presidents, headed by Speaker Clay and Secretary of the Treasury William Harris Crawford. General Andrew Jackson's name was included, on whose authority is unclear. The Rev. Robert Finley was also added. The real work of the society would be carried out by a board of managers, among whom were Francis Scott Key and several clergymen. Elias Caldwell was named the executive secretary. Although Charles Fenton Mercer was not involved in the meetings forming the society, he was elected to the House of Representatives and became, as one historian noted, "the virtual leader of the society."[66]

The response, both in the North and South, was generally favorable. Free blacks, however, reacted unfavorably. One protest meeting in Philadelphia condemned the stigma cast upon them, declaring that the United States was their home. A similar meeting of free blacks in Richmond protested colonization in Africa, but they proposed a colony in the West beyond the Mississippi River. The Virginia legislature, led by Mercer, had already adopted resolutions favoring a federal scheme of colonization, and instructed their senators and congressmen to support the idea.[67] It was critical to gain the support of the federal government, and thus a memorial from the new society was introduced into the House by John Randolph on January 14, 1817, asking Congress to create a colony for free blacks in Africa.[68]

The report of the House Committee on the African Slave Trade on February 11, 1817, was a disappointment for the society. Timothy Pickering, reporting for the committee, suggested that instead of a separate colony the United States should make a proposition to the British to accept colonists in Sierra Leone, and if they refused, then they should negotiate with the British and other powers to guarantee the neutrality of any colony established by the United States on the African coast.[69]

When the British declined the proposition, the society again pressed Congress for such a colony, but despite the particular efforts of William Crawford and the support of President James Monroe, the federal government's contribution was indirect and limited. Not until the early 1820s was the society able to establish the colony of Liberia on the west coast of Africa, and it never met the expectations of its managers.[70] As late as 1830, less than 1500 free blacks had made the passage back to Africa. By the 1830s abolitionists questioned whether the colonization society was a benevolent association at all, because of its indifference to race prejudice and slavery, and it began a slow decline.[71] In truth, while it may have been born out of a humanitarian impulse, it not only failed to address the evil of slavery, it also did not confront the ultimate question of racism. The colonization society's basic premise, that the two races could not live together, led to an unrealistic solution that was destined to fail.

The humanitarian impulse displayed by Americans in 1816, while creditable, did not challenge the basic structure of their republican experiment. Essentially, reformers saw their community as fundamentally good but flawed, and they sought to improve and make it better. Clearly, there was also a strong element of social control emanating from these efforts. While citizens increasingly exercised their collective influence in the nation's social sphere, their involvement in national politics remained defined primarily by regional and self-interest. Americans in 1816 had begun to grapple with the implications of a growing participation in the governance of their society, such as their reaction to the Compensation Act of 1816, but the presidential election of 1816 captured no such notice from the average citizen.

Chapter 12

Election of 1816

Historians have found little excitement during the 1816 presidential campaign. One writer characterized it as "dull as dishwater." Nor have other historians had much to say about this election; it has been largely ignored.[1] Nevertheless, the race was hardly devoid of interest. Opposition to the mode of nomination by party caucus, which became a major issue in 1824, was strongly articulated in 1816. The caucus in 1816 began and ended in intrigue. William Harris Crawford probably lost his opportunity to be president because he was reluctant to grasp it, while the nomination went to James Monroe, whose primary qualification seemed to be that he was, like three candidates before him, a Virginian.

The Federalist Party was reeling from criticism of their conduct against the War of 1812. Until its final days, the War of 1812 had seemed a boon to the Federalist cause. They had enjoyed marked success in the 1814 elections, gaining majorities in the legislatures of New England, Maryland, and Delaware, and strong minorities in New York, Pennsylvania, and New Jersey. However, Andrew Jackson's incredible victory over the British at New Orleans and the Treaty of Ghent, which ended the war, turned the tide against the Federalists. They were further tarnished by the anti-war, potentially secessionist Hartford Convention in late 1814, which turned public opinion strongly against them and saddled Federalists with the brand of "treason." Ultimately, they declined even to field a candidate for president. Although newspapers and political pamphlets kept issues boiling, the public seemed far more interested in other matters, such as the weather in the summer of 1816 and the Compensation

Act, than in who was to be the new Chief Magistrate. The outcome was more an "acclamation" than an election.

Another nail in the Federalist coffin was when Republicans in the Fourteenth Congress seemed to appropriate the Federalist political agenda for themselves. President James Madison, his popularity restored by the favorable outcome of the war, recommended Federalist measures such as a stronger military and a recharter of the Bank of the United States. The Republican response of strengthening the army and the navy, passing a protective tariff, and rechartering a Second Bank of the U.S., caused Federalists at first to express their delight at this turn-around, but they soon came to see that they had in fact been politically preempted. Ex-President John Adams observed, "Our two great parties have crossed over the valley and taken possession of each other's mountain."[2]

The nomination of James Monroe by the Republicans was by no means a certainty as the new year of 1816 approached. In fact, the prevailing political mood in Washington was apathy and a lack of partisan acrimony. On December 9, 1815, Albert Gallatin, just returned from a visit to Washington D.C., wrote John Quincy Adams, "There is at this moment less apparent party agitation than I had known for a long time; but," he added, "it will be sufficiently renewed by the Presidential election."[3] Indeed, the election was beginning to stir interest. A former governor of New York, Morgan Lewis, speculated to New York congressman John W. Taylor that James Madison might be enticed to run for a third term. The most important reason was that it would "give us a man from the Ancient Dominion for four years instead of eight; or more probably sixteen." Madison, he noted, was only a little older than Monroe, and staying in the presidency would make Monroe too advanced in age to be his successor. Moreover, Lewis added, "Madison is quick, temperate and clear. Monroe slow, passionate and dull. Madison's word may always be relied on . . . I am sorry to say I cannot bear the same testimony to Monroe."[4]

Monroe had been denied in his bid to "leap-frog" Madison eight years previously. He had patched up his differences with Madison and was admitted back into the good graces of the administration. In fact, Monroe as secretary of state had added strength and resolve to Madison's presidency. During the War of 1812 Monroe had intrigued for a military appointment. At one point he contrived to replace Gen. Henry Dearborn on the Northern front. Then he sought to replace Gen. William Hull on the Western frontier, only to be frustrated by Kentucky's appointment of Gen. William Henry Harrison. Monroe perceived Secretary of War John Armstrong Jr. as a rival for the presidency, and he fretted when Armstrong went to observe operations on the Northern front in 1813. While he was away, Monroe actively undercut Armstrong in the War Department, and he carried on a secret correspondence with Armstrong's generals. The capture of Washington, D.C., in August 1814 ruined Armstrong's reputation. Monroe's conduct during the British attack on Washington, D.C., was responsible more than he would admit, for the fall of Armstrong. Henry Adams, with some exaggeration, characterized Monroe's actions during this period as "a *coup d'etat*."[5] Monroe replaced Armstrong as secretary of war in the last months of the war. He confided to his son-in-law, George W. Hay, regarding his bustling activity during this period, "I hoped to place myself most distinctly on my own ground, not only, as to the part I had acted, in regard to the defence of this city, but certain traits of character, on which I set some value, and which it required some exertion on my part to bring into view."[6]

Monroe enjoyed solid support from Virginia, and a state caucus had already chosen electors favorable to him. Care had been taken to avoid a personal endorsement; no doubt they were aware of the stigma developing against another "Virginia candidate." The Washington D.C. *Daily National Intelligencer*, although strongly in Monroe's camp, nevertheless printed a jibe from the *Green Mountain Farmer* giving six reasons why Monroe must be the next president: "1st. He was born in Virginia. 2nd. He was educated in Virginia. 3rd. He lives in Virginia. 4th. Washington, Jefferson and Madison were and are of Virginia. 5th. He is a friend of Virginia. 6th. The last two Presidents lived in Virginia."[7]

Thomas Jefferson said of his friend Monroe, in an oft-quoted remark, that his "soul might be turned wrong side outwards without discovering a blemish to the world." Yet in 1816 many were aware that this observation was from 1786 and referred to a far younger and less adroit political man than now sought the succession. His mental powers were not generally admired; one-time Vice President Aaron Burr declared in a letter to his son-in-law on the impending nomination of Monroe that he found him "stupid and illiterate . . . improper, hypocritical, and indecisive."[8] Burr preferred Andrew Jackson.

A potential rival to Monroe was New York Governor Daniel D. Tompkins, who was being touted by friends in New York for the presidency. Tompkins had been an effective war governor, despite a lack of funds and militia failures. One drawback was his lack of experience at the federal level and no name recognition outside his state. Congressman Jonathan Fisk of New York doubted that Tompkins was up to the job. He noted in a letter to John W. Taylor on December 31, 1815, that while Tompkins was "honest, patriotic, and well attached to the Constitution," he was "too young, and even too volatile, for the gravity, dignity, and vast responsibility of that elevated station." Fisk believed De Witt Clinton's friends were promoting Tompkins to remove him from the state and pave the way for Clinton to become governor. Fisk asserted that "the great mass of the party in this city and state" were satisfied with Monroe. "He is certainly the most prominent public character;" he wrote, "public opinion centers upon him."[9]

Nevertheless, on February 14, the Republicans of the New York legislature formally nominated Tompkins for the presidency. A week later, lacking a viable alternative, the legislature also renominated Tompkins for governor—an event that caused the *Daily National Intelligencer* to comment archly: "We thought the Republican members of the Legislature of New York had recommended Mr. Tompkins as a candidate for the Presidency of the U. States. Perhaps this was an error."[10] In truth, though fully backing their governor, New York Republicans found little interest in him outside the state, and he had no support south of the Potomac. Jabez Hammond, a congressman and historian, suggested to Martin Van Buren that the best way to promote Tompkins' interest was "to divide the southern interests" by initially supporting William Harris Crawford of Georgia over Monroe. In fact, Van Buren was leaning towards Crawford anyway in hopes of a Crawford/Van Buren ticket in the future.[11]

According to a "confidant," three days before the congressional caucus, Tompkins stated that he had little hope of his own success, and he had already ruled out accepting the post of secretary of state. He was said to be certain to accept the vice presidency under Crawford, and he might do so under Monroe, although in the latter case he would prefer to remain as governor.[12]

William Harris Crawford, by Asher Brown Durand. National Portrait Gallery, Smithsonian Institution, Washington, D.C.

Crawford was a far more formidable rival, around whom the opposition to Monroe began to coalesce. The big, impressive secretary of war enjoyed substantial strength in the South and West. Jonathan Fisk, although he supported Monroe, admitted, "I am not insensible to the commanding merits of Mr. Crawford. . . . His age and experience render him, not a candidate of equal claim to Mr. Munro . . . yet I am the decided friend of Mr. C. I know him to be a man of pure principles, great mind and capabilities of the best achievements."[13]

On February 9, the Federalist *New York Evening Post* reported that a "letter from Washington" had informed the paper that an early determination by House members of the likely caucus choices were Rufus King and Langdon Cheves for the Federalists and William H. Crawford and Daniel D. Tompkins for the Republicans.[14] Four days later, the *Daily National Intelligencer* quoted a letter from Boston to the effect that Federalists, despairing of a candidate of their own, might better support Crawford. This administration newspaper, of course, urged the Republican Party not to let the opposition dictate its choice. However, whether this was part of any "divide and conquer" strategy, Federalist as well as Republican support began to swing Crawford's way.[15]

Through February the Georgian seemed to be consistently gaining strength. Several newspapers declared that he could have the nomination if he would only stretch forth his hand to grasp it. It was suggested that Kentucky and Pennsylvania were in Crawford's corner, and once its "favorite son" was denied, New York would also support Crawford strongly over Monroe.[16]

All of this came despite the fact that Crawford had apparently withdrawn as a candidate in January. The *Daily National Intelligencer* reported this fact on January 17 and applauded it as "the disinterestedness of a virtuous and firm republican." On February 1, it published a letter by Georgia Senator William W. Bibb, who claimed to speak for Crawford. The Georgian, he said, "did not consider himself among the number of those from whom the selection ought to be made, and that he was unwilling to be held up as a competitor for that office."[17]

Bibb's statement was apparently fully authorized by Crawford, who also told Erastus Root of New York that if elected he would not serve. Yet the people of the country did not fully credit these statements, and no clarifications or re-statements were forthcoming. The reason, it appears, was that the non-candidate was having second thoughts.[18]

Crawford, personally friendly to Monroe, had obviously been subjected to great pressures to allow the Virginian his turn at the helm. He was young enough to wait eight years, at which time he would enjoy undivided Republican support. Swayed by this reasoning and by appeals to party loyalty, Crawford had authorized the disavowals of his candidacy and assured Monroe of his personal support. The continued and growing public support for him, however, left him uncertain how to respond.[19]

On February 8, the *New York Patriot* trumpeted a letter that seemed to confirm its earlier assertion that Crawford's withdrawal was not to be credited, that Bibb spoke only for himself. The *Washington City Weekly Gazette* noted wryly: "Those who support Mr. Crawford for the presidency cannot be accused of being political infants. They have no occasion for a *bib*."[20]

While many debated who the caucus nominee would be, others were attacking the caucus mode of nomination. Perhaps the most influential was a pamphlet extracted from the best-selling book of the era, Mathew Carey's *The Olive Branch*. Carey denied the claim of caucus defenders that anything but the caucus method would lead to anarchy, calling it a "flimsy covering." He detailed four objections to the system: first, that the caucus was "unequal and unjust;" second, that it turned the nation's capital into "a scene of intrigue;" third, that it represented a dangerous "mixture" of the executive and the legislative branches; and fourth, that the caucus was "blatantly unconstitutional."[21] An appendix included an extract from the *Louisville Correspondent*, dated December 11, 1815, in which the editor lamented that the people seemed to be awaiting a nomination from Washington, D.C., and cited the "pernicious consequences of the growing usurpation of the Washington *palace* nomination." He suggested the Kentucky legislature should step in "Roman like, between the Republic and destruction."[22]

Many newspapers attacked the caucus, but none exceeded the Annapolis *Maryland Gazette*, a Federalist paper, which kept up a steady stream of anti-caucus articles throughout the year.[23] Federalists may have attacked the caucus to discredit the Republican candidate, but even the *Daily National Intelligencer*, the administration paper, called for some other means than one often "subject to the influence of conditions which ought to have no bearing on the question."[24] Also, there was growing unease about a caucus nomination among members of Congress. John W. Taylor, for example, wrote privately to his wife Jane that he had always been opposed to congressional caucuses, as "The management & electioneering which generally precedes them organize factions of the most dangerous character."[25] Fellow New Yorker Thomas P. Grosvenor expressed the view of many congressmen when he declared, "the Executive finds no difficulty in designating his successor with greater certainty than could the first tyrants of imperial Rome."[26]

In Monroe's papers in the Library of Congress there is a private memorandum he wrote discussing the virtues of the caucus system of nomination. It was to be preferred, he wrote, over other methods, such as a convention. Members of Congress might exceed their constitutionally delegated powers, he argued, "but they act, under a responsibility to their constituents," and their conduct would be approved or not "as it corresponds or opposes their sentiments & views."[27] Even after the caucus was used to nominate Monroe, it remained an issue throughout the campaign. The administration press felt it necessary to respond to defend the system. The *Muskingum* (OH) *Messenger*, for example, claimed that the caucus had merely "confirmed" a selection already made by the people, while the *New York Patriot* saw the caucus nomination as only a "recommendation" and thus as no "usurpation." When the *Catskill* (NY) *Recorder* revealed that its initial misgivings about the caucus had been assuaged by the choice of the perfect candidates, the *Daily National Intelligencer* could not resist asking why in that case the New York delegation had gone so strongly for Crawford.[28]

While criticism of the caucus system of nomination appeared with increasing frequency in the press, the reaction of the *Nashville Whig* in early February no doubt expressed the views of many when they asked why had nothing been done so far to call a caucus? One possible reason for delay was that Monroe would have preferred to forego the caucus, which might have favored Crawford. Glowing recommendations of Monroe by pro-administration newspapers, however, seemed to have stemmed the groundswell for Crawford.[29]

On March 10, "an unknown person" posted a notice to Republican members of both houses, announcing a caucus meeting on the twelfth to consider nominations for president and vice president. No one professed to know the author of the call, but when only fifty-eight of the 141 Republican members arrived for the meeting, it was obvious no nomination could be made that would command popular respect. Senator Jeremiah Morrow of Ohio then suggested a formal call for a meeting on March 16.[30]

The Federalist *New York Evening Post*, which had derided the coming caucus as a virtual "coronation," seemed amused that the postponement had been necessary when it was discovered that the "Crawfordites outnumbered the Monroeites."[31] It is very possible that the anonymous notice had come from supporters of Crawford, although almost certainly without his knowledge. The Monroe forces, taken aback, had boycotted the meeting to rally their people in the intervening time before the sixteenth.

When the caucus met on that date, all but twenty-two of the Republican members were present. That this system of nomination was under attack can be clearly seen in the initial resolution proposed by Henry Clay: "That it is inexpedient to make in Caucus, any recommendation to the good people of the United States, of persons, in the judgment of this meeting, fit and suitable to fill the offices of President and Vice-President of the United States."[32] Clay's resolution, and a similar one proposed by John W. Taylor, were voted down. It was obvious that the eventual winner would not escape a certain stigma.

Georgia's two senators, following instructions from Crawford, passed the word among their fellow legislators that the secretary of war had been persuaded to postpone his candidacy until 1824. As a result, several Crawford supporters absented themselves from the caucus. When the first (and only) tally showed sixty-five for Monroe and fifty-four for Crawford, the effect was surprise, even shock. The votes of Virginia (eleven votes) comprised the margin of Monroe's victory over a man who had withdrawn his name two months earlier.

Although he received a "torrent of ridicule and abuse" for having allowed his name to be proposed in opposition to Monroe, Crawford had never been "officially" a candidate at all. He had, in fact, specifically instructed his managers that in the event he should lose in the caucus vote, they were to issue a statement that his name had been presented without his consent. That they neglected to do so, Crawford always felt, led to the lack of administration support for his candidacy eight years later.[33]

After New York's Tompkins was endorsed for the vice presidency by eighty-five votes to thirty for Pennsylvania Governor Simon Snyder, the caucus adjourned, and the press (and historians) were left to speculate on what might have been. Several papers noted that Crawford would certainly have been nominated had he made even the slightest effort on his behalf, or if the caucus had been held the previous month. *Niles' Weekly Register* sought to blunt the argument of the Crawfordites by estimating that of the members not attending the caucus, "more than three-fourths" would have supported Monroe.[34]

Crawford was very displeased that his supporters had "bungled" their efforts. Several historians have focused on Crawford having given his word personally to Monroe that he wished only a sufficient show of strength to be credible as the successor in 1824. When his support appeared to be stronger than he had imagined, he was loath, as an honorable man to be seen as breaking his word. When, shortly after the caucus, Crawford was offered the Treasury appointment, he initially wavered, as he might potentially become a member of Monroe's cabinet. Monroe, he believed, "should at least be given an opportunity of manifesting his displeasure, if I have incurred it."[35]

In some quarters, there was an impression that Crawfordites had tried to "bully" the caucus into choosing their man over the choice of the people. This was answered by a charge that Monroe's friends had packed the room with all of his supporters and that they "were in a *moveable* condition and made use of several proxies."[36] One pamphlet of the time asserted that the Virginians would not go into the caucus until they were certain of success, and they were known to be pledged to support Monroe even if the caucus nominated someone else.[37]

What little thought Federalists had given to fielding a candidate against Monroe centered around New York Senator Rufus King. A member of the Constitutional Convention, one of New York's first Senators, and Minister to England during the John Adams's presidency, King had also been Alexander Hamilton's second in the fatal duel with Aaron Burr. King was also the vice presidential nominee of the Federalists with Charles C. Pinckney in 1808, and he was the

Rufus King, by Gilbert Stuart. National Portrait Gallery, Smithsonian Institution, Washington, D.C.

surprise choice of the New York legislature for senator in 1813. Widely admired after thirty years of political involvement, he nevertheless evoked little personal warmth or affection.[38]

Interestingly, King had supported earlier a proposed amendment to the Constitution which would have allowed the choosing of electors by district and popular vote, an implicit attack upon the caucus. King reminded his colleagues in the Fourteenth Congress that he was the only member among them that had sat in the Constitutional Convention, and he well knew what the Founding Fathers had intended. The proposed amendment, however, was not passed.[39]

Unfortunately, any hope for King or for his party fielding a credible presidential candidate in 1816 was ended by the action of the New York Federalist Party caucus in February. Meeting to select their choice in the gubernatorial race against the apparently unbeatable incumbent Tompkins, the legislators quickly settled on State Supreme Court Judge William W. Van Ness. That gentleman, however, stunned the caucus by refusing to run, citing his fear that his successor on the bench would be a Republican. After three days of vainly attempting to change Van Ness's mind, the exhausted Federalists unanimously named Rufus King as their gubernatorial nominee.[40]

Cognizant that King's reaction would certainly be negative, eight caucus members composed letters urging King's acceptance as a necessary sacrifice. The caucus, he was told, had been on the verge of breaking up in disarray when his name gained unanimous support. His patriotism was appealed to, as well as his party loyalty. Theodore Dwight wrote that if Federalists could not gain control of New York, "we cannot expect to have any effectual agency in the presidential election. If we cannot make any impression upon the presidential election . . . I see no hope for the future."[41] Stephen Van Rensselaer, stated frankly to King that Tompkins might win, but no one could make a better show against him than King, ensuring that quality candidates for the legislature would join his ticket. King was even urged to accept to counter the opposition charge that the Federalists had known that King would not accept the nomination, which was intended to cover a design to join hands with De Witt Clinton later. Only one writer, Gouverneur Morris, demurred, declaring that the office was not worthy of a first rate man.[42]

For more than two weeks, King hesitated before reluctantly accepting the nomination. To his son, Edward, he wrote, "I entertain little expectation of being elected and no personal desire to be so."[43] Reflecting his ambivalence, King did not put much effort into the campaign. He did attempt to discover whether Tompkins would indeed seek to run for governor and vice president concurrently, wondering whether any political advantage might be made out of that situation. His correspondent, Thomas J. Oakley, replied that Tompkins would almost certainly be a candidate for both offices because the Republican Party in New York "would not unite cordially on any other candidate." If Tompkins being a candidate for two places at once operated at all in favor of the Federalists, he added, it would be by exciting apprehensions among Republicans hostile to De Witt Clinton that he might regain the governorship in the election next spring. "Many would prefer the success of even the Federal candidate to any prospect of C.'s restoration to power."[44]

The New York gubernatorial campaign was not a high-minded affair. Tompkins was presented as a "patriot" during the late war, while the "subversive activities" at the Hartford Convention tarred all Federalists. Selective extracts from King's correspondence were used by the Republican press to suggest pro-British leanings by King during the conflict.[45] King was also unpopular with Irish voters. At a gathering of the Society of St. Patrick, a toast declared that King "preferred the favor of the British Cabinet to the glorious privilege of granting the patriots of your country an asylum from oppression. (Empty glasses.)" This was, no doubt, a reference to King's protest to the British government in 1798, while United States Minister to England, against their plan to banish Irish patriots, such as Thomas Addis Emmett, to America.[46]

A Federalist counterattack accused Tompkins of misusing public funds, a charge that would later be effectively resurrected by the Clintonians. More telling was the criticism of running for two offices simultaneously. If (as seemed likely) Tompkins succeeded in being elected vice president, who would become the new governor of New York? The *New York Evening Post* on April 16 accused the governor of having decided to accept the national nomination, but also requesting the word to be kept quiet until the gubernatorial election date was past. In fact, however, the written acceptance of the vice presidential selection had come ten days before and had been reported in several newspapers.[47]

In addition to fighting uphill odds, King was further handicapped by having to remain in Washington, D.C., through most of the gubernatorial campaign, due to Congress being in session. When he was finally ready to return to his home state, he was informed of an assassination threat made against him. Forced to take a circuitous route north, he was in Pennsylvania when he learned that Tompkins had defeated him by a vote of 45,412 to 38,647.[48]

Although the showing was actually quite respectable, it was nevertheless devastating to Federalist hopes for a King candidacy for president. The *New York Evening Post* bitterly blamed the defeat on "Apostates, Coodies, and Drunkards" (the middle term referring to defectors who had gone over to the Republican side). King himself thought he had seen the future. His analysis was that the Federalist effort had united the several factions of the Republican Party. "Personally," he wrote Christopher Gore, "I am satisfied no event could have been less agreeable to me than to have been elected Governor of the State." He added, "I presume that the failure will, as I think it should, discourage the Federalists from maintaining a fruitless struggle . . . Federalists of our age must be content with the past."[49] To another correspondent, King wrote, "The federal party in the sense of a party aiming at political power no longer exists." He also reiterated to his son that Federalists were "out of the question as a rival Party," and he suggested that as the Republicans were sure to divide among themselves, the best course for Federalist strategy (which in due course actually became the strategy of the remnants of the Federalist Party) would be to give their influence "to the least wicked Section of the Republicans."[50]

The setback in New York was thus fatal to the Federalist party. King's pessimism merely reflected the general mood of the party throughout the union. Thomas Ritchie, editor of the *Richmond Enquirer*, gloated in an editorial in May 1816 that the Federalists were finished. "Why waste your talents in fruitless opposition," he asked. He added, "Whatever new party distinctions may arise in the bosom of the republic; whatever new combinations may be formed from the elements of *local interest* or *constitutional doctrine*, this one fact seems to be clear, that the federal sun of the party of Pickering and Otis has set forever."[51] In truth, the party was so splintered and in such disarray that no Federalist caucus was ever called, and they never even fielded a presidential candidate for this election. It has often been stated that Rufus King was the last Federalist candidate for president, but he certainly had no knowledge of it. Nothing in King's correspondence nor in Federalist newspapers indicated that he was thought of (or thought of himself) as a candidate after the loss in New York in April.

Notwithstanding, the Republican Party was less than confident of its own unity. The editor of the *Savannah Republican* felt it necessary to declare that not a single Georgia elector would cast a vote for Crawford over Monroe. Some Federalist newspapers, such as the Philadelphia *True American*, urged party support for Crawford as an acceptable alternative to Monroe, while the *New York Courier* warned against this action, noting that "experience has been to us, a cruel teacher; but therefore a successful one." The *New York Evening Post*, while denying that Crawford had ever sought an alliance with the Federalists, gleefully noted that Monroe had definitely done so eight years before in his fight against Madison.[52]

Monroe was extremely sensitive to the latter charges, and he drew up a defense of his earlier actions. He actually sent a copy of his defense to his son-in-law, George W. Hay, but he also expressed doubts whether the document should be published. In the paper, Monroe stated, "Between me & the Federalists there was no connections."[53] There is no indication that Monroe's defense was ever published, even anonymously.

One attack upon Monroe attracted a lot of attention during the summer of 1816. On June 1, the influential editor, Hezekiah Niles noted the appearance of an anonymous pamphlet entitled *Exposition of Motives for Opposing the Nomination of Mr. Monroe for the Office of President of the United States*. Niles noted that, "If the articles were not anonymous it would, of course, have a place in the WEEKLY REGISTER, as belonging to the political history of our times."[54]

Other newspapers, however, did reprint the tract, as one Federalist paper said, "for the amusement of our readers."[55] The pamphlet became for some time a topic of much discussion. Purporting to explain the reasons why so many caucus members had voted against Monroe, it was actually an attack upon the party nominee on several points. Among the charges was that "the whole weight of the republican party, for fifteen years past, [has] been artfully wielded [by the Virginians] to *cut off* from popular respect and estimation the most distinguished characters in other parts of the United States." As support, it was noted that both Jefferson and Madison had chosen as vice presidents men so old and feeble they could never contest for the presidency. (Both George Clinton and Elbridge Gerry had in fact died in office.) John Quincy Adams, another potential rival, had been dispatched to Russia to keep him out of the public eye.[56]

James Monroe, on the other hand, had been "popularized" by glossing over his differences with Madison and had been brought into the State Department as heir-apparent. The pamphlet concluded with several references to the candidate's lack of qualifications: "slow of comprehension," "lust for power," and certain to be surrounded by incompetents.[57] It was widely speculated that this pamphlet was the work of Crawfordites or Clintonians, but it was actually penned by John Armstrong, Jr., one of Monroe's old rivals and one of the men Monroe was accused of "thwarting."[58]

Armstrong had intended the piece for the *Albany Argus*, but the editor, Jesse Buel, considered it too strong. It was eventually published in Washington, which explains why the author was not discovered by contemporaries. Charles Pinckney, who wrote a reply to the pamphlet, stated ten thousand copies of the *Exposition* were published and circulated.[59] In Ohio, the *Muskingum Messenger* felt compelled to denounce the *Exposition* as the work of a cabal of Crawfordites who saw a chance to resurrect their man's chances upon the ruins of Monroe's reputation.[60]

Aside from this early summer controversy, the interest of the people, as reflected in their newspapers, lay in other areas than the presidential election. While the bizarre weather of the summer attracted a great deal of attention, the major issue involving the American people, by far, was the Compensation Act (see chapter 5). The people were more interested in turning out self-aggrandizing public servants than with choosing a new president.

Nevertheless, party spirit was alive at the state level, as a sampling of political pamphlets from 1816 reveal. From time to time Federalists issued broadsides on behalf of local or state candidates, but none even mentioned the presidential election. A broadside in Lancaster, Pennsylvania, did declare that Federalist unity was "vital to the salvation of the party," which was "on the brink of destruction."[61] Most of the broadsides, however, dealt with local issues. A Federalist election circular in Salem, Massachusetts, for example, called the party faithful, "To your Posts!" Referring to the politics of gerrymandering under former governor, Elbridge Gerry, the broadside asked, "Are you ready to trust the ballot boxes in the hands of that party which attempted by force and violence to crush them to pieces and scatter your votes to the winds?" Voters were asked to scorn the Republican Party of "hollow *hypocrisy*, false pretensions, and flagrant inconsistencies!" All of this rhetoric, apparently, was poured out to elect a slate of town officers (selectmen, assessors, and overseers of the poor).[62] The concern of the Federalists in Salem was warranted. Salem, which had always been Federalist by considerable margins, elected Republican town officers by a margin of about 50 votes. Gloucester, another Federalist stronghold, also turned out the Federalists by a small margin.[63]

A similar Federalist pamphlet, addressed to the freemen of Connecticut, noted that for twenty years they had, in opposition "to the progress of error . . . always been victorious." Friends of the administration, the author assured Republicans, had nothing to fear. Federalists were willing to concede the national offices to the Republican Party. The Virginia dynasty, he declared, was too well established to fear their efforts. While Federalists believed neither in Monroe's talents or integrity, they intended "no opposition. We submit to this political visitation as to many mysterious dispensations of Providence in the natural world."[64]

Federalists were particularly sensitive to charges that their party was disloyal prior to and during the War of 1812. They were well aware these attacks were damaging to their party. At a Washington birthday celebration, William Darling informed a Washington Benevolent Society in Columbia County, New York, that the people were told the war was for free trade and sailor's rights. Three years of death followed, ending with "an ignominious peace." "Everybody knew," he said, "that not one single object, for which it was professedly waged, had been obtained—unless such attainment consisted in wasting the blood and treasures of the nation." Why then did the Federalists have no claim to the confidence of the people? True, they opposed the war, but "Standing on the verge of the Constitution, and pointing to that gulf into which their country was about to be plunged, they warned democracy of the consequences which *have* followed." The remedy, he warned, was in their hands, through the elective franchise, "the only hope between liberty and slavery."[65]

Conversely, on the Republican side, William Plumer's address to the freemen of New Hampshire laid out the Republican critique of Federalist conduct. Plumer asserted that the administration experienced a powerful and undeviating opposition in the New England States, and that the opposition "induced England to persevere in her piratical orders in council." Federalists also "attempted to bankrupt the Government, and give a death blow to our national credit," and they endeavored "to excite the most bitter local prejudices and antipathies between the North and South, the East and the West." The Hartford Convention, he alleged, was calculated "to destroy our union, destroy our Constitution, and consummate the views of the opposition leaders," but they were frustrated when peace came. Plumer nevertheless invited Federalists to come over to the Republican side. "Let them make a confession of their faults, promise to offend no more, and join in political communion with the patriotic part of the nation."[66]

Some young Federalists did come over to the Republican side. One example was John Kilbourn, an aspiring politician in Ohio. No doubt, he was well aware of the lack of prospect for a Federalist to gain office in heavily Republican Ohio. He informed the inhabitants of Columbus in June 1816 of his change in political identity, and he asked thereafter to be designated as a Republican. He entered, however, "a caveat against the supposition that I have changed one tittle of my former ideas and views." He was aware that his enemies might attribute his declaration to some unworthy motive, especially since a vast majority of the people of Ohio were Republican. He insisted the term republican more accurately reflected the principles he had always professed and supported, and he declared that he had no aversion "to adopting a name more consonant to the feelings of the majority of the people, where no sacrifice of principle is involved."[67]

The Federalists operated under severe handicaps. They were not as adept as their adversaries at manipulation through the patronage power, nor in subsidizing party newspapers. They had no organized pamphlet campaign, and their organization beyond the state level was practically non-existent. There was no coordination between

Federalist members of state legislatures, and they had no national committee.[68] As a result, the Federalist Party failed to even field a slate of electors in Rhode Island, Vermont, Ohio, New Jersey, Pennsylvania, or in any state south of the Potomac. A circular letter sent out in late August by William Milnor, a former Federalist congressman who had been named to head a Committee of Correspondence to look into the coming election, almost plaintively asked for advice as to whether it would be "expedient" at that late date to draft a presidential candidate, or whether to support a Republican in opposition to Monroe.[69]

A revealing article in the *Boston Daily Advertiser* pointed out the complacency felt in those areas of the Northeast thus far unchallenged by Republicans. Federalists, it was alleged, safe in their own region tended to slumber, hoping that if the encroachments of the Republicans ever came too near, there would always be time to save themselves.[70] The Boston *Columbian Centinel*, as if to confirm the *Daily Advertiser* article, declared that as Monroe was certain of election, Federalists were "indifferent whether his majority of supporters in the House were ten or a hundred."[71]

The election was essentially a non-event. John Randolph claimed that in Virginia "there was no election for Burgesses to the General Assembly which had not caused ten times the excitement that had been caused by the election of the President of the United States."[72]

Monroe's putative opponent, Rufus King, wrote to Christopher Gore that "so certain is the result . . . that no pains are taken to excite the community on the subject." He added, "It is quite worthy of remark, that in no preceding election, has there been such a calm respecting it, and it is equally so, that the candidate does not possess the full respect & confidence of either party."[73] The consensus among historians is that the voter turn-out was the lowest of any presidential election in American history.

What interest there was in the presidential election, with the outcome of the election not being in doubt, was who would be appointed to Monroe's Cabinet. Jonathan Fisk asserted to John W. Taylor that New York would not be forgotten in forming the next Cabinet, and he speculated that the Navy Department would be given to a New Yorker.[74] Gen. Andrew Jackson took the time to recommend to Monroe that Col. William Drayton of South Carolina be appointed secretary of war to replace William H. Crawford, who was moving to the Treasury Department.[75] Rufus King reported with dread that John Quincy Adams was to be recalled to become secretary of state under Monroe.[76]

Shortly before the Electoral College met in December, there was still much speculation on who would receive the ballots of the Federalist electors. Thirty-four electors from the states of Massachusetts, Connecticut, and Delaware, cast their ballots for Rufus King. The other 183 went to Monroe who, according to Rufus King, "had the zealous support of nobody, and he was exempt from the hostility of Everybody."[77] Christopher Gore assured King that in Massachusetts "no personal influence was necessary to attain the result of our Election. The Legislature sufficiently indicated their sentiments by their choice of Electors, and, among these, there was not a single question of hesitation as to the first officer, nor was there ever in the public mind."[78]

There was still one problem to be resolved. When the two houses of Congress met in joint session on February 12, 1817, to count the electoral vote and certify the results, John W. Taylor objected to counting the Indiana electoral vote on the grounds that Indiana had not been officially admitted to the Union until December, and the electors had been chosen prior to Indiana being declared admitted. Speaker Clay ruled that while acting as a joint session they could not consider any proposition nor conduct any business not prescribed by the Constitution.[79]

The Senate then withdrew, and the House took up Taylor's objection. Daniel Cady of New York noted the Senate had seated the Senators from Indiana, and he argued that the moment the constitution of the state was accepted she was entitled to all the privileges of the other states. Solomon P. Sharp from Kentucky moved to declare the votes of the electors of Indiana "were properly and legally given, and ought to be counted." Taylor countered with an amendment declaring the votes illegal. William Gaston of North Carolina opposed, but he also objected to the form of Sharp's motion—a proposed joint resolution of both houses.[80]

The sentiment in the House was clearly in favor of counting the Indiana vote. William Hendricks, the newly elected representative from Indiana, stated that the same authority that "gave him the right to vote in this House, gave them [Indiana] also a right to vote for President and Vice President of the United States." Samuel D.

Ingham of Pennsylvania moved to postpone indefinitely (thereby defeating) both Sharp's and Taylor's motions, which was agreed to almost unanimously. When the two houses reconvened, Speaker Clay informed the joint session that the House "had not seen it necessary to come to any resolution, or to take any order on the subject which had produced the separation of the two Houses." The count then proceeded, with the Indiana vote officially certified.[81]

The failure to contest the presidential election of 1816 confirmed the obvious fact that the Federalist Party was its death throes. The outward manifestation was a decline in partisan rancor, or as Christopher Gore phrased it, "a dead calm in our political atmosphere."[82] Federalist politicians had to accommodate themselves to the new realities. Rufus King observed with bemused detachment, "Those who have for some time desired emancipation, are considered free to pursue their respective courses, so that such as were the most zealous, or most noisy men in opposition, will now soften or wholly change their note—with what profit to themselves, is more than any one as yet pretends to determine."[83]

The Republicans, too, were confronted with a new situation. Shorn of their opposition, there was little reason to maintain party unity, and soon they fell into factionalism. Nevertheless, for one brief moment in 1816 there was truly an "Era of Good Feelings," a period of good will and cooperation in the political life of the nation—more than there ever had been or would be again.

Epilogue

In his inaugural address on March 4, 1817, the new president, James Monroe, welcomed the "increased harmony of opinion which pervades our Union," and he promised that his administration would do everything possible to advance that object. He added, with a touch of hyperbole, "If we persevere in the career in which we have advanced so far and in the path already traced, we can not fail . . . to attain the high destiny which seems to await us."[1] Monroe, in fact, entered the office intending to play the role of a conciliator and unifier. Earlier, in December 1816, he had written Gen. Andrew Jackson that "the chief magistrate of the country, ought not to be the head of a party, but of the nation itself." It was not his opinion, he said, that parties were necessary for free governments to exist. He intended to adopt a policy of moderation toward the Federalist party and hopefully "exterminate all party divisions in our country."[2]

In keeping with that resolve, Monroe conducted a tour of nearly sixteen weeks in the summer of 1817 that took him up the east coast to New England and thence to the West as far as Detroit before returning to Washington, D.C. Ostensibly, the purpose of his tour was to inspect the state of military fortifications and, to his credit, he was diligent in carrying out such inspections along the way.[3] Monroe's primary motive, however, was to promote national unity. In this regard, his trip was a great success. At every stop general good will prevailed. Major stops along the tour included Baltimore, Philadelphia, New York, Boston (where a Federalist paper referred to an "Era of Good Feelings"), Detroit, and Pittsburgh.

There is little doubt that Federalists, in particular, counted Monroe's visit as an important event, one that gave them an opportunity to ingratiate themselves with the chief magistrate of the nation. Christopher Gore related to Rufus King in May 1817, prior to Monroe's trip, that in Massachusetts great plans were being made to receive Monroe "with great splendour & respect. It is said to be necessary to show all party spirit done away, & to attain the favour of the Gov't."[4] Undoubtedly, one such favor included payment of Massachusetts' militia claim, which amounted to approximately $850,000. Monroe did a lot of "fence-mending" on his trip. He visited with many prominent Federalists and played down references to party; at one point when Republican members of the Massachusetts legislature attempted to address him saying it was from their party, he declared "that he knew no Party."[5]

Historian Shaw Livermore offered the view that Federalists after the War of 1812 pursued a "soft" line in hopes of splitting the Republican ranks.[6] Indeed, that may have been a motivation for some Federalists who still hoped to revive and maintain a Federalist party. But it seems more likely that those formerly designated as Federalists were realistically willing to accept the demise of the Federalist party and were seeking to accommodate themselves to the new political realities. The real reason may have been self-preservation. New England, the locus of Federalist power, was declining in political and economic influence, particularly due to the tide of emigration flowing out of all of the New England states, and it was not too difficult to see that the West's influence on national affairs would grow. George Sullivan had warned in his Fourth of July oration in 1816, that the growth of the Western country should be viewed as a threat to New England. His section and the Federalists generally had "wrongs to pardon and forget," and he urged them to repair their relations with the other states.[7] Similarly, Rufus King wrote, "How much with these prospects and apprehensions, are the courses and policy of late pursued and adopted to be regretted. How much to be desired is a wise influence of the Eastern States upon the general administration of our affairs."[8] Consciously or unconsciously, it would appear that the response to Monroe's visit was a positive step in that direction.

Other factors, no doubt, influenced Federalists to accept the dominance of the Republican party. As Rufus King wrote to a correspondent in June 1816, "the practice of the Republicans now is the same as that of the Federalists formerly," noting the Republican turnabout on such things as taxes, and the army and navy. He added, "I remain the same, and if others change & do what I did, and still contend that I was wrong in doing, as they now do, it is for them to make out their own consistency."[9] King's claim of constancy on his part and inconstancy on the part of the Republicans was exaggerated. In fact, Federalists also modified their political stances as well. As Norman K. Risjord pointed out, for example, Virginia Federalists after the War of 1812 supported internal improvements, education, and even franchise reform and were practically "indistinguishable from Republican nationalists."[10]

Monroe's policy of inclusion aptly suited the needs of New England and the followers of the prostrate Federalist party, particularly those who feared the alternatives of proscription and isolation from political power. They shrewdly calculated that Monroe was the political leader that would best serve the interests of their section. Many Republicans, however, were mortified by the attention Monroe showered upon Federalists, indicating that the healing process would take time. Monroe knew that he must go slowly in welcoming former Federalists back into the fold. As Livermore noted, Monroe was "confused about his role as president. He was attracted to wistful fancies of a country unsullied by internal conflicts, yet he understood that he had assumed practical responsibilities as a party leader."[11] It was undoubtedly naive of Monroe to believe that he could eradicate party spirit, particularly with the rise of popular politics epitomized by the public response to the Compensation Act and the broadened franchise. Moreover, the very success of the nationalist program raised alarms among many politicians who feared that it portended a growth of the federal government and a decline in states' rights. It was not long before American politics resumed a more natural division between those who believed that the federal government could be used to advance the interests of the nation and those who believed the interests of the country would be best served if that government's ability to interfere in American life was limited. One wing of the Republican Party took a nationalist stance that more closely approached the Federalist ideology while another wing reverted to the traditional conservative, states' rights philosophy of the Republicans. Within a short time the Republican Party began to collapse into factions, as dominant personalities within the party began to jockey for the presidency.

In retrospect, the Republicans in 1816 were influenced by the public's desire for reconciliation and for a decline of partisan rancor. As a consequence, they were inclined to support measures where they sensed popular support but which often ran contrary to their party's ideology. As Rufus King astutely observed, the decline of the Federalist Party allowed the dominant Republican Party to act outside of party constraints and to consult the best interests of the country instead. They had been swept up in the tide of nationalism of the postwar era. They had been influenced by the crisis atmosphere of the postwar period, where renewal of war seemed a real possibility, to retain a larger army and a strong navy for defense, and maintain high taxes to address the debt problem, as well as to meet new needs for an improved transportation infrastructure. They had also been persuaded to recharter the Second Bank of the United States to place the nation's currency on a sound basis and to give protection to infant manufacturing to meet the challenge of British dumping tactics.

There is little doubt that the legislative program of Congress in 1816 was one of the most productive and progressive periods in the history of the early republic. The success of this program grew out of a developing sense of nationalism and the confused state of political affairs after the War of 1812. The general good will that prevailed in 1816 offered a unique opportunity to forge a political agenda that was based on a consensus rather than partisan ideology. Ultimately, as the future was to show, it was an unrealistic expectation that political parties could be supplanted by a nonpartisan political system. The political Era of Good Feelings in 1816, in the final analysis, was one response to the sense of ambivalence in the nation at the end of the War of 1812. Like a change in the weather, the nation was on the cusp of political, economic, and social change, looking toward the emergence of a modern political system.

Notes

Abbreviations

AHR	*American Historical Review*
Annals	*Annals of Congress: Debates and Proceedings in the Congress of the United States, 1789-1824,* 42 vols., Washington, D.C., 1834-1856
ASPCN	*American State Papers: Commerce and Navigation,* 2 vols., Washington, D.C., 1832-1834
ASPMA	*American State Papers: Military Affairs,* 7 vols., Washington, D.C., 1832-1861
ASP, Misc.	*American State Papers: Miscellaneous,* 2 vols., Washington, D.C., 1834
DAB	Dumas Malone, et al., *Dictionary of American Biography* (New York: Charles Scribner's Sons), 20 vols.
JAH	*Journal of American History*
JER	*Journal of the Early Republic*
JSH	*Journal of Southern History*
LC	Library of Congress, Washington, D.C.
MHS	Massachusetts Historical Society, Boston, Mass.
NYHS	New York Historical Society, New York, N.Y.
NYPL	New York Public Library, New York, N.Y.
PMHB	*Pennsylvania Magazine of History and Biography*
RSUS	Records of the States of the United States
WMQ	*William and Mary Quarterly*

Introduction

1. Andrew Burstein, *America's Jubilee: How in 1826 a Generation Remembered 50 Years of Independence* (New York: Knopf, 2001); Louis P. Masur, *1831: Year of Eclipse* (New York: Hill and Wang, 2001).

2. Gaillard Hunt, *Life in America One Hundred Years Ago* (New York: Harper & Brothers, 1914).

3. Fred Somkin, *Unquiet Eagle: Memory and Desire in the Idea of American Freedom, 1815–1860* (Ithaca, NY: Cornell University Press, 1967), 53.

4. *Annals*, 14th Cong., 2nd Sess. (House), 854.

5. *Annals*, 14th Cong., 1st Sess. (House), 729.

Chapter 1. Year Without a Summer

1. Jefferson to Gallatin, Sept. 8, 1816, in Paul Leicester Ford, ed., *The Writings of Thomas Jefferson* (10 vols., New York 1892–1899), 10:64–65. The summer of 1816 has been written about mostly as a curiosity and has received little serious study by historians or meteorologists. Treatments in the journalistic vein would include Charles M. Wilson, "The Year Without a Summer," *American History Illustrated*, 5 (June 1970), 24–29; A. Devoe, "Year Without a Summer, 1816," *American Mercury*, 45 (Nov. 1938), 353–56; G.S. Fichter, "Eighteen-hundred-and-froze-to-death: Snow-filled summer of 1816," *Science Digest*, 69 (Feb. 1971), 62–66. From the meteorological point of view, the most valuable study is Willis I. Milham, "The Year 1816: The Causes of Abnormalities," *Monthly Weather Review*, 52 (Dec. 1924), 563–70. An intriguing but ultimately disappointing study is H.E. Landsberg and J.M. Albert, "Summer of 1816 and Volcanism," *Weatherwise*, 27 (April 1974), 63–66. Henry Stommel and Elizabeth Stommel, "The Year Without a Summer," *Scientific American*, 240 (June 1979), 176–86, has some useful historical data, but cites volcanism as the only causation. For an earlier version of this chapter, see C. Edward Skeen, "The Year Without A Summer: A Historical View," JER, 1 (Spring 1981), 51–67.

2. *Richmond Enquirer*, March 20, 1816. All temperatures are given in Fahrenheit.

3. Reported in the Washington, D.C., *Daily National Intelligencer*, April 20, 1816.

4. David Thomas, *Travels through the Western Country in the Summer of 1816: Including Notices of the Natural History, Topography, Commerce, Antiquities, Agriculture, and Manufactures: With a Map of the Wabash Country now Settling* (Auburn, NY: David Rumsey, 1819), EAI, #49585, 16, 32. The report of snow in Albany is from the Philadelphia *United States Gazette*, May 22, 1816.

5. *Niles' Weekly Register*, 11 (Sept. 7, 1816), 31.

6. Milham, "The Year 1816," 564; Hartford *Connecticut Courant*, June 11, 18, 25, 1816; *Richmond Enquirer*, July 3, 1816.

7. Milham, "The Year 1816," 564.

8. *Albany Argus*, June 11, 1816.

9. The account of Cape May frosts is from a letter to the editor of *Freeman's Journal* and is cited in the *American Beacon* (Norfolk, VA), July 4, 1816. The report on the destruction of the fruit trees in the West is from Thomas, *Travels through the Western Country*, 73, 105.

10. *Richmond Enquirer*, June 12, 1816.

11. *Charleston Courier*, July 3, 1816.

12. Letter to the *Daily National Intelligencer*, July 23, 1816, cited in the *American Beacon*, Aug. 19, 1816.

13. *Trenton True American*, June 27, 1816, quoted in *American Beacon*, July 2,

1816; *Richmond Enquirer,*July 3, 1816, and *Norfolk Herald,*July 1, 1816, both quoted in *Charleston Courier,*July 9, 1816.

14. Boston *Columbian Centinel*, July 15, 1816, quoted in *Daily National Intelligencer,*July 24, 1816.

15. These reports are gathered from the *United States' Gazette* (Philadelphia), July 20, 24, 27, Aug. 10, 1816; *Richmond Enquirer*, July 13, 1816; *Scioto Gazette* (Chillicothe, OH), July 9, 1816.

16. *Charleston Courier,*April 3, July 3, 1816; *Southern Patriot* (Charleston), March 29, 1816, quoted in *American Beacon,*April 5, 1816.

17. *NewYork Columbian*, May 1, 1816, quoted in *Charleston Courier,*May 11, 1816.

18. See, for example, the *Connecticut Courant,* June 11, 1816; *American Beacon*, Sept. 16, 1816, quoting the *Raleigh Star*, Sept. 13, 1816.

19. *Richmond Enquirer,*Aug. 31, 1816.

20. *Georgetown Gazette* [Sept. 1816], quoted in *American Beacon,*Sept. 16, 1816.

21. *Augusta Chronicle* [Sept. 1816], quoted in *Richmond Enquirer*, Oct. 2, 1816.

22. *Farmer's Register,*July 23, 1816, quoted in *Richmond Enquirer*, Oct. 2, 1816.

23. *Albany Argus,*July 19, 1816.

24. Ibid., Aug. 6, 23, 1816.

25. This information is gathered from the *Daily National Intelligencer,*Aug. 30, Sept. 3, 5, 9, 1816, and the *United States' Gazette*, Sept. 11, 1816. The Petersburg report is in the *Daily National Intelligencer*, Sept. 3, 1816, and from Richmond, in the *Richmond Enquirer*, Sept. 4, 1816.

26. *Richmond Enquirer*, Sept. 14, 1816.

27. *Albany Argus*, Sept. 20, 24, 1816.

28. *Daily National Intelligencer*, Sept. 17, 1816.

29. Emmanuel Le Roy Ladurie, *Times of Feast, Times of Famine: A History of Climate Since the Year 1000*, trans. Barbara Bray (Garden City, NY: Doubleday, 1971), 64, 94. A recent study, Michael E. Mann, Ed Gille, Ramond S. Bradley, Malcolm K. Hughes, Jonathan Overpeck, Frank T. Keimig, and Wendy Gross, "Global Temperature Patterns in Past Centuries: An Interactive Presentation," *Earth Interactions*, 4 (2000), 21 22, stated that the year 1816 "was an anomalously cold year only in Europe and parts of North America. In fact, conditions in the Middle and Near East were warmer than normal by twentieth century standards." The entire paper is on the web at http://www.ngdc.noaa.gov/paleo/ei/ei_cover.html.

30. Ladurie, *Times of Feast, Times of Famine*, 64–65.

31. *Charleston Courier,*July 20, 1816; *Albany Argus*, Sept. 3, Oct. 29, 1816. The quotation is from the *Maryland Gazette* (Annapolis), Oct. 17, 1816, citing a letter from the *Boston Daily Advertiser*, Oct. 9, 1816.

32. *Daily National Intelligencer*, May 1, 3, 7, 9, June 27, July 16, 24, 26, Aug. 29, 1816; *Richmond Enquirer*, May 1, 4, June 15, Aug. 31, 1816; *United States' Gazette*, May 9, Sept. 17, 1816; *Maryland Gazette*, May 9, 16, 1816.

33. Boston *Columbian Centinel,*July 15, 1816, quoted in *Daily National Intelligencer*, July 24, 1816; *Boston Daily Advertiser*, n.d., quoted in *United States' Gazette,*July 31, 1816. On sunspots, see *Daily National Intelligencer*, May 3, 7, July 26, August 29, 1816; *Maryland Gazette*, May 16, 1816; *Richmond Enquirer*, May 8, 1816.

34. *United States' Gazette*, July 31, 1816; *Daily National Intelligencer*, May 13, 1816; *Charleston Courier*, May 18, 23, 1816; *American Beacon*, Oct. 1, 1816.

35. Petersburg (VA) *Intelligencer*, n.d., quoted in *Daily National Intelligencer*, Sept. 30, 1816. An article in *Niles' Weekly Register*, 10 (Aug. 10, 1816), 385–385, rejected the sunspot theory but gave some credence to the earthquake factor.

36. Stommel and Stommel, "The Year Without a Summer," 186.

37. *American Beacon*, Oct. 1, 1816.

38. *United States' Gazette*, July 31, 1816.

39. An example of an eruption influencing the weather was the explosion of Huaynaputina in Peru in February 1600. A study in 1998 suggested that Europe's summer of 1601 was the coldest in the past six hundred years. David M. Pyle, "How did the Summer Go?" *Nature*, 393 (June 4, 1998), 415.

40. Milham, "The Year 1816," 564; Stommel and Stommel, "The Year Without a Summer," 176; Fred Mason Bullard, *Volcanoes of the Earth* (Austin: University of Texas Press, 1976), 512. The latest studies on the influence of volcanism are Shanaka L. de Silva and Gregory A. Zielinski, "Global Influence of the AD 1600 Eruption of Huaynaputina, Peru," *Nature*, 393 (June 4, 1998), 455–58; and K.R. Briffa, P.D. Jones, F.H. Schweingruber, and T.J. Osborn, "Influence of Volcanic Eruptions on Northern Hemisphere Summer Temperature over the past 600 Years," *Nature*, 393 (June 4, 1998), 450–54. The latter study suggests the 1600 eruption had a greater effect than Tambora on low tree ring density in the Northern Hemisphere. A fascinating eye-witness account from a ship captain in the vicinity of the eruption is in the *Albany Argus*, May 31, 1816.

41. *Daily National Intelligencer*, May 1, 1816; *American Beacon*, May 9, 1816.

42. Boston *Columbian Centinel*, July 15, 1816, quoted in *Daily National Intelligencer*, July 24, 1816.

43. Landsberg and Albert, "Summer of 1816 and Volcanism," 63–66.

44. Stommel and Stommel, "The Year Without a Summer," 176.

45. Milham, "The Year 1816," 566–567, has a useful discussion of the factors that influence the weather. On volcanism and the weather, see Bullard, *Volcanoes*, 511–31, especially 516–17.

46. Le Roy Ladurie, *Times of Feast, Times of Famine*, 62–64.

47. *Charleston Courier*, Sept. 11, 1816; *United States' Gazette*, July 31, 1816.

48. *Journal of the General Assembly of the State of Vermont, at their Session begun and held at Montpelier, in the County of Washington on Thursday, the Tenth of October, A.D. 1816* (Rutland: Fay & Davison, 1816), EAI, SS#39662.

49. *At the General Assembly of the State of Rhode Island and Providence Plantations begun and holden . . . at Providence* (Providence: Brown & Wilson, 1816), EAI, SS#38795 (June Session), 4; ibid. (Oct. Session), 39.

50. Jefferson to Gallatin, Sept. 8, 1816, in Ford, ed., *Jefferson Writings*, 10:65.

51. *Richmond Enquirer*, Sept. 4, 1816.

52. *United States' Gazette*, July 20, 24, Aug. 28, 1816; *Connecticut Courant*, Aug. 6, 1816; *Richmond Enquirer*, Nov. 19, 1816; *American Beacon*, Sept. 4, 1816.

53. Stommel and Stommel, "The Year Without a Summer," 180–82. All prices are in contemporary dollars.

54. John J. McCusker, *How Much is That in Real Money?* (Worcester, MA:

American Antiquarian Society, 1992), from *Proceedings of the American Antiquarian Society*, 101 (Oct. 1991), 343–344.

55. *Albany Argus*, Oct. 22, 1816.

56. *Richmond Enquirer*, Sept. 18, 1816.

57. *Albany Argus*, Nov. 6, 29, 1816.

58. Ibid., Nov. 26, 1816.

59. See also, Henry Adams, *History of the United States of America During the Administrations of Jefferson and Madison* (9 vols., New York: Charles Scribner's Sons, 1889–1891), 9:138. The statistics are based on a comparison of the two Congresses in *A Biographical Directory of the American Congress, 1774–1949* (Washington, D.C. 1950), 110–21.

60. See, for example, Helmut E. Landsberg, *Weather and Health: An Introduction to Biometeorology* (New York: Doubleday, 1969), chapter 9.

61. Cited in *Charleston Courier*, Sept. 10, 1816.

62. *Daily National Intelligencer*, Nov. 11, 1816.

63. Quoted in Stommel and Stommel, "The Year Without a Summer," 182.

64. Cited in *United States' Gazette*, June 26, 1816. See also *Connecticut Courant*, July 23, 1816.

65. *Niles' Weekly Register* (Baltimore), 12 (May 10, 1817), 167–68.

66. Gustavus A. Weber, *The Weather Bureau: Its History, Activities and Organization* (New York: D. Appleton, 1922), 2–6. A more recent work, Donald R. Whitnah, *A History of the United States Weather Bureau* (Urbana: University of Illinois Press, 1961), 5–6, devoted only two sentences to the summer of 1816 and failed to link this summer to the actions of either Meigs or Lovell.

Chapter 2. Legacy of the War of 1812

1. *United States Gazette*, Aug. 10, 1816.

2. *Albany Argus*, Dec. 13, 1816.

3. *Niles' Weekly Register*, 10 (Aug. 17, 1816), 401. Editor Jesse Buel, similarly confirmed this impression. He noted, "It seems probable that the number of emigrants to our shores this year will be greater than at any former period." *Albany Argus*, July 23, 1816.

4. *Boston Recorder*, n.d., in *Niles' Weekly Register*, 10 (June 1, 1816), 232. Census figures are conveniently found in *Historical Statistics of the United States, 1789–1945* (Washington, D.C.: U.S. Government Printing Office, 1949).

5. "Exports for Year Ending September 30, 1815," A.J. Dallas to House, Feb. 14, 1816, 14th Cong., 1st Sess. (House), ASPCN, Doc. 196, 2:20–24; "Exports for the Year Ending September 30, 1816," W.H. Crawford to House, Feb. 3, 1817, 14th Cong., 2nd Sess. (House), ASPCN, Doc. 205, 2:52–57; "Imports for the Year Ending September 30, 1815," W.H. Crawford to House, Feb. 28, 1817, 14th Cong., 2nd Sess. (House), ASPCN, Doc. 208, 59–86; "Imports for the Year Ending September 30, 1816," W.H. Crawford to House, April 15, 1818, 15th Cong., 1st Sess. (House), ASPCN, Doc. 216, 118–52. See also, Bureau of the Census, *Historical Statistics of the United States, 1789–1945* (Washington, D.C.: U.S. Government Printing Office, 1949), Series M, 42–55, 244–45.

6. Curtis P. Nettels, *The Emergence of a National Economy, 1775–1815* (1962, reprint New York: Harper & Row, 1969), 340, 275–77.

7. *An Address to the Electors of the State of New York by the Republican Members of the Legislature, April 10, 1815* (Albany: J. Buel, 1815), EAI, SS#33786, unpaged.

8. Orsamus C. Merrill, *An Oration, Delivered at the Meeting House in Burlington, Vermont, on the Sixteenth of August* (Bennington, VT: Darius Clark, Aug. 1815), EAI, SS#35263, 18, 19, 25–26. Merrill's partisanship is revealed in his Fourth of July orations of 1804 and 1806, both of which, but particularly the latter, intemperately denounced the Federalists. See O.C. Merrill, *The Happiness of America: An Oration, Delivered at Shaftsbury, on the Fourth of July, 1804* (Bennington, VT: Anthony Haswell, 1804), EAI, SS#6771, 27 pp.; O.C. Merrill, *An Oration, Delivered at the Meeting-House in Bennington, on the 4th of July, 1806* (Bennington, Vt.: Benjamin Smead, 1806), EAI, SS#10861, 56 pp. Merrill was one of those who benefitted from the backlash against the Compensation Act. He was elected as a Representative from Vermont to the Fifteenth Congress.

9. Sage to Taylor, Jan. 27, 1816, John W. Taylor Papers, NYHS.

10. *Address to the Independent Electors of Massachusetts, by a Meeting of Citizens from Every Part of the State, Holden in Boston, 27 February 1815* (Boston: Russell & Cutler, 1815), EAI, SS#33789, n.p.

11. This information is derived primarily from Kenneth W. Rowe, *Mathew Carey: A Study in American Economic Development* (Baltimore: The Johns Hopkins Press, 1933), The Johns Hopkins University Studies in Historical and Political Science, series 51, no. 4, chapter 1, 9–31. See also, "Mathew Carey," DAB, 3:489–491.

12. Adams to Alexander H. Everett, Nov. 23, 1817, "Letters of John Quincy Adams to Alexander Hamilton Everett, 1811–1837," AHR, 11 (Oct. 1901), 110.

13. Mathew Carey, *The Olive Branch: or Faults on Both Sides, Federal and Democratic. A Serious Appeal on the Necessity of Mutual Forgiveness and Harmony*, 7th ed. (Middlebury, VT: William Slade, Jr., Jan. 1816), 13, 37.

14. 14. Ibid., 268–76, 323 (quotation), 444–45.

15. [William McKean,] *An Answer to Certain Parts of a Work Published by Mathew Carey, entitled "The Olive Branch" . . . by a Federalist* (New York: n.p., Dec. 1816), EAI, SS#36749, v, 31, 93. A Virginian also vindicated Federalists and the "purity of their motives," and he absolved them "from any design to destroy the state governments." "A Citizen," *A Candid Appeal to the Present Ruling Party of the United States* (Alexandria, VA: Samuel Snowden, 1816), EAI, SS#37163, 6, 47.

16. *A Candid Appeal to the Present Ruling Party in the United States. By A Citizen* (Alexandria, VA: Samuel Snowden, 1816), EAI, SS#37163, 4–5, 6, 44.

17. "A Citizen of Vermont," *The Crisis: On the Origin and Consequences of our Political Dissensions . . .* (Albany: E.E. Hosford, 1815), EAI, SS#34476, 17, 71.

18. See Richard Gabriel Stone, *Hezekiah Niles as an Economist* (Baltimore: The Johns Hopkins Press, 1933), The Johns Hopkins University Studies in Historical and Political Science, series 51, no. 5, chapter 2, 33–56. See also, "Hezekiah Niles," DAB, 13:521–522.

19. "The Prospect Before Us," *Niles' Weekly Register*, 9 (Sept. 2, 1815), 1–3.

20. *Albany Argus*, June 11, 1816.

21. *Otsego* (NY) *Herald*, May 23, 1816.

22. Seventh Annual Message, Dec. 5, 1815, James D. Richardson, ed., *A Compilation of the Messages and Papers of the Presidents, 1788–1897*, 10 vols., (Washington, D.C.: Government Printing Office, 1897–1900), 1:568.

23. *Annals*, 14th Cong., 1st Sess. (House), 466, 466–67.

24. Robert L. Meriwether, ed., *The Papers of John C. Calhoun*, 26 vols. to date (Columbia, SC: University of South Carolina Press, 1959–2001), 1:288.

25. *Annals*, 14th Cong., 1st Sess. (Senate), 222; *Annals*, 14th Cong., 2nd Sess. (House), 339.

26. Connor to John Davis, April 22, 1816, Lewis Williams to Robert Martin, April 25, 1816, Dickens, "To the Citizens of the Counties of Orange, Wake and Person," March 4, 1817, Noble E. Cunningham, Jr., ed., *Circular Letters of Congressmen to their Constituents, 1789–1829*, 3 vols. (Chapel Hill: Institute of Early American History and Culture, 1978), 2:973, 980, 1007.

27. *Annals*, 14th Cong., 1st Sess. (House), 438–43 (quotations on 439, 441, 443).

28. Ibid., 446–48 (quotations on 446, 447).

29. Charles R. King, ed., *The Life and Correspondence of Rufus King*, 6 vols. (New York: G.P. Putnam's Sons, 1894–1900), appendix 7, 5:563.

30. Carl E. Prince, "Patronage and a Party Machine: New Jersey Democratic-Republican Activists, 1810–1816," *WMQ*, 3rd Ser., 21 (Oct. 1964), 578.

31. Message of Governor Plumer, June 6, 1816, *Journal of the Honorable Senate, of the State of New Hampshire, at their Session, Begun and Holden at Concord, on the First Wednesday of June . . . 1816* (Concord: Isaac Hill, Aug. 1816), EAI, SS#38392, 14; Message of Gov. William Jones, Feb. 19, 1816, *At the General Assembly of the State of Rhode Island and Providence Plantations begun and holden . . . at Providence . . . on the third Monday of February . . . 1816* (Providence: Brown & Wilson, 1816), EAI, SS#38793, 3; Speech of Gov. Galusha, Oct. 11, 1816, *Journals of the General Assembly of the State of Vermont, at their Session Begun and held at Montpelier . . . on Thursday, the Tenth of October, A.D. 1816* (Rutland: Fay & Davison, 1816), EAI, SS#39662, 15, 16.

32. Message of Gov. Miller, Nov. 22, 1815, *Journal of the North Carolina House of Commons . . . begun and held in the City of Raleigh, on the twentieth day of November . . . one thousand eight hundred and fifteen* [Raleigh: n.p., 1816], EAI, SS#38479, 9.

33. Message of Gov. Snyder, Dec. 8, 1815, *Journal of the Senate of the Commonwealth of Pennsylvania . . .* (Harrisburg: Christian Gleim, 1815 [sic 1816]), EAI, SS#38581, 12–13.

34. Gallatin to Jefferson, Sept. 6, 1815, Albert Gallatin Papers (microfilm), reel 28.

35. Adams to A.H. Everett, March 16, 1816, "Letters of John Quincy Adams to Alexander Hamilton Everett, 1811–1837," *AHR*, 11 (Oct. 1905), 103.

36. Speech on the Revenue Bill, Jan. 31, 1816, Meriwether, ed., *Papers of John C. Calhoun*, 1:321.

37. [Benjamin Waterhouse] *A Journal, of a Young Man of Massachusetts, Late a Surgeon on Board an American Privateer, who was Captured at Sea by the British in May, Eighteen Hundred and Thirteen, and was Confined First, at Melville Island, Halifax, then at Chatham, in England, and Last at Dartmoor Prison. Interspersed with Observations, Anecdotes and Remarks tending to Illustrate the Moral and Political Characters of*

Three Nations. To Which is Added, A Correct Engraving of Dartmoor Prison, Represent-
ing the Massacre of American Prisoners (Boston: Rowe and Hooper, 1816), EAI,
SS#39719, 166–171, 187–215, 227–30 (quotation on 227). This book was well
received, and by the end of 1816, at least three new editions had been published.
See EAI, SS#39720, SS#39721, and SS#39722. On the Dartmoor incident, see
Annals, 14th Cong., 1st Sess. (House), appendix, doc. 4, 1506–1601, which includes all the documents generated by the investigation. An excellent analysis of
the Dartmoor Prison is Robin F.A. Fabel, "Self-Help in Dartmoor: Black and
White Prisoners in the War of 1812," *JER*, 9 (Summer 1989), 165–190. A popularly written account is Reginald Horsman, "The Paradox of Dartmoor Prison,"
American Heritage, 26 (Feb. 1975), 12–17, 85.

38. *Annals*, 14th Cong., 1st Sess. (House), 452, 817, 976, 1015, 1090, 1249,
1263.

39. Quoted in *The Reviewers Reviewed; or Remarks on the Edinburgh Review. By*
an American (Baltimore: Benjamin Edes, 1816), EAI, SS#38790, 58.

40. On Smith, see Robert E. Spiller, "The Verdict of Sydney Smith," *American*
Literature, 1 (March 1929), 3–13. Walsh wrote his book "to repel actively, and, if
possible, to arrest, the war which is waged without stint or intermission, upon
our national reputation." Quoted in Merle Curti, "The Reputation of America
Overseas," *American Quarterly*, 1 (Spring 1949), 66. Walsh's book was entitled *An*
Appeal from the Judgments of Great Britain Respecting the United States of America . . .
and Strictures Upon the Calumnies of British Writers (Philadelphia 1819).

41. *Annals*, 14th Cong., 1st Sess. (House), 1153–54.

42. Shamrock Society of New York, *Hints to Emigrants from Europe, Who Intend*
to Make a Permanent Residence in the United States (New York: Van Winkle & Wiley,
1816), EAI, SS#38924, 22pp. The president of the society was listed as "Mr.
Emmet," undoubtedly Thomas Addis Emmett, who fled Ireland in the troubles
of ninety-eight and became a prominent Republican leader. Members of the
committee that drew up the pamphlet included William James MacNevin, who
was described as a "gentleman of finest culture." Another member was a Mr. Irvine,
possibly William Irving, the congressman for New York City, or perhaps John T.
Irving, a Bucktail Democrat and the brother of novelist Washington Irving.

43. Cited in "Westward!" *Niles' Weekly Register*, 8 (August 12, 1815), 420.

44. *Annals*, 14th Cong., 2nd. Sess. (House), 253, 268–69, 408–9.

45. Wendover to ?, Feb. 13, 1817, March 24, 1818, in website http://
www.geocities.com/flag_of_usa/history_of_the_american.flag.

Chapter 3. The Fourteenth Congress Begins

1. *Annals*, 14th Cong., 1st Sess. (House), 380–381; ibid. (Senate), 10–11, 19, 21.

2. Report of Library Committee, Feb. 20, 1815, 13th Cong., 3rd Sess. (Senate), ASP, Misc., Doc. 387, 2:274; Report of House Committee, Jan. 26, 1816,
14th Cong., 1st Sess. (House), ibid., Doc. 396, 2:279–82. Watterson's nationality is
listed in a report of Secretary of State James Monroe to Congress, Dec. 2, 1816,
ibid., Doc. 410, 2:311. The proposal for a library building is in *Annals*, 14th Cong.,
2nd Sess. (Senate), 131, 144.

3. Latrobe to Samuel Lane (Commissioner of Public Buildings), Nov. 28, Dec. 3, 1816, ASP, Misc. (Doc. 431), 2:427–29. See also, Samuel Lane to Rufus King, Oct. 24, 1815, King Papers, NYHS, regarding Senate alterations. King brought in a report on the alterations to the Senate on April 3, 1816, and the report was approved on April 5. *Annals*, 14th Cong., 1st Sess. (Senate), 296–297. A good description of the damage to both the Capitol and the President's House is in Anthony S. Pitch, *The Burning of Washington* (Annapolis, MD: Naval Institute Press, 1998), 103–21.

4. Lane to Condict, Feb. 15, 1817, ASP, Misc. (Doc. 431), 2:438.

5. Taylor to Jane Taylor, Dec. 29, 1816, Taylor Papers, NYHS.

6. Hoban to Lane, Dec. 3, 12, 1816, ASP, Misc. (Doc. 431), 2:429–30.

7. Hunt, *Life in America*, 4; Noble E. Cunningham, Jr., *The Presidency of James Monroe* (Lawrence: The University Press of Kansas, 1996), 28–29.

8. Lane to Condict, Feb. 15, 1817, ASP, Misc. (Doc. 431), 2:434.

9. See, ASP, Misc. (Docs. 459, 461, 484), 2:528–30, 531–33, 577–80.

10. Seventh Annual Message, Dec. 5, 1815, Richardson, ed., *Messages and Papers*, 1:562–69.

11. Adams, *History*, 9:106, 138.

12. The standing committees (with chairs) were: Elections (Taylor, NY); Ways and Means (Lowndes); Public Lands (Robertson, LA); Commerce and Manufacturing (Newton, VA); Claims (Yancey, NC); Post Office and Post Roads (Ingham, PA); District of Columbia (Tucker, VA); Pensions and Revolutionary Claims (Chappell, SC); Judiciary (Nelson, VA); Public Expenditures (Murfree, NC); Accounts (McLean, OH); Revised and Unfinished Business (Condict, NJ). Select Committees (with chairs) were: Foreign Affairs (Forsyth); Uniform National Currency (Calhoun); Military Peace Establishment, Corps of Invalids, Fortifications, Military Academy (Johnson, KY); Naval Affairs (Pleasants, VA); Roads and Canals (Creighton, OH); National Seminary of Learning in D.C. (Wilde, GA); Militia Classification (Clark, KY); Unpaid Militia Expenses (Wright, MD).

13. Coleman to King, Jan. 14, 1816, Giles to King, Jan. 15, 1816, Rufus King Papers, NYHS, vol. 15.

14. Charles King (London) to King, Jan. 30, 1816, ibid.

15. *Annals*, 14th Cong., 1st Sess. (House), 419–20, 454–55 (Forsyth), 456 (Gaston), 457 (Clay), 457 (Forsyth).

16. Ibid., 478 (Forsyth), 479–80 (Barbour).

17. Ibid., 526–32 (quotations on 529).

18. James C. Jewett to Gen. H.A.S. Dearborn, Feb. 5, 1817, "The United States Congress of 1817 and Some of its Celebrities," WMQ, 17 (Oct. 1908), 140.

19. [Francis Walker Gilmer] *Sketches of American Orators. By Anonymous. Written in Washington*. (Baltimore: Fielding Lucas, Jr., 1816), 9. EAI, SS#37711.

20. *Annals*, 14th Cong., 1st Sess. (House) 533–38 (quotations on 533, 536, 538).

21. See, for example, the speeches of Elijah H. Mills (MA), ibid., 540–42, and Benjamin Hardin (KY), ibid., 543–45. The vote is on 545–46.

22. Ibid., 554–56 (Cuthbert quotation on 555), 558–64 (Tucker quotations on 559, 563).

23. [Gilmer] *Sketches of American Orators*, 25–26.

24. *Annals*, 14th Cong., 1st Sess. (House), 564–79 (quotations on 567, 575).

25. Ibid., 593–94 (Forsyth quotation on 594), 594–95 (Pickering quotation on 595), 595–99.

26. Ibid., 599–604 (Wright quotation on 600), 604–5 (Lowndes quotation on 605).

27. Ibid., 616–23 (quotations on 621, 622, 623).

28. Ibid., 672–71 (quotations on 662, 663).

29. Ibid., 639–51 (quotation on 640).

30. Ibid., 674.

31. *Annals*, 14th Cong., 1st Sess. (Senate), 46–57 (quotations on 47, 49).

32. Ibid., 57–62.

33. Ibid., 57, 74–78, 65–70 (Roberts quotations on 66, 69, 70).

34. Ibid., 88.

35. *Annals*, 14th Cong., 1st Sess. (House), 719–20.

36. "John Forsyth," DAB, 6:533–535.

37. *Annals*, 14th Cong., 1st Sess. (House), 884.

38. Ibid., 884–96 (quotations on 885, 890).

39. Ibid., 897–98.

40. *Annals*, 14th Cong., 1st Sess. (Senate), 129.

41. The House report was discussed by Forsyth on Feb. 19, ibid. (House), 1018–1023. King's report to the Senate is in ibid. (Senate), 160–61.

42. The House vote is in ibid. (House), 1057–1058.

43. King, ed., *Correspondence of Rufus King*, Appendix VII, 5:562. The vote on the Forsyth report is in *Annals*, 14th Cong., 1st Sess. (House), 1057–1058. The Act of March 1, 1816, is in ibid., 1798.

44. Ibid., 958–59, 999–1006 (quotations on 1000, 1006).

45. Ibid., 1034, 999, 1006–1014, 1030–1037, 1048.

46. Ibid., 986–94, 996. A motion on February 20, to reinstate the bounty proposal was defeated, 77–59. The bill was then read a third time and passed on February 24. Ibid., 1038–1051, 1058.

47. North Carolina's amendment was introduced by Israel Pickens (NC) on Jan. 5, 1816, and Massachusetts's proposal by Timothy Pickering (MA), on March 6, 1816, *Annals*, 14th Cong., 1st Sess. (House), 461–62, 1150–1151. The Massachusetts resolutions rejecting the North Carolina amendment and adopting an alternative are in *Resolves of the General Court of the Commonwealth of Massachusetts, Passed at their Session, which Commenced on Wednesday, the Tenth Day of January . . . 1816* (Boston: Russell, Cutler and Co., 1816), chapter 166, 155–58.

48. Varnum's amendment, submitted on Feb. 27, 1816, is in *Annals*, 14th Cong., 1st Sess. (Senate), 158. King's statement is in ibid., 216.

49. Speech of James Barbour (VA), March 20, 1816, ibid., 213–14.

50. *Albany Argus*, Dec. 27, 1816.

51. *Annals*, 14th Cong., 2nd Sess. (House), 256–57, 302–11, 323–36 (quotations at 326, 330).

52. Ibid., 338–56, 451.

53. *Annals*, 14th Cong., 1st Sess. (Senate), 94, 106, 132, 143, 147, 163.

54. Ibid., 170–171, 177, 182, 208–9, 212, 298. The vote was 19–7.

55. *Annals*, 14th Cong., 2nd Sess. (House), 268.

56. *Annals*, 14th Cong., 2nd Sess. (Senate), 30–31.

57. Ibid., 696–98 (quotations on 696, 696).

58. Ibid., 699, 699–718 (quotations on 699, 700).

59. Ibid., 1291–1292 (quotation on 1292). The committee on rules and orders was discharged on April 22. Ibid., 1412.

Chapter 4. A Tariff and a Bank

1. "William Lowndes (1782–1822)," DAB, 11:473–474.

2. The report may be found in *Annals,* 14th Cong., 1st Sess. (House), 516–22.

3. Ibid., 720–23 (quotation on 721).

4. Ibid., 723–25.

5. Ibid., 734–35.

6. Ibid., 737–46.

7. Ibid., 737–57 (quotations on 747, 752, 754). Randolph's characterization of Hardin is quoted in Claude G. Bowers, *Jefferson in Power: The Death Struggle of the Federalists* (Boston: Houghton Mifflin Company, 1936), 104.

8. *Annals,* 14th Cong., 1st Sess. (House), 772–76.

9. Ibid., 776–92.

10. Ibid., 792–802 (quotation on 800).

11. Ibid., 804–17.

12. Ibid., 822–28.

13. Ibid., 829–39 (quotation on 829).

14. Ibid., 840–46 (quotation on 841).

15. Ibid., 846 (quotation on 847).

16. Ibid., 864–66.

17. Ibid., 864, 867–75.

18. Ibid., 875, 900–908 (quotations on 904). Atherton's statement contradicts Rufus King, who wrote Gouverneur Morris that the slaveholding states disliked the land tax and that the Western states evaded all taxes. King to Morris, March 9, 1816, King, ed., *King Correspondence,* 6:11.

19. *Annals,* 14th Cong., 2nd Sess. (House), 909–17 (quotations on 909, 910, 911, 915).

20. Ibid., 922–39, 949–52.

21. Ibid., 976, 1134–136. A separate bill relating to household furniture, gold and silver watches, and stills was passed on March 20. Ibid., 1188–89, 1226–28, 1233–34.

22. Ibid., 675–76 (quotation from Wright of MD on 676).

23. Ibid., 676–678, 684–87 (quotations on 685, 687).

24. *Niles' Weekly Register,* 9 (Jan. 27, 1816), 365.

25. Douglas C. North, *The Economic Growth of the United States, 1790–1860* (New York: W. W. Norton & Company, Inc., 1966), 61–63.

26. *Annals,* 14th Cong., 1st Sess. (House), 877–80.

27. Ibid., 880–84, 898, 918–22, 976–77.

28. Dallas's letter, dated Feb. 12, 1816, with proposed tax rates, is in ibid., Appendix, 1674–98. Newton's report is on 960–67.

29. Ibid., 1234, 1237.

30. Ibid., 1237–38, 1239–46.

31. Ibid., 1247, 1258–1261 (quotation on 1261).

32. Ibid., 1262–63.

33. *Baltimore Patriot,* April 30, 1816, in *Richmond Enquirer,* May 4, 1816.

34. *Annals,* 14th Cong., 1st Sess. (House), 1270–73 (quotations on 1270, 1272, 1273).

35. Rates were increased on lump sugar, lead bars, iron and steel wire, clocks and clock parts, cotton lace and cotton yarn, and gunpowder. Efforts to raise duties on copper sheets and in plates were defeated. Attempts to reduce duties on imported tallow, cocoa, and on iron bars also failed. The tax on imported iron, however, was reduced from seventy-five cents to forty-five cents, and the duties on Russian and Holland sail-duck and gold leaf were also reduced. Woolen blankets and rugs were exempted from the 25 percent duty until June 30, 1819, and then put at 20 percent. Ibid., 1268–85.

36. Ibid., 1287, 1288.

37. Ibid, 1313–14.

38. Ibid., 1314–15.

39. Ibid., 1317–26 (quotations on 1317–1321).

40. Ibid., 1327–29.

41. Ibid., 1328–29.

42. Ibid., 1329–36 (quotation on 1335).

43. Ibid., 1350–52.

44. Ibid., (Senate), 311, 321, 324, 326–31, 348.

45. Ibid. (House), 1415, 1438.

46. Norris W. Preyer, "Southern Support of the Tariff of 1816: A Reappraisal," *The Journal of Southern History,* 25 (Aug. 1959), 306–22.

47. F.W. Taussig, *The Tariff History of the United States* (1892, reprint New York: Capricorn Books, 1964), 18., 30, 35 (quotation on 68).

48. [Anonymous,] *Brief Remarks on the Proposed New Tariff...* (New York: Van Winkle & Wiley, 1816), 15–16.

49. *Niles' Weekly Register,* 9 (Oct. 9, 1815), 96. Niles did suggest that manufacturers provide some education to the children and their term of work be limited to four years. In return, to compensate the employer for his expense, Niles suggested that either workers at his mill be exempted from militia service or his property be exempted from taxation.

50. *American Beacon,* July 1, 1816.

51. Wolcott to King, April 2, 1816, King Papers, NYHS.

52. Richardson, ed., *Messages and Papers,* 1:566. For Dallas's letter, see *Annals,* 14th Cong., 1st Sess. (House), 494–505.

53. *Annals,* 14th Cong., 1st Sess. (House), 494–505.

54. See Robert V. Remini, *Andrew Jackson and the Bank War* (New York: W.W. Norton & Company, 1967), 25–26. Raymond G. Walters Jr., "The Origins of the Second Bank of the United States," *The Journal of Political Economy,* 53 (June 1945), 115–131, cites the influence of financiers such as John Jacob Astor, David Parish, Stephen Girard, and Jacob Barker in pushing for the Second BUS. See

also, Ralph C.H. Catterall, *The Second Bank of the United States* (Chicago: The University of Chicago Press, 1903), the old standard history of the Second Bank, and the superb work by Bray Hammond, *Banks and Politics in America, From the Revolution to the Civil War* (Princeton: Princeton University Press, 1957).

55. Madison's veto message may be found in Richardson, comp., *Messages and Papers of the Presidents,* 1:555–57. For a discussion of the currency debate in 1814, see Adams, *History,* 8:239–62.

56. Jewett to Gen. H.A.S. Dearborn, Feb. 5, 1817, "The United States Congress of 1817 and Some of Its Celebrities," *WMQ,* 17 (Oct. 1908), 143.

57. *Annals,* 14th Cong., 2nd Sess. (House), 1060–66 (quotations on 1062, 1063, 1066).

58. Ibid., 1066.

59. See the speech of Samuel Smith (MD), ibid., 1070–74.

60. Ibid., 1074–81 (quotation on 1075).

61. See the arguments of Jonathan Ward and Henry St. George Tucker, ibid., 1082–88.

62. Ibid., 1091–94.

63. Ibid., 1096–94.

64. The vote on Sergeant's motion is in ibid., 1108. Calhoun's statement is in ibid., 1152.

65. Ibid., 1109–19 (vote on 1119).

66. Ibid., 1136.

67. Ibid., 1137–48.

68. Ibid., 1139–1151.

69. Ibid., 1153–55 (quotation on 1153).

70. Ibid., 1201.

71. Clay's speech on March 9 was not recorded, but an address delivered to his constituents on June 3 in Lexington, Kentucky, reportedly contained the substance of his remarks in committee of the whole, and was included in ibid., 1189–95. The speech is also pubished in James F. Hopkins, ed., *The Papers of Henry Clay,* 11 vols. (Lexington: The University Press of Kentucky, 1959–1992), 1:199–205.

72. *Annals,* 14th Cong., 2nd Sess. (House), 1200–1204 (quotation on 1203).

73. Ibid., 1204–1205.

74. Ibid., 1205–1206, 1207–1208. Jackson's war on the BUS was strongly abetted by New York politicians and financiers.

75. Ibid., 1209.

76. Ibid., 1209–11.

77. Ibid., 1212–19.

78. *Annals,* 14th Cong., 1st Sess. (Senate), 204–205, 231, 235–41 (quotations on 238, 239).

79. Ibid., 241–46.

80. Ibid., 246–54.

81. Ibid., 253–58.

82. Ibid., 258–74.

83. Ibid., 276–81.

84. *Annals,* 14th Cong., 1st Sess. (House), 1327–28, 1337–38 (quotation on 1338).

85. Ibid., 1338–39.

86. Ibid., 1339.

87. Ibid., 1339–44 (quotation on 1343).

88. Ibid., 1345–46, 1356–57, 1361, 1365, 1382–88 (quotation on 1387).

89. Ibid., 1382, 1388–94.

90. Ibid., 1394–1401, 1405, 1413, 1416–17.

91. Ibid., 1417.

92. Ibid., 1418, 1429–31.

93. Ibid., 1432–37 (quotation on 1433). Prior to the defeat of Calhoun's proposal, Mathew Carey denounced the measure. He argued that there was far more paper money in circulation than specie to redeem it. The result, he said, would be "general bankruptcy." Carey doubted there would be for some time an adequate supply of specie. Congress, he asserted, "may do the nation more injury after a debate of a few hours, than the British government were able to effect in a whole year." Mathew Carey, *Letter to the Hon. Mr. Calhoun, Chairman of the Committe on a National Currency* (Philadelphia: M. Carey, 1816), EAI, SS#37172, 12.

94. *Annals,* 14th Cong., 1st Sess. (House), 1440–48 (quotation on 1447).

95. Ibid., 1449–51, 1466.

96. Adams, *History,* 9:128.

97. Ibid., 129.

98. Ibid., 130–131.

99. *Annals*, 14th Cong., 2nd Sess. (House), 431–436, 454–459, 1053.

100. Adams, *History,* 9:131–132; *To President and Directors of the Bank of the United States. The Memorial of the Citizens of the Town of Lexington* [Lexington, Ky.: n.p., September 14, 18160, 16pp., EAI, SS#38070; chapter 91, Approved, December 13, 1816 (effective June 1, 1817), *Laws of the Commonwealth of Massachusetts, Passed by the General Court, at their Session, which Commenced on Wednesday the 13th of November, and Ended on the 14th of December, 1816* (Boston: Russell, Cutler and Co., 1816), EAI, SS#38166, 345–346. Default incurred a 2 percent fine per month.

101. See Leon M. Schur, "The Second Bank of the United States and the Inflation After the War of 1812," *The Journal of Political Economy,* 68 (April 1960), 118–134.

Chapter 5. Compensation Act of 1816

1. Most of the analysis of the first party system has been on its origins. See, for example, Joseph Charles, *The Origins of the American Party System* (Williamsburg, VA: Institute of Early American History and Culture, 1956); William Nisbet Chambers, *Political Parties in a New Nation: The American Experience, 1776–1809* (New York: Oxford University Press, 1963); and Noble Cunningham, Jr., *The Jeffersonian Republicans: The Formation of Party Organization, 1789–1801* (Chapel Hill: University of North Carolina Press, 1957). The only work dealing more than tangentially with the decline of the first party system is Richard P. McCormick, *The Second Party System: Party Formation in the Jacksonian Era* (Chapel Hill: University of North Carolina Press, 1966), ch. 2. George Dangerfield's two books,

The Era of Good Feelings (New York: Harcourt, Brace, & World, Inc., 1952), and *The Awakening of American Nationalism, 1815–1828* (New York: Harper & Row, Publishers, 1965), scarcely notice the details of the transition of politics in this period. More pertinent are Paul Goodman, "The First American Party System," in *The American Party Systems: Stages of Political Development*, ed. William Nisbet Chambers and Walter Dean Burnham (New York: Oxford University Press, 1967), 56–89; Norman K. Risjord, *The Old Republicans: Southern Conservatism in the Age of Jefferson* (New York: Columbia University Press, 1965); Shaw Livermore, Jr., *The Twilight of Federalism: The Disintegration of the Federalist Party, 1815–1830* (Princeton: Princeton University Press, 1962), and to some extent, David Hackett Fischer, *The Revolution of American Conservatism: The Federalist Party in the Era of Jeffersonian Democracy* (New York: Harper & Row, Publishers, 1965). It is generally agreed that Andrew Jackson was the beneficiary of the democratic brand of politics, and not the creator of this "new politics." The best statement of this view is Edward Pessen, *Jacksonian America: Society, Personality, and Politics* (Homewood, IL: The Dorsey Press, 1969). See also Robert V. Remini's two works, *The Election of Andrew Jackson* (Philadelphia: J.B. Lippincott Company, 1963), and *Martin Van Buren and the Making of the Democratic Party* (New York: W.W. Norton & Company, 1951). For an earlier version of this chapter, see C. Edward Skeen, "*Vox Populi, Vox Dei*: The Compensation Act of 1816 and the Rise of Popular Politics," JER, 6 (Fall 1986), 253–74.

2. William Nisbet Chambers, ed., *The First Party System: Federalists and Republicans* (New York: John Wiley & Sons, 1972), preface; Richard P. McCormick, "Political Development and the Second Party System," in Chambers and Burnham, eds., *American Party Systems*, 91; Walter Dean Burnham, "Party Systems and the Political Process," ibid., 289–92; Ronald P Formisano, "Deferential-Participant Politics: The Early Republic's Political Culture, 1789–1840," *American Political Science Review*, 68 (June 1974), 484.

3. Lynn L. Marshall, "The Strange Stillbirth of the Whig Party," AHR, 72 (Jan. 1967), 461; Chambers, *Political Parties in a New Nation*, 107.

4. Fischer, *Revolution in American Conservatism*, 49.

5. Michael Wallace, "Changing Concepts of Party in the United States: New York, 1815–1828," AHR, 74 (Dec. 1968), 453–91.

6. William Nisbet Chambers, "Party Development and Party Action: The American Origins," *History and Theory*, 3 (1963), 116. On the growth of suffrage, see two articles by Richard P. McCormick, "Suffrage Classes and Party Alignments: A Study in Voter Behavior," *Mississippi Valley Historical Review*, 46 (Dec. 1959), 397–410, and "New Perspectives on Jacksonian Politics," AHR, 65 (Jan. 1960), 288–301. See also Chilton Williamson, *American Suffrage: From Property to Democracy, 1760–1860* (Princeton: Princeton University Press, 1960).

7. McCusker, *How Much is That in Real Money?*, 325–327. The base years were 1700–1702.

8. *Annals*, 13th Cong., 3rd Sess. (House), 1131–1132.

9. Ibid., 14th Cong., 2nd Sess. (House), 593; *Niles' Weekly Register*, 9 (Jan. 20, 1816), 350–51; *Daily National Intelligencer*, Jan. 26, 1816; *Baltimore American*, Jan. 26, Feb. 15, 1816.

10. *Annals*, 14th Cong., 1st Sess. (House), 1127–30. The comment was by Lewis Condict (NJ), ibid., 14th Cong., 2nd Sess. (House), 680.

11. Ibid., 14th Cong., 1st Sess. (House), 1158.

12. Ibid., 1158–1176. See John McLean, *The Following Letter on the Compensation Bill, was addressed by Mr. McLean, a Member of Congress, to a Friend . . .* (n.p., 1816), EAI, #38129, 7.

13. *Annals*, 14th Cong., 1st Sess. (House), 1159–69.

14. Randolph's remarks are ibid., 1169; Pickering's, ibid., 1176; and Wright's, ibid., 1180–82.

15. Ibid., 1182–83 (Grosvenor), 1183–84 (Calhoun).

16. The House vote is in ibid., 1188. The committee of the whole vote is from John Culpepper's speech (NC), ibid., 14th Cong., 2nd Sess., 586. The debate in the Senate is ibid., 14th Cong., 1st Sess. (Senate), 184–204 (vote on 203–204).

17. Taylor to Jane Taylor, March 26, 1816, John W. Taylor Papers, NYHS.

18. Act of March 19, 1816, in Richard Peters, ed., *Public Statutes at Large of the United States of America* (Boston 1848), III, 257–58. *Annals*, 14th Cong., 1st Sess. (House), 1305–1306, 1307.

19. *Annals*, 14th Cong., 2nd Sess. (House), 1310–11.

20. Pickering to Coleman, Apr. 17, 1816, Timothy Pickering Papers, MHS, XV, 116–17; Coleman to Pickering, Apr. 21, 1816, ibid., XXXI, 105.

21. See the comments of Jesse Buel in the *Albany Argus*, Apr. 19, 1816. In the House, 39 Federalists and 41 Republicans voted for the bill and 14 Federalists and 52 Republicans voted against it. In the Senate, 7 Federalists and 14 Republicans voted for the measure, while 3 Federalists and 8 Republicans voted against it. Thus 46 Federalists (of 63 casting votes), or 73 percent voted for the bill, and 55 Republicans (of 115 casting votes), or 47.8 percent supported the measure. Not included are the votes of 2 non-party men (John Randolph and Richard Stanford of North Carolina), the first voting for the bill and the latter opposing it.

22. *Daily National Intelligencer*, Mar. 19, 20, 1816. For other letters on the same issue, see ibid., Mar. 25, 26, Apr. 23, 24, 1816. A clever parody, circulated widely around the country, was entitled "A New Song," which repeated the chant, "Twelve dollars a day, Twelve dollars a day, Twelve dollars a day's the dandy O!" For examples, see Annapolis *Maryland Gazette*, Aug. 18, 1816, and *Charleston* (SC) *Courier*, Aug. 10, 1816.

23. Johnson's statement is in *Annals*, 14th Cong., 2nd Sess. (House), 237. See also the statement of Philip P. Barbour (VA), ibid., 517, and the comment of Thomas Ritchie in the *Richmond Enquirer*, July 13, 1816. Jefferson's comment is quoted in Leonard D. White, *The Jeffersonians: A Study in Administrative History, 1801–1829* (New York: The Macmillan Company, 1951), 401.

24. Committee members of New York resolutions were checked with the lists of candidates for local and state offices, as well as congressional candidates, and no candidates for office were found. Lists in other states bear out this conclusion.

25. The first resolutions are from Canajoharie, NY, in the *Albany Argus*, July 16, 1816. The second set are from Saratoga, NY, in the Ballston Spa (NY) *Independent American*, July 17, 1816. New York was an especially fertile ground for town meetings denouncing the Compensation Act. See, for example, the *Albany Argus*,

June 21, Oct. 14, 18, 22, 1816; the *Independent American*, June 12, 19, Aug. 7, Sept. 26, Oct 2, 16, 23, 1816; and the *Otsego Herald*, Nov. 21, 1816. For reports of meetings and resolutions from other parts of the country, see *Daily National Intelligencer*, July 25, 1816; *Pittsburgh Gazette*, June 8, 1816; Lexington *Kentucky Gazette*, July 15, 1816.

26. Quoted from the *New York Columbian* in *Niles' Weekly Register*, 10 (July 20, 1816), 340. A sampling of toasts is conveniently gathered in the *Daily National Intelligencer*, July 13, 19, 22, 1816. For other toasts, see *Albany Argus*, July 9, 12, 1816.

27. See two articles by Robert E. Shalhope: "Toward a Republican Synthesis: The Emergence of an Understanding of Republicanism in American Historiography," WMQ, 3rd Ser., 29 (Jan. 1972), 49–80; "Republicanism and Early American Historiography," ibid., 39 (Apr. 1982), 334–56. On the ideology and rhetoric of republicanism, see Bernard Bailyn, *The Ideological Origins of the American Revolution* (Cambridge, MA: Belknap Press, 1967); Gordon S. Wood, *The Creation of the American Republic, 1776–1787* (Chapel Hill: University of North Carolina Press, 1969); J.G.A. Pocock, *The Machiavellian Moment: Florentine Political Thought and the Atlantic Republican Tradition* (Princeton: Princeton University Press, 1975); and Lance Banning, *The Jeffersonian Persuasion: Evolution of a Party Ideology* (Ithaca, NY: Cornell University Press, 1978). Banning suggests (274) that only after the War of 1812 was it "possible to say that the ideas received by revolutionary thinkers from the English eighteenth century had ceased to exercise a guiding influence on American affairs." Clearly, however, these ideas held a strong sway over American thought in 1816 and for many years thereafter.

28. A good example of a document encompassing most of these arguments is the eight resolutions adopted at Galway, NY. See *Independent American*, Oct. 2, 1816.

29. "Spirit of Pennsylvania," printed in ibid., May 1, 1816.

30. Richard Hofstadter, *Anti-Intellectualism in American Life* (New York: Knopf, 1963), ch. 6.

31. "Yankee," *Independent American*, Aug. 21, 1816. See also "A Citizen," in Hartford *Connecticut Courant*, May 21, 1816, in support of the salary law.

32. *Daily National Intelligencer*, Mar. 19, 1816.

33. Ibid., June 13, 1816.

34. Quoted in *Connecticut Courant*, July 2, 1816.

35. *Annals*, 14th Cong. 2nd Sess. (House), 502.

36. *Daily National Intelligencer*, June 13, 1816.

37. *Annals*, 14th Cong., 2nd Sess. (House), 546–48, quotation 547.

38. Only Virginians Henry St. George Tucker and John Randolph did not accept the increased salary. Ibid., 519.

39. Webster to William Sullivan, Jan. 2, 1817, G.F. Hoar Papers, MHS.

40. The letter was published in *Daily National Intelligencer*, Nov. 13, 1816.

41. *Annals*, 14th Cong., 2nd Sess. (House), 681–82.

42. John A. Munroe, *Louis McLane: Federalist and Jacksonian* (New Brunswick, NJ: Rutgers University Press, 1973), 210.

43. Clayton's letter, dated Aug. 12, was first published in the *Delaware Gazette*. See Philadelphia *United States Gazette*, Aug. 24, 1816.

44. Bibb's letter was widely reprinted. See *Daily National Intelligencer*, Sept. 7, 1816; *Richmond Enquirer*, Sept. 11, 1816; and *Albany Argus*, Sept. 13, 1816.

45. *Annals*, 14th Cong., 2nd Sess. (House), 601.

46. Ibid., 237. The *Kentucky Gazette* was full of letters in the summer of 1816 from candidates dutifully stating their opposition to the Compensation Act. See, for example, June 3, 10, 17, 24, July 1, 15, 29, 1816.

47. *Annals*, 14th Cong., 2nd Sess. (House), 533. Samuel McKee and Micah Taul also declined renomination.

48. Ibid., 669. The representative was Peter Wendover (NY).

49. These figures include congressmen who resigned or died during the 14th Congress, with the exception of Nathaniel Macon (NC), who resigned and became a Senator on Dec. 13, 1815. He was replaced by Weldon N. Edwards, who took his seat on Feb. 7, 1816, and voted on the Compensation Bill. Edwards is counted as if he were originally elected to the 14th Congress. By way of comparison, non-returnees of the 13th Congress to the 14th was 51 percent and non-returnees from the 15th to the 16th was also 51 percent. Further analysis, such as age differential, sheds little light. The average age at election of the 14th Congress (170 of 181 cases) was 43.68 and for the 15th Congress (175 of 184 cases) was 43.13. Average age of the newcomers in the 15th Congress was 41.22 (101 of 106 cases). Occupations were not noticeably different. In the 14th Congress, 54.14 percent were lawyers, while 51.09 percent were lawyers in the 15th Congress. No other occupation (merchant, farmer, planter, soldier) was statistically significant.

50. At least 24 congressmen declined to run, 9 resigned, and 4 died during the session. Forty-five can be identified who were defeated, and the status of 43 can not be determined. Over half of this group (22) did vote for the bill and probably also declined to run.

51. McLean, *Letter on the Compensation Bill*, 5.

52. Ibid., 3–4, 12.

53. Boston *Columbian Centinel*, Nov. 13, 1816.

54. Wright's statement is in *Annals*, 14th Cong., 2nd Sess. (House), 527; Johnson's, ibid., 237.

55. Ibid., 637. Cyrus King (MA), disagreed with Clay, noting the people could distinguish between form and substance. Ibid., 504.

56. See, for example, *Maryland Gazette*, Aug. 8, 15, 1816. It is conjectural whether the weather affects the attitude of people. Some studies suggest it does. See Helmut E. Landsberg, *Weather and Health*, especially ch. 9. An account of the weather of 1816 is given in chapter 1.

57. *Annals*, 14th Cong., 2nd Sess. (House), 613–14.

58. George Rogers Taylor, *The Transportation Revolution, 1815–1860* (New York: Harper & Row, Publishers, 1951), 334, stated a postwar boom lasted "nearly to the end of 1818," but Paul W. Gates, *The Farmer's Age: Agriculture, 1815–1860* (New York: Harper & Row, Publishers, 1960), ch. 2, shows, the prosperity was unevenly distributed. See also Douglass C. North, *The Economic Growth of the United States, 1790–1860* (New York: W.W. Norton & Company, 1966), 181, and the wholesale price index chart for these years in Lance E. Davis et al., *American*

Economic Growth: An Economist's History of the United States (New York: Harper & Row, 1972), 364.

59. Clement Eaton, "Southern Senators and the Right of Instruction, 1789–1860," JSH, 18 (Aug. 1952), 303–305. For a comprehensive discussion of the doctrine of instruction, see C. Edward Skeen, "An Uncertain Right: State Legislatures and the Doctrine of Instruction," *Mid-America*, 73 (January 1991), 29–47.

60. The committee report may be found in *Annals*, 14th Cong., 2nd Sess. (House), 312–20. See also, *Report of the Committee Appointed on the 4th Instant, to Inquire into the Expediency of Repealing or Modifying the Law Passed at the Last Session, Changing the Mode of Compensation to the Members of Congress (December 18, 1816)* [Washington 1816], EAI, #39589.

61. Ibid., 242.

62. Ibid., 488–93 (Desha), 495 (Clay). Clay's remarks are ironic; he ignored the state instructions in 1825 during the House vote on the presidential election of 1824. He denied at that time the power of state legislators to instruct him.

63. Ibid., 503–507. See also the comments of Benjamin Hardin (KY), ibid., 532.

64. Hulbert's statement is ibid., 549, and Wright's comments are ibid. 527–29. The Wright characterization by Randolph is found in Bowers, *Jefferson in Power*, 104.

65. *Annals*, 14th Cong., 2nd Sess. (House), 528–29 (Connor), 537–39 (Parris).

66. Pickering to Brooks, Dec. 14, 1816, Pickering Papers, MHS, reel 38.

67. *Annals*, 14th Cong., 2nd Sess. (House), 574–82, quotations, 576–77.

68. Ibid., 619 (Tyler), 693 (Harrison).

69. Grosvenor's speech is ibid., 621–37.

70. Ibid., 686–91.

71. Ibid., 657.

72. Adams, *History*, 9:138.

73. *Annals*, 14th Cong., 2nd Sess. (House), 484.

74. Ibid., 486–87, 498–503, 705.

75. Ibid., 714. The Senate vote is ibid., 14th Cong., 2nd Sess. (Senate), 92. See also Act of Feb. 6, 1817, Peters, ed., *Public Statutes at Large*, III, 345.

76. Act of Jan. 22, 1818, Peters, ed., *Public Statutes at Large*, III, 404–405.

77. Gore to King, Jan. 26, 1817, Rufus King Papers, NYHS, vol. 15.

78. *Daily National Intelligencer*, Sept. 7, 1816.

79. M.J. Heale, *The Making of American Politics, 1750–1850* (London: Longman, Inc., 1977), 123.

80. *Niles' Weekly Register*, 13 (Dec. 20, 1817), 259–60; ibid., 13 (Jan. 10, 1818), 313.

81. Nathaniel H. Carter and William L. Stone, comps., *Reports of the Proceedings and Debates of the Convention of 1821 . . . of the State of New York* (Albany: E. & E. Hosford, 1821), 421.

82. Ibid., 423.

Chapter 6. Internal Improvements

1. John Lauritz Larson, "'Bind the Republic Together': The National Union and the Struggle for a System of Internal Improvements," JAH, 74 (Sept. 1987), 363–66, 368–69. See also Larson's broader study of this issue, *Internal Improvement:*

National Public Works and the Promise of Popular Government in the Early United States (Chapel Hill:The University of North Carolina Press, 2001).Another useful study on internal improvements is George Rogers Taylor, *The Transportation Revolution: 1815–1860* (NewYork: Rinehart, 1957). See also, Carter Goodrich, "American Development Policy:The Case of Internal Improvements," *Journal of Economic History*, 16 (Dec. 1956), 449–60; and "Internal Improvements Reconsidered," ibid., 30 (June 1970), 289–311.

2. Ibid., 370.

3. Richardson, ed., *Messages and Papers*, 1:409.

4. Gallatin's report is found in many places, most conveniently in *ASP, Misc.*, Doc. 250, 1:724–41.Appendixes for this report are in ibid., 742–921.

5. *Niles' Weekly Register*, 10 (Aug. 3, 1816), 381.

6. Hunt, *Life in America*, 49–50, 52.

7. *Memorial to the President on the Subject of the National Road* (Philadelphia: n.p., 1816), SS#38360, 1–8 (quotation on 6).

8. Billy Joe Peyton, "Surveying and Building the National Road," in Karl Raitz, ed., *The National Road* (Baltimore:The Johns Hopkins University Press, 1996), 128–33. See also, Balthasar Henry Meyer, *History of Transportation in the United States before 1860* (ForgeVillage, MA: Peter Smith, 1948), 12–17;Taylor, *Transportation Revolution*, 22–23.

9. *Message from the President of the United States, transmitting a Report of the Secretary of the Treasury on the Subject of the Cumberland Road; with a Statement of Past Appropriations, with an Estimate of Required Appropriations (March 13, 1816)* (Washington:William A. Davis, 1816), SS#39559, 1–8 (quotation on 8).The report is also in ASP, Misc., Doc. 403, 2:296–98.

10. Ibid., 9–11.

11. *Annals*, 14th Cong., 1st Sess. (House), 1250–54 (quotation on 1252).

12. Ibid., 1307. See also,ASP, Misc., Doc. 406, 2:300–302.

13. Peyton, "Surveying and Building the Road," 142.

14. Joseph A. Durrenberger, *Turnpike: A Study of the Toll Road Movement in the Middle Atlantic States and Maryland* (1931, reprint, Cos Cob, CN: John E. Edwards, 1968), 54–58.

15. Raitz, ed., *National Road*, 119. The author of this felicitous phrase was Joseph S.Wood.

16. Taylor, *Transportation Revolution*, 61–63.

17. Hunt, *Life in America*, 50.

18. Murphey's report is in *Journal of the Proceedings of the Senate of North Carolina . . .* (Raleigh: T. Henderson, 1816), 22–32. See, *Laws of the State of North Carolina, enacted in theYear 1815* (Raleigh:Thomas Henderson, 1816), chapters 13, 14, and 15, 12–18.

19. The entire report is in Carter Goodrich, ed., *The Government and the Economy, 1783–1861* (Indianapolis: Bobbs-Merrill Company, 1967, 59–77 (quotations on 61, 73).

20. *Journal of the Senate of the Commonwealth of Virginia . . .* (Richmond:Thomas Burling, 1815, *sic* 1816), EAI, SS#39684, 3–5, 41–42; "Act to Create a Fund for Internal Improvement," chapter 17, February 5, 1816, *Acts Passed at a General*

Assembly of the Commonwealth of Virginia . . . (Richmond: Thomas Ritchie, 1816), EAI, SS#39680, 35–39.

21. *Acts of the Commonwealth of Virginia*, 71–73, 78–80, 85–86, 94–103, 104–28, 141–90.

22. Message of Gov. Mitchell, Nov. 5, 1816, *Journal of the Senate of the State of Georgia* . . . (Milledgeville: B. & F. Grantland, 1816), EAI, SS#37701, 6; *Journal of the Senate of the Commonwealth of Pennsylvania* . . . (Harrisburg: Christian Gleim, 1815, *sic* 1816), EAI, SS#38581, 372–75; *Governor's Message, December 5, 1816* (Harrisburg: James Peacock, 1816), EAI, SS#38580, 1

23. Governor Shelby's message of Dec. 5, 1815, in *Journal of the House of Representatives, of the Commonwealth of Kentucky* . . . (Frankfort: Gerard & Berry, 1815, *sic* 1816), EAI, SS#37990, 12. The proposed Ohio resolution is in *Journal of the House of Representatives of the State of Ohio* . . . (Zanesville: David Chambers, 1815, *sic* 1816), EAI, SS#38504, 371–73 (quotations on 371, 372). The Ohio Resolution (Feb. 23, 1816) is in *Acts passed at the First Session of the Fourteenth General Assembly of the State of Ohio* . . ., vol. 14 (Chillicothe: Nashee & Denny, for John Bailhache, 1816), EAI, SS#38502, 458–59.

24. *Annals*, 14th Cong., 1st Sess. (Senate), 107–124 (quotations on 109, 110).

25. Ibid., 300, 303, 330, 332.

26. James S. and Margaret Cawley, *Along the Delaware and Raritan Canal* (Rutherford, NJ: Farleigh Dickinson University Press, 1970), 16, 23.

27. Carter Goodrich, *Government Promotion of American Canals and Railroads, 1800–1900* (New York: Columbia University Press, 1960), 41, 63.

28. Julius Rubin, "An Innovating Public Improvement: The Erie Canal," in Carter Goodrich, ed., *Canals and American Economic Development* (New York: Columbia University Press, 1961), 15–44; George E. Condon, *Stars in the Water: The Story of the Erie Canal* (New York: Doubleday & Company, 1974), 19–27.

29. Condon, *Stars in the Water*, 28.

30. Dixon Ryan Fox, *The Decline of Aristocracy in the Politics of New York, 1801–1840* (1919; reprint New York: Harper and Row, 1965), 153–56; Rubin, "Innovating Public Improvement," 43–54.

31. De Witt Clinton, *Circular Letter, 13 January 1816*, [New York 1816], EAI, SS#37270.

32. [De Witt Clinton,] *To the Legislature of the State of New-York. The Memorial of the Subscribers, in favor of a Canal Navigation between the Great Western Lakes and the Tidewaters of the Hudson. In Assembly, Feb. 21, 1816*, [Albany: n.p., 1816], EAI, SS#38427 (quotations on 4, 6, 12, 13).

33. [De Witt Clinton,] *Remarks on the Proposed Canal, from Lake Erie to the Hudson River. By Atticus* (New York: Samuel Wood & Sons, 1816), quotations on 7, 11.

34. "A Friend to His Country," *A Serious Appeal to the Wisdom and Patriotism of the Legislature of the State of New York; on the Subject of A Canal Communication between the Great Western Lakes and the Tidewaters of the Hudson* (n.p. 1816), EAI, SS#38912, 19. On the title page is handwritten, "By F. Pell."

35. *Journal of the Assembly, of the State of New York: At their Thirty-Ninth Session, Begun and Held at the City of Albany, the Thirtieth Day of January, 1816* (Albany: J. Buel, 1816), EAI, SS#38436, 12.

36. Ibid., 269–79. Examples of memorials petitioning for a canal are from Buffalo, Seneca, Geneva, Reading, Watervliet, and Troy, and the counties of Genesee and Cayuga on 166, 260, 290.

37. *Journal of the New York Assembly*, 393.

38. Ibid., 393–94. The report included James Geddes' statement on the route from Black Rock to the Cayuga marshes at the Canandaigua outlet and Benjamin Wright's from Cayuga to Rome, 394–96. See also, *The Joint Committee on that Part of his Excellency the Governor's Speech, which Relates to Canals and Roads, Report. In Assembly, March 21, 1816* (Albany: n.p., 1816), EAI, SS#38428, which also includes the bill proposed by the committee, 6–12.

39. *Journal of the New York Assembly*, 519–21.

40. Ibid., 631–32.

41. Rubin, "Innovating Public Improvement," 60–61.

42. Ibid., 633–36.

43. *Journal of the Senate of the State of New York at their Thirty-Ninth Session, Begun and held at the City of Albany, the Thirtieth Day of January, 1816* (Albany: J. Buel, 1816), EAI, SS#38437, 295–99, 308–13.

44. *Journal of the New York Assembly*, 690, 692–93, 707; *Journal of the New York Senate*, 316, 320. The law is found in Act of April 17, 1816 (chap.237), *Laws of the State of New York, Passed at the Thirty-Ninth Session of the Legislature, Begun and Held at the City of Albany, the Thirtieth Day of January, 1816* (Albany: J. Buel, 1816), EAI, SS#38438, 295–96.

45. Morris to King, March 15, 1816, Rufus King Papers, NYHS, vol.15.

46. Rubin, "Innovating Public Improvements," 59.

47. *Memorial of the Commissioners of the State of New York, in behalf of said State; Praying the Aid of the General Government in opening a Communication between the Navigable Waters of Hudson River and the Lakes (December 11, 1816)* (Washington: William A. Davis, 1816), EAI, SS#39544

48. "To the Members of Congress from the State of New York," January 22, 1817, Taylor Papers, NYHS. De Witt Clinton signed as the president of the Canal Commissioners.

49. Condon, *Stars in the Water*, 53, 73, 93; Goodrich, ed., *Canals and American Economic Development*, 263 n79.

50. Taylor, *Transportation Revolution*, 34, 339.

51. Richardson, ed., *Messages and Papers*, 1:576.

52. *Annals*, 14th Cong., 2nd Sess. (House), 297, 361.

53. Ibid., 851–58 (quotations on 854, 857, 858).

54. Ibid., 858–59, 861, 865.

55. Ibid., 866–68.

56. Ibid., 869–70.

57. Ibid., 874, 875–76.

58. Ibid., 876–78.

59. Ibid., 878–80.

60. Ibid., 880–86 (quotation on 886).

61. Ibid., 899–910 (quotation on 903).

62. Ibid., 910–12.

63. *Annals*, 14th Cong., 2nd Sess. (House), 465, 466.

64. Ibid., 913–14 (quotations on 913).

65. Ibid., 918–22 (quotations on 920).

66. Ibid., 922, 875, 922.

67. Ibid., 922, 933–34.

68. *Annals*, 14th Cong., 2nd Sess. (Senate), 120–22.

69. Ibid., 165–80. Daggett was supported by Nathaniel Macon (NC) and Eli P. Ashmun (MA), and opposed by Martin D. Hardin (KY).

70. Ibid., 186–88.

71. *Annals*, 14th Cong., 2nd Sess. (House), 1043, 1052.

72. Clay to [Madison], March 3, 1817, Hopkins, ed., *Papers of Henry Clay*, 2:322.

73. *Annals*, 14th Cong., 2nd Sess. (House), 1060–61. See also, Richardson, ed., *Messages and Papers*, 1:584–85.

74. *Annals*, 14th Cong., 2nd Sess. (House), 1062–63.

75. See, for example, Dangerfield, *Era of Good Feelings*, 103, and *The Awakening of American Nationalism*, 19–20.

76. For an excellent analysis of these points see, Larson, "Bind the Republic Together," 382–87.

Chapter 7. Fourth of July Celebrations

1. See, for example, *Richmond Enquirer*, July 3, 1816. In fact, Adams was referring to July 2, not to July 4. See John Richard Alden, *The American Revolution, 1775–1783* (New York: Harper & Row Publishers, 1954), 81–82.

2. The description of the celebration is based on many newspaper accounts for this year. Several works have surveyed the Fourth of July celebrations, the parades, and the symbolic significance of these events. See, for example, David Waldstreicher, *In the Midst of Perpetual Fetes: The Making of American Nationalism, 1776–1820* (Chapel Hill: The University of North Carolina Press, 1997); Len Travers, *Celebrating the Fourth: Independence Day and the Rites of Nationalism in the Early Republic* (Amherst: University of Massachusetts Press, 1997); Susan Davis, *Parades and Power: Street Theater in Nineteenth Century Philadelphia* (Philadelphia: Temple University Press, 1986); and Mary Ryan, "The American Parade: Representations of the Nineteenth-Century Social Order," *The New Cultural History*, ed. Lynn Hunt (Berkeley: University of California Press, 1989). See also, Burstein, *American Jubilee*.

3. *Charleston* (S.C.) *Times*, July 3, 5, 1816; *Southern Patriot*, July 1, 5, 1816; *Charleston Courier*, July 3, 1816. In Albany, NY, beams of a church floor gave way under the celebrating citizens, injuring two. *Daily National Intelligencer*, July 6, 1816.

4. *New York Evening Post*, July 3, 1816.

5. *Washington City Weekly Gazette*, July 13, 1816.

6. *Daily National Intelligencer*, July 4, 1816.

7. Newark (NJ) *Centinel of Freedom*, July 9, 1816.

8. *New York Evening Post*, July 3, 1816.

9. *Merrimac Intelligencer*, July 13, 1816; *Boston Gazette*, July 4, 1816.

10. All toasts cited are in *Charleston Times*, July 5, 1816.

11. *Richmond Enquirer*, July 6, 1816 (Brown and Scott); *Charleston Times*, July 5, 1816 (Macomb and Macdonough).

12. *Daily National Intelligencer*, July 6, 1816 (Decatur and Pike); *Charleston Courier*, July 6, 1816 (Greene).

13. Philadelphia *Gazette of the United States*, July 17, 1816.

14. See, for example, ibid.

15. *Kentucky Gazette*, July 8, 1816; *Gazette of the U.S.*, July 17, 1816; *Daily National Intelligencer*, July 6, 8, 1816.

16. Toast in Boston reported in *Albany Argus*, July 12, 1816; toast in Virginia in *Richmond Enquirer*, July 6, 1816.

17. *Daily National Intelligencer*, July 6, 1816; *Albany Argus*, July 12, 1816; *Charleston Courier*, July 6, 1816.

18. Both toasts are reported in *Daily National Intelligencer*, July 6, 1816.

19. Quoted from the *New York Columbian* in *Niles' Weekly Register*, 9 (July 20, 1816), 340.

20. *Kentucky Gazette*, July 8, 1816. Another toast reported in the *Daily National Intelligencer*, July 6, 1816, was: "Indiana—A speedy admission into the American family."

21. Hallowell (ME) *American Advocate*, July 4, 1816. The cryptic allusion to "five ninths" is discussed in chapter 9.

22. Cosan E. Bartlett, *An Oration, Pronounced before the Franklin Society, and a respectable Assembly of Citizens, in the City of Hartford, 4 July, 1816* (Hartford: Benjamin L. Hamlen, 1816), EAI, SS#36886, 10.

23. Alexander MacLeod, *An Oration, Delivered at Georgetown (S.C.) on the 4th Day of July, 1816* (Georgetown, S.C.: E. Waterman, 1816), EAI, SS#38131, 8; 22–23. Selleck Osborn, *An Oration in Commemoration of American Independence, Pronounced at Windsor, Vt., July 4, 1816* (Windsor: Jesse Cochran, 1816), EAI, SS#38536, 17–18.

24. Leonard Moody Parker, *An Oration, Pronounced at Charlestown, Massachusetts, on the Fourth of July, A.D. 1816, by the Request of the Republican Citizens of Middlesex County . . .* (Boston: Rowe & Hooper, 1816), EAI, SS#38556, 7; Asher Ware, *An Oration, Delivered Before the Washington Society, in Boston, on Fourth of July, 1816* (Boston: Rowe and Hooper, 1816), EAI, SS#39705, 11; Benjamin D. Pardee, *An Oration, Delivered at the Baptist Church in Cincinnati, Before the Tammany Society or Columbian Order; Wigwam No. III, of the State of Ohio . . .* (Cincinnati: Looker, Palmer, and Reynolds, 1816), 19.

25. Parker, *An Oration*, 8–9.

26. Ware, *An Oration*, 16; Zenas Lockwood Leonard, *An Oration, Pronounced at Southbridge, Massachusetts, July 4th, 1816, in Commemoration of American Independence* (Worcester: Henry Rogers, 1816), EAI, SS#38055, 18.

27. [John D'Wolf,] *An Address Delivered to the Citizens of Bristol (R.I.), July 4, 1816, and published at their request* (Warren, RI: Samuel Randall, 1816), EAI, SS#37441, 17; John Davis, *An Oration, Pronounced at Worcester (Mass.), on the Fortieth Anniversary of American Independence* (Worcester: William Manning, July 1816), EAI, SS#37403, 14.

28. "An Oration Delivered at the Celebration of Our National Indepen-

dence, at the City of Washington, July 4, 1816, by Benjamin L. Lear," *Daily National Intelligencer,* July 9, 1816.

29. *Camden* (SC) *Gazette,* July 11, 1816. See also, *Daily National Intelligencer,* July 6, 1816.

30. Daniel Clarke Sanders, *An Address, Delivered in Medfield, 4th July, 1816* (Dedham, MA: Abel D. Alleyne, 1816), EAI, SS#38868, 17; Henry Collins Flagg, *An Oration, Delivered before the Harmony Society, in New-Haven, on the Fortieth Anniversary of American Independence* (New Haven: T.G. Woodward, 1816), EAI, SS#37611, 14; William Lincoln, *An Oration, Pronounced at Worcester, Massachusetts, July 4th, 1816 . . . Before an Assembly of Youth* (Worcester: Henry Rogers, 1816), EAI, SS#38079, 4.

31. Charles G. Ferris, *An Oration Delivered Before the Tammany Society, or Columbian Order, Hibernian Provident, and Columbian Societies, the Union Society of Shipwright's & Caulker's, Tailors, Journeymen House Carpenters, and Mason's Societies, in the City of New York on the Fourth Day of July, 1816* (New York: Thomas P. Low, 1816), EAI, SS#37529, 14. Information on the Tammany Society may be found in Alan Leander MacGregor, "Tammany: The Indian as Rhetorical Surrogate," *American Quarterly,* 35 (Autumn 1983), 398–399.

32. Osborn, *An Oration,* 22–23.

33. Davis, *An Oration,* 15.

34. Ibid., 21–23.

35. George Sullivan, *An Oration, Pronounced on the Fourth July, 1816, before the Inhabitants of the Town of Boston, at the Request of the Selectmen* (Boston: C. Stebbins, 1816), EAI, SS#39032, 17, 20–24 (quotations on 17, 22).

36. Gilmer, *An Oration,* 9–10; Lincoln, *An Oration,* 5; MacLeod, *An Oration,* 16.

37. John Test, *An Oration Delivered . . . 4th of July, A.D. 1816, in Brookville, Indiana* (Brookville: Keen [1816]), EAI, SS#39069, 21; Ferris, *An Oration,* 14; Francis W. Gilmer, *An Oration, Delivered at the Presbyterian Church in Winchester, on the Fortieth Anniversary of American Independence* (Winchester, VA: J. Foster, 1816), EAI, SS#37712, 3; Sanders, *An Address,* 12; Pardee, *An Oration,* 21.

38. Gilmer, *An Oration,* 4; Osborn, *An Oration,* 20; Parker, *An Oration,* 7; Sullivan, *An Oration,* 12; Pardee, *An Oration,* 22.

39. Ware, *An Oration,* 4–5; William Lance, *An Oration, Delivered on the Fourth of July, 1816, in St. Michael's Church, S.C. by Appointment of the '76 Association* (Charleston: Office of the Southern Patriot, 1816), EAI, SS#38029, 21.

Chapter 8. National Defense

1. Sources on the militia in the early republic include: Lawrence D. Cress, *Citizens in Arms: The Army and Militia in American Society to the War of 1812* (Chapel Hill: The University of North Carolina Press), 1981); John K. Mahon, *The American Militia: Decade of Decision, 1789–1800* (Gainesville: University of Florida Press, 1960). For the militia in the War of 1812, see C. Edward Skeen, *Citizen Soldiers in the War of 1812* (Lexington: The University Press of Kentucky, 1999).

2. Message of December 5, 1815, *Journal of the House of Representatives, of the*

Commonwealth of Kentucky . . . (Frankfort: Gerard & Berry, 1815 [sic 1816]), EAI, SS#37990, 12.

3. Message of December 5, 1815, *Journal of the Senate of the State of Ohio, being the Fourteenth General Assembly, begun and held in the town of Chillicothe* . . . (Zanesville: David Chambers, 1815 [sic 1816]), EAI, SS#38505, 16–17.

4. *Journal of the House of Representatives of the State of Ohio, being the Fourteenth General Assembly, begun and held in the town of Chillicothe on Monday the fourth day of December 1815* . . . (Zanesville: David Chambers, 1815 [sic 1816]), EAI, SS#38504, 197–98; Resolution of Feb. 1, 1816, *Acts passed at the First Session of the Fourteenth General Assembly of the State of Ohio* . . ., vol. 14 (Chillicothe: Nashee & Denny, 1816), EAI, SS#38502, 475–76.

5. *Journal of the Twenty-Sixth House of Representatives of the Commonwealth of Pennsylvania* . . . (Harrisburg: James Peacock, 1815 [sic 1816]), EAI, SS#38582, 212–14.

6. Ibid., 232, 236, 240, 245, 248–49.

7. Act of March 19, 1816, *Acts of the General Assembly of Pennsylvania* (Philadelphia: n.p., 1816), 220–30, RSUS, Session Laws, PA, reel 6.

8. *Pennsylvania. Governor's Message, Dec. 5, 1816* (Harrisburg: James Peacock, 1816), EAI, SS#38580, 4–5.

9. *Journal of the Senate of the Commonwealth of Virginia, Begun and Held at the Capitol, in the City of Richmond, the Fourth Day of December, One Thousand Eight Hundred and Fifteen* (Richmond: Thomas Burling, 1815 [sic 1816]), EAI, SS#39684, 4.

10. *Journal of the Honorable Senate, of the State of New Hampshire, at their Session, Begun and Holden at Concord* . . . (Concord: Isaac Hill, August 1816), EAI, SS#38392, 15; *Journal of the Senate of the State of Georgia, at an Annual Session of the General Assembly, Begun and Held at Milledgeville, the Seat of Government, in November and December, 1816* (Milledgeville: B. & F. Grantland, 1816), EAI, SS#37701, 6; *Journal of the House of Representatives of the State of Louisiana. Second Session, Second Legislature: Begun and Held at the City of New Orleans* . . . (New Orleans: P.K. Wagner, 1816), EAI, SS#38102, 5–6.

11. *Journal of the House of Representatives of the State of Delaware* . . . (Wilmington: M. Bradford, 1816), 54, 59, 75–76, 76–79, 144–146, 185, RSUS, Legislative Records, DE, reel 4; *Journal of the Senate of the State of Delaware* . . . (Wilmington: M. Bradford, 1816), 57, 62–63, 89, 92, 97–98, 137, RSUS, Legislative Records, DE, reel 2.

12. W. Kennedy (Adj. DE) to Daniel Parker (Adj. and Insp. Gen., U.S.), Dec. 22, 1820, ASPMA, Doc. 208, 2:320.

13. Richardson, ed., *Messages and Papers*, 1:564, 566.

14. *Annals*, 14th Cong., 1st Sess. (House), 1408–1409.

15. *Annals*, 14th Cong., 1st Sess. (Senate), 157, 162, 169–70, 193, 207, 210, 227–28, 282.

16. *Annals*, 14th Cong., 1st Sess. (House), 402, 418–19, 421–22 (quotation on 422).

17. Ibid., 423–24, 425.

18. Ibid., 427–29 (quotation on 427).

19. Ibid., 430–35.

20. Ibid., 435.

21. Ibid., 436–37.

22. Ibid., 448–49.

23. Ibid., 449–50.

24. Ibid., 1235.

25. *Annals*, 14th Cong., 2nd Sess. (House), 245, 267, 1025.

26. White, *The Jeffersonians*, 251–60. The Act of April 29, 1816, is in Peters, ed., *Statutes at Large*, 3:321.

27. Crawford to Johnson, Dec. 27, 1815, ASPMA, Doc. 146, 1:636.

28. C. Edward Skeen, *John Armstrong, Jr., 1758–1843: A Biography* (Syracuse: Syracuse University Press, 1981), 127–28; White, *The Jeffersonians*, 233–35.

29. *Annals*, 14th Cong., 1st Sess. (House), 1234–39, 1250, 1410–11.

30. William B. Skelton, "The Commanding General and the Problem of Command in the United States Army, 1821–1841," *Military Affairs*, 34 (Dec. 1970), 117, suggested that the ambition of Secretary of War Calhoun was the primary factor. A supreme military commander would create both a "superfluous and a potential rival."

31. Jackson to Monroe, May 12, 1816, Harold D. Moser, ed., *The Papers of Andrew Jackson*, 4 vols. to date (Knoxville: The University of Tennessee Press, 1994), 4:28–30.

32. Crawford's full report may be found in *Daily National Intelligencer*, April 13, 1816.

33. Robert V. Remini, *Andrew Jackson and the Course of American Empire, 1767–1821* (New York: Harper & Row, 1977), 324–31. A map on 396 shows the extent of the purchases.

34. Ibid., 344. See also, Herbert Aptheker, *American Negro Slave Revolts* (1943, reprint, New York: International Publishers, 1969), 31.

35. Crawford to Jackson, March 15, 1816, Jackson to Gaines, April 8, 1816, Jackson to Zuniga, April 23, 1816, Amelung to Jackson, June 4, 1816, John Spencer Bassett, ed., *Correspondence of Andrew Jackson*, 7 vols., (Washington, D.C.: Carnegie Institution of Washington, 1926–1935), 2:236–37, 239, 241–43; Aptheker, *Slave Revolts*, 259.

36. Jackson to Graham, Jan. 14, 1817, Graham to Jackson, Feb. 1, 1817, Division Order, April 22, 1817, Moser, ed., *Papers of Andrew Jackson*, 4:84–87, 113–14. Jackson also appealed to the new President James Monroe on March 4, 1817, but he received no reply, prompting him to issue his division order. Ibid., 93–98.

37. Emory Upton, *The Military Policy of the United States* (1904, reprint New York: Greenwood Press, 1968), 146–47. See also, White, *The Jeffersonians*, 240–45.

38. Graham to Speaker Clay, Dec. 13, 1816, ASPMA, Doc. 149, 1:642–44.

39. Harrison Report, Jan. 17, 1817, ibid., Doc. 152, 663–64.

40. *Annals*, 14th Cong., 2nd Sess. (House), 845, 1041.

41. *Albany Argus*, March 7, 1815.

42. *Annals*, 14th Cong., 1st Sess. (House), 747–57.

43. Ibid., 720–23.

44. Ibid., 758–62.

45. Ibid., 829–39 (quotation on 833).

46. Ibid., 804–17 (quotations on 809, 816).

47. *Annals*, 14th Cong., 2nd Sess. (House), 459–62.

48. Ibid., 969, 971, 980–88, 990, 994, 997, 1000–1002, 1013–15.

49. *Annals*, 14th Cong., 2nd Sess. (Senate), 124–30, 152–64.

50. The Army Reduction Act of March 2, 1821, is discussed in depth in C. Edward Skeen, "Calhoun, Crawford, and the Politics of Retrenchment," *The South Carolina Historical Magazine*, 73 (July 1972), 141–55.

51. *Annals*, 14th Cong., 1st Sess. (Senate), 130, 161 (quotation by Mason, 130).

52. *Annals*, 14th Cong., 1st Sess. (House), 442.

53. Seventh Annual Message, Dec. 5, 1815, Richardson, ed., *Messages and Papers*, 1:566–67.

54. Report of James Pleasants, April 13, 1816, *Annals*, 14th Cong., 1st Sess. (House), 1367–69. The best discussion of the struggle to build an American navy is Craig Symonds, *The Navalists and Anti-Navalists: The Naval Policy Debate in the United States, 1785–1827* (Newark: University of Delaware Press, 1980). Symonds focuses on the anti-navalists, but they were less anti-navy than he asserts and were concerned more with retrenchment of government expenses.

55. Ibid., 829–39.

56. Ibid., 843.

57. Ibid., 1369–74, 1439, 1453.

58. K. Jack Bauer, "Naval Shipbuilding Programs, 1794–1860," *Military Affairs*, 29 (Spring 1965), 34.

59. See Michael S. Fitzgerald, "'Nature Unsubdued': Diplomacy, Expansion and the American Military Buildup of 1815–1816," *Mid-America*, 77 (Winter 1995), 28–29.

60. Based on appropriation figures taken from the U.S. Statutes at Large for the five-year period from 1817 to 1821.

Chapter 9. State Developments

1. John M. Shirley, *The Dartmouth College Causes and the Supreme Court of the United States* (1895, reprint New York: De Capo Press, 1971), 81–85; Richard N. Current, "The Dartmouth College Case," in John A. Garraty, *Quarrels That Have Shaped the Constitution* (New York: Harper & Row, 1962), 15–19; Francis N. Stites, *Private Interest and Public Gain: The Dartmouth College Case, 1819* (Amherst, MA: University of Massachusetts Press, 1972).

2. The trustees report citing the allegations against Wheelock, as well as the resolutions adopted by them are in Shirley, *Dartmouth College Causes*, 97–100.

3. Lynn W. Turner, *William Plumer of New Hampshire, 1759–1850* (Chapel Hill: University of North Carolina Press, 1962), chapters 9–11.

4. *Journal of the Honorable Senate, of the State of New Hampshire, at their Session, Begun and Holden at Concord, on the First Wednesday of June, Anno Domini, 1816* (Concord: Isaac Hill, August, 1816), EAI, SS#38392, 9–28 (quotations on 26, 27).

5. Jefferson to Plumer, July 21, 1816, quoted in Shirley, *Dartmouth College Causes*, 107.

6. *Documents Relative to Dartmouth College* (Concord: n.p., 1816), EAI, SS#38391, 38pp.

7. *Journal of the New Hampshire Senate*, 104–107 (quotation on 106).

8. *Journal of the House of Representatives of the State of New Hampshire at their Session, Begun and Holden at Concord, June Session, 1816* (Concord: Isaac Hill, Aug. 1816), EAI, SS#38393, 129–32, 171–73, 175–77.

9. Ibid., 194–99, 235–41 (quotations on 235, 236, 238).

10. *Journal of the New Hampshire Senate*, 138–43; "An Act to Amend the Charter and Enlarge and Improve the Corporation of Dartmouth College," (chap. 35), *Laws of the State of New Hampshire. June Session, 1816* [Exeter? 1816], EAI, SS#38394.

11. The trustee's position was outlined in Plumer's message to the legislature on Nov. 20, 1816. See *Speech of His Excellency, the Governor of New Hampshire, Before the Legislature. November Session, 1816* [n.p., 1816], EAI, SS#38396, 4.

12. Turner, *Plumer*, 263–66; Shirley, *Dartmouth College Causes*, 110–15.

13. Ibid., 5.

14. Garraty, ed., *Quarrels that Shaped the Constitution*, 22–25.

15. See the editorial note discussion of this case in Charles F. Hobson, ed., *The Papers of John Marshall*, 9 vols. to date (Chapel Hill: University of North Carolina Press, 1995), 8:217 23 (quotation on 221).

16. Garraty, ed., *Quarrels that Shaped the Constitution*, 29.

17. See the editorial note and associated documents in Hobson, ed., *Marshall Papers*, 8:108–121, 121–126. See also, Alfred H. Kelly, Winfred A. Harbison, and Herman Belz, *The American Constitution: Its Origins & Development*, 6th ed. (New York: W.W. Norton & Company, 1983), 187–188.

18. Kelley, et al., *American Constitution*, 188–189.

19. The standard work is Ronald F. Banks, *Maine Becomes a State: The Movement to Separate Maine from Massachusetts, 1785–1820* (Middletown, CT: Wesleyan University Press, 1970). On the early movement, see esp. 5–17.

20. Ibid., 60.

21. Ibid., 69–73.

22. Ibid., 76–87, 35–36.

23. *Massachusetts General Court, 1816. Report of the Committee of Both Houses Upon the Return of Votes from the several towns in the District of Maine, and upon sundry memorials accompanying the same . . .* [Boston: n.p., 1816], EAI, SS#38173, 1–2, 4; "An Act Concerning the Separation of the District of Maine from Massachusetts Proper, and forming the same into a separate and Independent State," chap. 41, *Laws of the Commonwealth of Massachusetts, Passed by the General Court, At their Session, which Commenced on Wednesday, the twenty-ninth day of May, and ended on the twentieth of June, 1816*, EAI, SS#38165, 247–57.

24. *An Address to the People of Maine, On the Question of Separation. By the Convention of Delegates, Assembled at Brunswick, August 1, 1816* [n.p. 1816], EAI, SS#38135, 24 pp. (quotation on 13).

25. The figures are tallies by the Massachusetts legislature. The Brunswick Convention gave a different return, 11,969 to 10,347. See Table V-1 in Banks, *Maine Becomes a State*, 97.

26. *Proceedings of the Convention of Delegates, Held in Brunswick, Maine, 1816* [n.p. 1816], EAI, SS#38136, 10–12.

27. Ibid., 12–13.

28. Ibid., 15.

29. Ibid., 17–20. The apparent author of the protest was Josiah Stebbens.

30. *Report of the Committee . . . to Whom were Referred the Memorials and Documents . . . Concerning the Separation of Maine* (Boston: n.p., 1816), EAI, SS#38171, 3–5, 7–8.

31. Banks, *Maine Becomes a State*, 115, 124, 128, 135–37, 146, 152–53, 207.

32. ASP, Misc., 14th Cong., 2nd Sess. (House), Doc. 391, 2:276–77.

33. *Annals*, 14th Cong., 1st Sess. (House), 408, 413, 416–18, 1300–1301, 1373.

34. Ibid. (Senate), 31, 276, 280, 282, 312, 315, 352.

35. Ibid. (House), 1373. The enabling act of April 19 is in ibid., 1841–44. All of the documents relating to Indiana statehood are conveniently gathered at the website http://www.statelib.lib.in.us./html.

36. *Annals*, 14th Cong., 2nd Sess. (Senate), 21, 31–32; *Annals*, 14th Cong., 2nd Sess. (House), 252, 254.

37. *Annals*, 14th Cong., 2nd Sess. (House), 252, 358–60, 373. See also, ASP, Misc., 14th Cong., 2nd Sess. (House), Doc. 416, 2:407–408.

38. Ibid., 442, 565–66.

39. "Tempus Nunc," *An Address to the People of the Mississippi Territory Shewing the Policy and Expediency [of] Dividing the Territory Preparatory to the Formation of Two States, and that Now is the Time it May Be Done* (Natchez: Peter Isler, 1816), EAI, SS#36681, 6–7, 10, 33–35.

40. *Annals*, 14th Cong., 2nd Sess. (Senate), 71, 86–88, 91.

41. *Annals*, 14th Cong., 2nd Sess. (House), 801, 831, 1026–27, 1034; *Annals*, 14th Cong., 2nd Sess. (Senate), 184.

42. *Journal of the North Carolina House of Commons . . .* [Raleigh: n. p., 1816], EAI, SS#38479, 39–40.

43. Ibid., 57; *Journal of the Proceedings of the Senate of North Carolina . . .* [Raleigh: T. Henderson, 1816], EAI, SS#38480, 41, 45.

44. Report of Secretary of State M.D. Hardin, Jan. 3, 1816, *Journal of the House of Representatives, of the Commonwealth of Kentucky . . .* (Frankfort: Gerard & Berry, 1815 [sic 1816]), EAI, SS#37990, 89–91.

45. Ibid., 91–112. The report also enclosed a large amount of correspondence relating to the disputed boundary.

46. Ibid., 139.

47. Ibid., 182–83.

48. Ibid., 296, 309.

49. An Act for Adjusting the Boundary between this State and the State of Kentucky, chapter 157, Nov. 24, 1817; An Act to Adjust the Boundary Line between this State and the State of Kentucky, chapter 67, Nov. 23, 1819; A Convention Entered into between the States of Kentucky and Tennessee, Feb. 2, 1820; Resolution Giving the Consent of Congress to a Compact Concluded between the States of Kentucky and Tennessee for the Settlement of their Boundary Line, May 12, 1820, Henry D. Whitney, ed., *The Land Laws of Tennessee . . .* (Chattanooga: J.M. Dearborn, 1891), 641–47.

50. Ibid., chapter 128 (1844), 649–50; Resolution 20 (1848), 651; chapter 26

(1858), 652–53; chapter 79 (1860), 653–70. The 1860 law describes the line in minute detail. See also, chapter 21 (1875), 671–72. My thanks to Kent Moran for helping me understand these boundary lines.

51. *Journal of the Proceedings of a Convention Begun and Held at Staunton, the 19th day of August, in the Year 1816* [Staunton? 1816], EAI, SS#39683, 9, 15–16. See also, Julius F. Prufer, "The Franchise in Virginia from Jefferson Through the Convention of 1829," WMQ, 2nd Series, 8 (Jan. 1928), 25–26; J.R. Pole, "Representation and Authority in Virginia from the Revolution to Reform," JSH, 24 (Feb. 1958), 34–36; Norman K. Risjord, "The Virginia Federalists," JSH, 33 (Nov. 1967), 514–16.

52. Stuart to William Wirt, Aug. 25, 1816, quoted in Pole, "Representation and Authority in Virginia," 36.

53. Ibid.; Prufer, "The Franchise in Virginia," 25–27.

54. Edward B. Matthews, *The Counties of Maryland* (Baltimore: Johns Hopkins Press, 1907), 405–407; *Niles' Weekly Register*, 11 (Nov. 2, 1816), 147.

55. *Niles' Weekly Register*, 10 (Oct. 19, 1816), 127.

56. *Maryland Gazette*, July 23, 1816.

57. Matthew Page Andrews, *History of Maryland: Province and State* (1929; reprint ed., Hatboro, PA: Tradition Press, 1965), 450.

58. See Merrill D. Peterson, ed., *Democracy, Liberty, and Property: The State Constitutional Conventions of the 1820s* (Indianapolis: The Bobbs-Merrill Company, 1966). This work covers the Massachusetts, New York, and Virginia conventions.

Chapter 10. Crime and Punishment

1. Biographical information on Carson is found in *A Biographical Sketch of the late Captain John Carson, who was shot by Richard Smith, late a Lieutenant in the United States Army, on the 20th January, and who died on the 4th February, 1816* (Philadelphia: Thomas Desilver, June 14, 1816), EAI, #37011, 4–8.

2. *The Trials of Richard Smith, Late Lieutenant in the 23rd Regiment U. States Infantry, as Principal, and Ann Carson, Alias Ann Smith, as Accessory for the murder of Captain John Carson, on the 20th Day of January, 1816 . . .* (Philadelphia: Thomas Desilver, 1816), EAI, #39115, 44, 59.

3. Biographical information on Smith may be found in Richard Smith, *Confession and Repentance of Lieutenant R. Smith . . .* (Philadelphia: n.p., 1816), EAI, #38956, 2–5; *Account of the Execution of Lieutenant R. Smith for the murder of Capt. John Carson . . .* (Philadelphia: n.p., August 1816), EAI, #36667, 5.

4. *Account of the Execution of Lt. R. Smith*, 5–6. Mullany's statement is in *Trial of Richard Smith*, 60.

5. *Trial of Richard Smith*, 45.

6. *Interesting Trial! The Commonwealth of Pennsylvania vs. Lieut. Richard Smith, Charged with the late Murder of Captain John Carson, at Philadelphia* (Boston: N. Coverly, 1816), EAI, #37934, 3–4. See also, *Trial of Richard Smith*, 219.

7. *Trial of Richard Smith*, 130.

8. *Interesting Trial!*, 8; *Account of Execution*, 6–7; *Trial of Richard Smith*, 46.

9. *Trial of Richard Smith*, 28, 56.

10. Ibid., 48–49.

11. *Interesting Trial!*, 8–9.

12. *Biographical Sketch of John Carson*, 15.

13. *Trial of Richard Smith*, 22.

14. Ibid. (quotations on 22 and 32).

15. Ibid., 93. During a break in the trial, a member of the crowd, "made a blow at [Smith]," but no witness would identify who had done so. Ibid., 107.

16. *Interesting Trial!*, 1–5.

17. *Trial of Richard Smith*, 86–92. See the discussion on capital punishment in Samuel Riddle and Jonathan Walker, *A New Penal Code for Pennsylvania; or Mr. Ingersoll's Bill to Consolidate and Amend the Penal Laws of this Commonwealth* (Bedford, PA: n.p., 1816), 9–64, esp. 11.

18. Ibid., 157.

19. Ibid., 206.

20. Ibid., 160, 162.

21. Ibid., 208.

22. Ibid., 213–14.

23. Ibid., 232.

24. Ibid., 234–37.

25. *An Account of the Murder of Capt. J. Carson by Lieut. R. Smith, Late of the United States Army* (Philadelphia: n.p., 1816), EAI, #36670, 8.

26. *Trial of Richard Smith*, 237–39.

27. Ibid., 240.

28. Ibid., 247. The testimony in this case is on 242–247.

29. Ibid., 247. Ann was, however, obliged to give security to appear at the next mayor's court to answer the charge of bigamy. *Interesting Trial!*, 14.

30. Smith, *Confession*, 6, 7.

31. Ibid., 8.

32. *Account of Execution*, 3.

33. Ibid., 2. Another affecting account of the execution is from the Philadelphia *Democratic Press*, Aug. 12, 1816, in *Albany Argus*, Aug. 20, 1816.

34. *Albany Argus*, Aug. 20, 1816.

35. *Account of Execution*, 2. The Philadelphia *Democratic Press* account stated that at the moment of execution the crowd let out "a general and involuntary shriek of horror; sobs and groans were heard on every side, and fervent prayers were offered up." *Albany Argus*, Aug. 20, 1816.

36. David D. Field, *Warning Against Drunkenness, A Sermon Preached in the City of Middletown, June 20, 1816, The Day of the Execution of Peter Lung, for the Murder of his Wife, At the Request of the Sheriff of the County of Middlesex, and in Accordance with the Wishes of the Criminal, Together with a Short Sketch of the Life and Hopeful Repentance of said Lung* (Middletown: Seth Richards, 1816), EAI, #37596, 21–24.

37. Peter Lung, *A Brief Account of the Life of Peter Lung, Who is Sentenced to be Executed in June Next, and is now Confined in a Gloomy Dungeon, Loaded with Chains, Awaiting the Awful Execution of the Law, Given by Himself . . .* (Hartford: William S. Marsh, March 1816), EAI, #38112, 6–7.

38. Ibid., 8.

39. Ibid., 11–12.

40. Zephaniah Swift, *A Vindication of the Calling of the Special Superior Court, at Middletown, on the 4th Tuesday of August, 1815, for the Trial of Peter Lung, Charged with the Crime of Murder. With Observations on the Constitutional Power of the Legislature to Interfere with the Judiciary in the Administration of Justice* (Windham: J. Byrne, 1816), EAI, #39040, 3.

41. Ibid., 34, 39.

42. Field, *Warning Against Drunkenness*, 25–26.

43. Lung, *A Brief Account of the Life of Peter Lung*, 12.

44. Ibid., 13–14.

45. Ibid., 16–17.

46. Louis P. Masur, *Rites of Execution: Capital Punishment and the Transformation of American Culture, 1776–1865* (New York: Oxford University Press, 1989), 3–6 (quotation on 5–6).

47. Field, *Warning Against Drunkenness*, 27–28.

48. *A Citizen of Winyaw. Observations on the Penal Code. Addressed to the People of South Carolina* (Charleston: Office of the Southern Patriot, 1816), EAI, #38497, 33, 34–37, 45.

49. Samuel Riddle and Jonathan Walker, *A New Penal Code for Pennsylvania; or Mr. Ingersoll's Bill to Consolidate and Amend the Penal Laws of this Commonwealth* (Bedford, PA: n.p., 1816), EAI, #38813, 11.

50. "Philo Humanitas," *A Brief Review, of the Principles of Capital Punishments* (Philadelphia: Merritt, 1816), EAI, #37085.

51. Miner Babcock, *The Life and Confession of Miner Babcock: Who was Executed at Norwich, Connecticut, June 6th, 1816 . . .* (New London: Samuel Green, 1816), EAI, #36778, 6.

52. Ibid., 9–12.

53. Ibid., 14.

54. Ibid., 60.

55. *Trial of Perley Cutler and Ayers White on an Indictment for the Murder of Henry Holton, before the Hon. Supreme Judicial Court, of the Commonwealth of Massachusetts, at an Adjourned Term, Holden at Boston, in the County of Suffolk, on the Third Tuesday of July 1816* (Boston: Russell, Cutler, and Co., 1816), EAI, #39114, 2–4.

56. Ibid, 6–7, 13.

57. Ibid., 28–30.

58. Ibid., 31.

59. [Fred A. Packard,] *Report of the Trial of George Bowen for the Murder of Jonathan Jewett, Who Committed Suicide on the 9th of November, 1815, While Confined in the Common Gaol of the County of Hampshire, under sentence of Death for the Murder of his Father* (Northampton, MA: n.p., 1816), EAI, #38784, 30.

60. Ibid., 30, 50–56.

61. *Sketch of the Trial of George Coombs, for the Murder of Maria Henry, alias Maria Coombs, On the 15th of June, 1816* (Boston: T.G. Bangs, 1816), EAI, # 38939, 4–6.

62. Ibid., 8.

63. Ibid., 9–10.

64. Ibid., 10–11.

65. Ibid., 12–14.

66. Ibid., 18.

67. Ibid., 18.

68. Ibid., 22.

69. *Journal of the Assembly, of the State of New York: At their Thirty-Ninth Session, Begun and Held at the City of Albany, the Thirtieth Day of January, 1816* (Albany: J. Buel, 1816), EAI, #38436, 12, 72.

70. The affidavits are in ibid., 72–77.

71. Ibid., 78.

72. Ibid., 79–80, 83.

73. Ibid., 199, 252; *Journal of the Senate of the State of New York at their Thirty-Ninth Session, Begun and held at the City of Albany, the Thirtieth Day of January, 1816* (Albany: J. Buel, 1816), EAI, #38437, 152–153; *Journal of the New York House*, 511; *Journal of the New York Senate*, 183; Act of April 5, 1816 (chapter 76) *Laws of the State of New York, Passed at the Thirty-Ninth Session of the Legislature, Begun and held at the City of Albany, the Thirtieth Day of January, 1816* (Albany: J. Buel, 1816), EAI, #38438, 73.

74. *Sketch of the Trial of William Bevans, for the Murder of Peter Lunstrum, on Board the United States' Ship Independence, on the 6th of November, 1816* (Boston: Thomas G. Bangs, 1816), EAI, #38940, 5–9, 3.

75. Ibid, 25.

76. Ibid., 25, 33.

77. Hobson, ed., *Papers of John Marshall*, 8:181. The complete opinion is on 181–85.

78. Ibid., 181.

79. Ibid., 182, 184.

80. Ibid., 182–83.

81. Ibid., 183.

82. *Report of the Committee of the Society in Portland for Suppressing Vice and Immorality . . . April 27, 1816* (Portland: A. & J. Shivley, 1816), EAI, #38971, 7–8.

83. David Thurston, *A Sermon Delivered in Saco, June 26, 1816, Before the Maine Missionary Society, at their Ninth Annual Meeting* (Hallowell: N. Cheever, 1816), EAI, # 39087, 14; *Warning to the Intemperate*, 23. See also, John Winslow, *An Address, Delivered June 17th, 1816, Before the Association, for the Suppression of Intemperance, and the Promotion of Morality in the town of Hanover, Massachusetts* (Boston: Wells and Lilly, 1816), EAI, #39843. For the modern calculations of alcohol consumption (as well as an excellent study of the entire movement), see W.J. Rorabaugh, *The Alcoholic Republic: An American Tradition* (New York: Oxford University Press, 1979), Appendix 1, 225–36.

84. Rorabaugh, *Alcoholic Republic*, 191–92. The Methodist resolution is quoted in Alice Felt Tyler, *Freedom's Ferment: Phases of American Social History from the Colonial Period to the Outbreak of the Civil War* (Minneapolis: University of Minnesota Press, 1944, reprint New York: Harper and Row, 1962), 320.

85. Benjamin Rush, *Extracts from Dr. Benjamin Rush's Inquiry into the Effects of Ardent Spirits upon the Human Body and Mind* (Philadelphia: [Skerrett] for Benjamin & Thomas Kite, 1816), EAI, #38849. Rush's work was also extracted in *A*

Warning Voice to the Intemperate (New Brunswick, N.J.: Deare & Myer, Sept. 1816), EAI, #39707, 4–14. Weems retitled his work, *A Calm Dissausive against Intemperance; or An Awful View of the Horrors and Miseries of Drunkenness* (Philadelphia: Printed for Mason L. Weems, 1816), EAI, #37312.

86. [Rhode Island,] Message of Gov. William Jones, Oct. 28, 1816, *At the General Assembly . . . Last Monday of October 1816* (Providence: Brown & Wilson, 1816), EAI, SS#38796, 3. Gov. Snyder's message is cited in [Dr. Jesse Torrey, Jr.], *The Intellectual Flambeau, Demonstrating that National Happiness, Virtue and Temperance exist, in a Collateral Ratio, with the Dissemination of Philosophy, Science and Intelligence . . .* (Washington, D.C.: Daniel Rapine, 1816), EAI, SS#39105, 47.

87. Torrey, *Intellectual Flambeau*, 3, 60–61, 65, 101 (quotations on 3, 60–61).

88. *Annals*, 14th Cong., 1st Sess. (House), 922–31, 934–35 (quotation on 934).

89. Ibid., 932, 936–39 (quotation on 936–37).

90. Ibid., 949, 1233. The final vote was 118–13.

91. Adna Heaton, *War and Christianity Contrasted: With a Comparative View of Their Nature and Effects. Recommended to the Serious and Impartial Consideration of the Professors of the Christian Religion* (New York: Samuel Wood & Sons, 1816), EAI, SS#37821, 58. Heaton was citing a speech by Gov. D.D. Tompkins of New York.

92. Message of Gov. Jones, Oct. 28, 1816, EAI, SS#38796, 4.

93. *Journal of New York Assembly*, 39th Sess., 80.

94. Act of April 12, 1816, *Laws of the State of New York* (Chapter 85), 79–80.

95. See the discussion in Tyler, *Freedom's Ferment*, 274–83.

Chapter 11. The Humanitarian Impulse

1. Richard Storrs, *Union Among the Friends of Religious Order, A Sermon Preached 5th June 1816, before the Convention of Norfolk County at Dedham, for Encouraging the Due Observance of the Lord's Day* (Dedham: Abel D. Alleyane, 1816), EAI, SS#39018, 16.

2. *Remarks on the Existing State of the Laws of Massachusetts, Respecting Violations of the Sabbath* (Boston: Nathaniel Willis, 1816), EAI, SS#38777, 11–12.

3. David D. Field, *The Sabbath, A Sermon Preached at Hartford, on the Evening of May 15, 1816, before the Connecticut Society for the Promotion of Good Morals* (Hartford: Benjamin L. Hamlen, 1816), EAI, SS#37595, 12, 19. Other sabbatarian sermons printed in this year include: [Rufus Wyman,] *Remarks on the Observation of the Lord's Day, as a Moral, a Positive, and a Civil Duty, By a Tythingman* (Cambridge, MA: Hilliard and Metcalf, 1816), EAI, SS#39885; Daniel Clarke Sanders, *A Sermon, Preached 9th January 1816, before the Convention of Norfolk County at Dedham for Encouraging the Due Observance of the Lord's Day* (Dedham, MA: Gazette Office, 1816), EAI, SS#38869; Thomas Snell, *A Sermon, Preached before the Auxiliary Society for the Reformation of Morals, in Brookfield, April 15, 1816* (Brookfield: E. Merriam and Company, 1816), EAI, SS#38964.

4. Richard R. John, "Taking Sabbatarianism Seriously: The Postal System, the Sabbath, and the Transformation of American Political Culture," JER, 10 (Winter 1990), 520–35.

5. *Annals*, 14th Cong., 1st Sess. (House), 1123–26 (quotation on 1123). Examples of petitions introduced are on ibid., 679, 975, and *Annals*, 14th Cong., 2nd Sess. (Senate), 26, 28, 35, 41–42, 229.

6. Examples of petitions are in *Annals*, 14th Cong., 2nd Sess. (House), 419, 436, 472. The Mills committee report is on ibid., 1045–49 (Meigs quotation on 1047). See also, John, "Taking Sabbatarianism Seriously," 535–36.

7. Tyler, *Freedom's Ferment*, 400–402. Tyler's chapter 15 on the peace movement is outstanding. Merle Curti, *The American Peace Crusade, 1813–1860* (Durham, NC: Duke University Press, 1929), is the standard treatment.

8. *A Circular Letter from the Massachusetts Peace Society. Respectfully Addressed to the Various Associations, Presbyteries, Assemblies and Meetings of the Ministers of Religion in the United States* (Cambridge, MA.: Hilliard and Metcalf, 1816), EAI, SS#38190, 15–16. The constitution of the society was signed on Dec. 28, 1815, and may be found in ibid., 13–16.

9. Ibid., 3–13 (quotations on 6, 9).

10. Tyler, *Freedom's Ferment*, 402.

11. *Daily National Intelligencer*, June 12, 1816.

12. John Leland, *Free Thoughts on War* (Pittsfield: Phineas Allen, Dec. 1816), EAI, SS#38052, 1–23 (quotations on 8, 19, 21).

13. William Ellery Channing, *A Sermon on War: Delivered before the Convention of Congregational Ministers of Massachusetts, May 30, 1816* (Boston: Wells & Lilly, 1816), EAI, SS# 37207, iii, 21.

14. Adna Heaton, *War and Christianity Contrasted: With a Comparative View of their Nature and Effects. Recommended to the Serious and Impartial Consideration of the Professors of the Christian Religion* (New York: Samuel Wood & Sons, 1816), EAI, SS#37821, 50–51.

15. "Philo Pacificus," *The Friend of Peace, No. II, Containing a Review of the Arguments of Lord Kames in Favour of War* (Philadelphia: W. Brown for Kimber & Sharpless, 1816), EAI, SS#38628, 4–11, 12–18, 31–37 (quotations on 11, 17, 33).

16. *The Memorial of the Governors of the New-York Hospital* [Albany 1816], EAI, SS#38973.

17. *First Annual Report of the Philadelphia Orphan Society* (Philadelphia: William Fry, 1816), EAI, SS#38614, 3–4, 6–7, 10–14, 20; *Account of the Present State of the Asylum for the Relief of Persons Deprived of the Use of Their Reason* (Philadelphia: W. Brown, 1816), EAI, SS#37670, 1–6. The building was 60 feet square with wings 124 feet long.

18. Two works of Mason Locke Weems: *A Calm Dissuasive against Intemperance*, originally published in 1812, was republished in 1816, EAI, SS#37312, as was a fourth edition of *The Drunkard's Looking Glass*, EAI, SS#39765. The old standby, Richard Rush's *Enquiry into the Effects of Ardent Spirits . . .*, was widely circulated by the tract societies of the time. An example is [Dr. Jesse Torrey, Jr.], *The Intellectual Flambeau, Demonstrating that National Happiness, Virtue and Temperance exist, in a Collateral Ratio, with the Dissemination of Philosophy, Science and Intelligence . . .* (Washington, D.C.: Daniel Rapine, 1816), EAI, SS#39105, 79–89.

19. *The First Annual Report of the Philadelphia Female Tract Society, for the year 1816 . . .* (Philadelphia: Lydia R. Bailey, Dec. 26, 1816), EAI, SS#38609, 1, 5–11. An example of the tracts distributed is *A Present to Children at School* (Philadel-

phia: Lydia R. Bailey, 1816), EAI, SS#38610. The remaining thirteen tracts are found in EAI, SS#38611.

20. *The Fourth Annual Report of the New-York Religious Tract Society* (New York: J. Seymour, 1816), EAI, SS#38457, 5, 17–18. See Leigh Richmond, *The Dairyman's Daughter*, Parts 1 and 2 (Philadelphia: William Bradford, 1816), EAI, SS#38807 and SS#38808. Richmond wrote many other tracts distributed by the societies, such as: *The African Servant* (Andover, MA: Flagg & Gould, 1816), EAI, SS#38804, and *The Young Cottager* (Andover, MA: Flagg & Gould, 1816), EAI, SS#38809.

21. Eliza Bowen West, *The Awful Beacon; To the Rising Generation of Both Sexes or A Farewell Address to the Youths of and Final Adieu to the State of Massachusetts* (Boston: N. Coverly, Jr., 1816), EAI, SS#39742, 60pp. (quotations from 2, 45). Earlier parts one and two are in *The Female Marine or the Adventures of Miss Lucy Brewer* (Boston: n. p., Jan. 1816), EAI, SS#39743. Other versions by the same title are in ibid., SS#39744, SS#39745, SS#39746, SS#39748, and the fullest version (140pp.), containing parts one, two, and three, is ibid., SS#39747.

22. Rachel Sperry, *A Brief Reply to the Late Writings of Louisa Baker [alias Lucy Brewer], Late an inhabitant of West Boston Hill, and who in disguise served Three Years on board the Frigate CONSTITUTION* (Boston: M. Brewster, 1816), EAI, SS#38890, 3–4, 6, 9, 11–12, 23–24 (quotation on 9).

23. Almira Paul, *The Surprising Adventures of Almira Paul, A Young Woman who, garbed as a male, has for three of the last preceding years, actually served as a common Sailor, on board of English and American armed vessels, without discovery of her sex being made* (Boston: N. Coverly, Jr., 1816), EAI, SS#38563, 24pp.

24. See the introduction in Daniel A. Cohen, ed., *The Female Marine and Related Works: Narratives of Cross-Dressing and Urban Vice in America's Early Republic* (Amherst: University of Massachusetts Press, 1997), 1–45.

25. Information on Bible societies have been gleaned from many sources. See John Prince, *A Discourse Delivered in Salem, before the Bible Society of Salem & Vicinity on the Anniversary, June 12, 1816* (Salem: Thomas C. Cushing, 1816), EAI, SS#38707, 5–6; James Morss, *A Discourse Before the Merrimac Bible Society, On their 5th Anniversary, Preached in St. Paul's Church, Newburyport, July 31, 1816* (Newburyport: William B. Allen & Co., Aug. 1816), EAI, SS#38297, 16–17, 19; *Report of the Proceedings of the Ohio Bible Society, from its formation to November 1815* (Marietta: Office of the American Friend, 1816), EAI, SS#38511, 4; *The Fifth Report, of the Directors of the Oneida Bible Society, exhibited at their Annual Meeting in Utica, January 17, 1816* (Utica: George Camp, [1816]), EAI, SS#38528, 4–5.

26. *Second Report of the Board of Managers of the Louisiana Bible Society. Read and Approved the 21st May, 1816* (New Orleans: P.K. Wagner, 1816), EAI, SS#38104, 3, 6–8, 10.

27. *A Memoir On the Subject of a General Bible Society for the United States of America. By a Citizen of the State of New York* (New Jersey: n.p., 1816), EAI, SS#38226, 8, 10–16.

28. *Proceedings of a Meeting of the Citizens of New York and Others, Convened in the City Hall on the 13th of May, 1816; At the Request of the Board of Managers of the American Bible Society* (New York: J. Seymour, 1816), EAI, SS#38715, 14–15; *The Fourth Annual Report of the Board of Managers of the Otsego County Bible Society, June 13, 1816* (Cooperstown, NY: J.H. Prentiss, 1816), EAI, SS#38537, 6–7.

29. *Sixth Report of the Board of Managers of the New Jersey Bible Society, Read before the Society at their Annual Meeting held at Princeton, on the Twenty-eighth day of August, A.D. 1816* (Trenton: George Sherman, 1817), EAI, SS#38414; *Seventh Report of the Board of Managers of the New-York Bible Society: Presented and Read at the Annual Meeting of the Society, Held the 2d December, 1816* (New York: J. Seymour, 1816), EAI, SS#38449, 4; *Otsego County Bible Society Annual Report*, 7–8; *Fourth Report of the Vermont Bible Society, Communicated to the Society at Their Annual Meeting, at Montpelier, October 16, 1816* (Montpelier: Walton & Goss, October 1816), EAI, SS#39665, 8. Information on Boudinot's gift is in Morss, *A Discourse*, 19.

30. *Proceedings of a Meeting of Members of the Legislature, and Other Gentlemen from Different Parts of the State, Convened at the State-House in Boston, December 6, 1816, for the Purpose of Adopting Measures for Recommending the American Bible Society to the Patronage and Support of the Public* [Boston 1816]. EAI, SS#38716, 1–4.

31. *Report of the New York Bible Society*, 9; P.J. Staudenraus, *The African Colonization Movement, 1816–1865* (New York: Columbia University Press, 1961), 12.

32. Morss, *Discourse*, 14.

33. "A Clergyman," *Some Questions and Answers on the Subject of the American Bible Society* (New York: Van Winkle & Wiley, 1816), EAI, SS#38976, 4–7, 11, 14–15, 29, 33–35 (quotations on 4, 15, 33, 35).

34. John C. Rudd, *An Address, Delivered Before the Elizabethtown Female Bible and Common Prayer Book Society, at the Adoption of their Constitution, June 20, 1816* (Elizabethtown: J. & E. Sanderson, 1816), EAI, SS#38844, 6–7.

35. *The First Annual Report of the Providence Female Tract Society* (Providence: Miller & Hutchens, 1816), EAI, SS#38745, 22–24; *First Annual Report of the Providence Auxiliary Bible Society. With an Appendix* (Providence: Miller & Hutchens, 1816), EAI, SS#38743, 3–5.

36. John C. Rudd, *An Address, Delivered before the Elizabethtown Free-School Association, December 16, 1816* (Elizabethtown: Isaac A. Kullock, 1816), EAI, SS#38845, 3, 7–8.

37. Henry Ustick Onderdonk, *A Sermon, On General Education Delivered before the Female Charitable Society of Canandaigua, September 8, 1816* (Canandaigua, NY: J.D. Bemis, 1816), EAI, SS#38526, 9–10.

38. *Eleventh Annual Report of the Free-School Society of New York* (New York: Collins and Co., 1816), EAI, SS#37638, 1–2. In addition to Clinton, the Board included numerous prominent New Yorkers, such as John Murray, Jr. (vice-president), Henry Ten Brook, Thomas Eddy, Henry Rutgers, John E. Caldwell, Thomas L. Ogden, David L. Dodge, and others.

39. Massachusetts General Court, 1816. *Report of the Commonwealth of Massachusetts Legislature Regarding Actual State of Literary and Scientific Societies* [Boston: n.p., 1816], EAI, SS#38172, 3–6. The chair of the committee was Josiah Quincy.

40. Ibid., 9–10, 11, 13–16.

41. Charles W. Peale, *Address, Delivered by Charles W. Peale, to the Corporation and Citizens of Philadelphia, on the 18th Day of July, 1816, in Academy Hall, Fourth Street* (Philadelphia: For the Author, 1816), EAI, SS#38567, 4, 10, 15, 18–20, 22.

42. Charles Coleman Sellers, *Charles Willson Peale: Later Life (1790–1827)*, Part II (Philadelphia: The American Philosophical Society, 1947), 305–18.

43. William W. Freehling, "The Founding Fathers and Slavery," AHR, 77 (Oct. 1972), 81–91, argued that the Founding Fathers were anti-slavery. Paul Finkelman, *Slavery and the Founders: Race and Liberty in the Age of Jefferson* (Armonk, NY: M.E. Sharpe, 1996), has a contrary view.

44. Herbert Aptheker, *American Negro Slave Revolts* (1943, reprint New York: International Publishers, 1969), 255–58. The Camden incident is found in *Camden* (SC) *Gazette*, July 4, 1816.

45. *An Address from the Manumission Society of Tennessee to the Free Men of the State, on Account of the Oppressed Africans Therein* (Rogersville, TN: P. Carey, 1816), 3–5, 8, 11–12.

46. "Philo Justitia," *Circular. To the Advocates of African Emancipation* . . . (St. Clairsville, OH: n.p., Jan. 4, 1816), broadside.

47. *Minutes of Proceedings of the Fourteenth American Convention for Promoting the Abolition of Slavery, and Improving the Condition of the African Race* . . . (Philadelphia: W. Brown, 1816), 9, 12, 24–25, 30–33.

48. *United States Gazette*, Aug. 10, 1816. An example of a slave being offered for sale is in the *Albany Argus*, March 19, 1816.

49. *Annals*, 14th Cong., 1st Sess. (House), 1115–16.

50. Ibid., 1116–17, 1465.

51. *Annals*, 14th Cong., 1st Sess. (House), 691–92. The concerns about free black colonies on the frontier are laid out by Robert Finley, *Thoughts on the Colonization of Free Blacks* [Washington, D.C.: n.p., 1816], EAI, SS#37606, 6–7.

52. Merton L. Dillon, *The Abolitionists: The Growth of a Dissenting Minority* (New York: W.W. Norton, 1979), 38.

53. George Bourne, *The Book and Slavery Irreconcilable, with Animadversions upon Dr. [Samuel Stanhope] Smith's Philosophy* (Philadelphia: J.M. Sanderson & Co., 1816), 3, 8–9, 14, 36, 65, 74–75, 122 (quotations on 3, 122, 74–75). On Bourne's influence, see for example, Dillon, *The Abolitionists*, 38.

54. *Constitution of the Columbian United Abolition Society, with the Minutes of a Meeting of the Society, Held at Eaton, on the 16th of the 8th Month, 1816; To Which is Prefixed, an Address to the People of the States of Ohio and Indiana, on the Subject of Slavery* (Cincinnati: Williams & Mason, 1816), EAI, SS#37307, 3, 4–5, 6–7.

55. *Journal of the Senate of the State of Ohio, being the Fourteenth General Assembly, begun and held in the Town of Chillicothe* . . . (Zanesville: David Chambers, 1815 [sic, 1816]), EAI, SS#38505, 235, 238, 241–43, 262–63; chapter 46, "An Act for the Relief of the Poor," (Feb. 10, 1816), *Acts Passed at the First Session of the Fourteenth General Assembly of the State of Ohio* . . ., vol. 14 (Chillicothe: Nashee & Denney, for John Bailhache, 1816), EAI, SS#38502, 199–201.

56. *The Constitution of the State of Indiana* (Vincennes: Elihu Stout, 1816), EAI, SS#37922, 19–20, 22. The question of slavery in the Northwest Territory, after 1787, is dealt with fully by Paul Finkelman, *Slavery and the Founders*, 57–79.

57. *An Address to the Public, on the Subject of the African School, lately established under the care of the Synod of New-York and New-Jersey. By the Directors of the Institution* (New York: J. Seymour, 1816), EAI, SS#38704, 3–5, 7–8. Earlier, in June 1816, Bishop James Kemp exhorted the Protestant Episcopal Church of Maryland to reach out to blacks, "part of our Lord's vineyard." *Journal of a Convention of the Protestant Episcopal Church of Maryland held in St. Anne's Church, Annapolis, June*

12th, 13th, & 14th, 1816 (Annapolis: Jonas Green, 1816), EAI, SS#38730, 16.

58. Mercer's role is persuasively argued by Douglas R. Egerton, "'Its Origin is Not a Little Curious': A New Look at the American Colonization Society," JER, 5 (Winter 1985), 463–80.

59. Gary B. Nash, *Forging Freedom: The Formation of Philadelphia's Black Community, 1720–1840* (Cambridge, MA: Harvard University Press, 1988), 100–101.

60. Henry Noble Sherwood, "Paul Cuffe," *Journal of Negro History*, 8 (April 1923), 198–99. A useful biography is Lamont D. Thomas, *Paul Cuffe: Black Entrepreneur and Pan-Africanist* (Urbana: University of Illinois Press, 1988). See also, Nash, *Forging Freedom*, 184–85, 235–39.

61. Henry Noble Sherwood, "The Formation of the American Colonization Society," *Journal of Negro History*, 2 (July 1917), 214.

62. Finley, *Thoughts on Colonization*, 4–6. See also, Staudenraus, *African Colonization Movement*, 19–22.

63. Staudenraus, *African Colonization Movement*, 23–27; Sherwood, "Formation of the American Colonization Society," 220–21.

64. Staudenraus, *African Colonization Movement*, 28–29.

65. Quoted in Staudenraus, *African Colonization Movement*, 29. Sherwood, "Formation of the American Colonization Society," 226, maintained "the colonization movement of 1816–17 was at that time sincere in its purpose and straightforward in its aims." That may have been true for some of the participants, but they were undoubtedly in the minority.

66. Sherwood, "Formation of American Colonization Society," 226–228; Staudenraus, *American Colonization Movement*, 29–30. The quotation is from Egerton, "The American Colonization Society," 479.

67. Staudenraus, *African Colonization Movement*, 32, 34.

68. *Annals*, 14th Cong., 2nd Sess. (House), 481–83.

69. Ibid., 939–41.

70. Staudenraus, *African Colonization Movement*, 48–68.

71. The struggles of the colonization society are detailed in Charles I. Foster, "The Colonization of Free Negroes, in Liberia, 1816–1835," *Journal of Negro History*, 38 (Jan. 1953), 41–66.

Chapter 12. Election of 1816

1. Paul F. Boller, Jr., *Presidential Campaigns* (New York: Oxford University Press, 1984), 29. Boller devoted only two pages (of 420) to the 1816 election. Lynn W. Turner's article, "Elections of 1816 and 1820," in Arthur Schlesinger, Jr., ed., *History of American Presidential Elections, 1789–1968*, 4 vols. (New York: Chelsea House Publishers, 1971), 1:299–346, is the only one that combines two elections. More space is devoted to the latter, in which Monroe received all but one electoral vote, than is given to the former (10 pages).

2. Quoted in Shaw Livermore, Jr., *The Twilight of Federalism: The Disintegration of the Federalist Party, 1815–1830* (Princeton: Princeton University Press, 1962), 14–15.

3. Gallatin to Adams, Dec. 9, 1815, Albert Gallatin Papers (microfilm), reel 28.

4. Lewis to Taylor, Dec. 22, 1815, John W. Taylor Papers, NYHS.

5. Adams, *History*, 8:159. See also, C. Edward Skeen, "Monroe and Armstrong: A Study in Political Rivalry," *The New-York Historical Society Quarterly*, 57 (April 1973), 121–47, esp. 126–40.

6. Monroe to Hay, Sept. 7, 1814, James Monroe Papers, NYPL.

7. Harry Ammon, *James Monroe: The Quest for National Identity* (New York: McGraw Hill, 1971), 353–54; quotation cited in *Daily National Intelligencer*, March 6, 1816.

8. Quoted in Turner, "Elections of 1816 and 1820," 1:304. See also, J.E.D. Shipp, *Giant Days, or, The Life and Times of William H. Crawford* (Americus, GA: Southern Printers, 1909), 141.

9. Fisk to Taylor, Dec. 31, 1815, Taylor Papers, NYHS.

10. Ray W. Irwin, *Daniel D. Tompkins: Governor of New York and Vice President of the United States* (New York: New York Historical Society, 1968), 202–203; *Daily National Intelligencer*, Feb. 17, 1816.

11. Chase C. Mooney, *William H. Crawford, 1772–1834* (Lexington: University Press of Kentucky, 1974), 214; Shipp, *Giant Days*, 143–44.

12. Irwin, *Tompkins*, 206–207.

13. Ibid.

14. *New York Evening Post*, Feb. 9, 1816.

15. *Daily National Intelligencer*, Feb. 13, 1816; *Eastern Argus*, cited in *Daily National Intelligencer*, March 6, 1816.

16. *Alexandria* (VA) *Gazette*, Jan. 27, 1816; *Savannah Republican*, cited in *Charleston Courier*, Feb. 6, 1816; *Raleigh Star*, March 8, 1816.

17. *Daily National Intelligencer*, Jan. 17, 1816, Feb. 1, 1816.

18. Mooney, *Crawford*, 218.

19. Ibid.

20. *New York Patriot*, cited in *Charleston Courier*, Feb. 8, 1816; *Washington City Weekly Gazette*, cited in *Charleston Times*, March 16, 1816.

21. [Mathew Carey,] *Historical Sketch of, and Remarks upon Congressional Caucuses for President & Vice-President, From the Olive Branch* (Philadelphia: Mathew Carey, January 1816). EAI, SS#37170.

22. Ibid., 35–36.

23. See for example, *Maryland Gazette*, April 16, June 20, Sept. 19, Oct. 31, Nov. 14, 1816. See also, *Pennsylvania Gazette*, March 30, Oct 18, 1816.

24. *Daily National Intelligencer*, April 9, 1816.

25. John W. Taylor to Jane Taylor, Feb. 28, 1816, Taylor Papers, NYHS. Taylor quoted the anti-caucus resolution he presented that was rejected by the caucus on March 16.

26. *Annals*, 14th Cong., 2nd Sess. (House), 352.

27. There are actually two undated memorandums, no doubt written in early March. The second appears to be a continuation of the first. James Monroe Papers, LC (Microfilm).

28. *Muskingum Messenger*, June 13, 1816; *New York Patriot*, cited in *Daily National Intelligencer*, March 29, 1816; *Catskill Recorder*, cited in *Daily National Intelligencer*, April 3, 1816.

29. *Nashville Whig*, cited in *Daily National Intelligencer*, Feb. 17, 1816; Turner, "Elections of 1816 and 1820," 1:302. Examples of pro-Monroe articles are found in the *Daily National Intelligencer*, Feb. 6, 8, 13, 16, 17, 19, 22, 24, 27, March 1, 4, 12, 1816.

30. Turner, "Elections of 1816 and 1820," 302.

31. *New York Evening Post*, March 13, 1816; Turner, "Elections of 1816 and 1820," 1:303.

32. Hopkins, ed., *Clay Papers*, 2:176–77. Although he objected to the caucus method, Clay voted for Monroe and Tompkins. Clay to Martin D. Hardin, March 18, 1816, ibid., 2:177.

33. Mooney, *Crawford*, 89; Ammon, *Monroe*, 354–55.

34. *Niles' Weekly Register*, 10 (March 23, 1816), 60.

35. Holmes Alexander, *The American Talleyrand: The Career and Contemporaries of Martin Van Buren, Eighth President* (New York: Harper & Brothers, 1935), 144; Shipp, *Giant Days*, 144; Mooney, *Crawford*, 220–21.

36. C.S. Thompson, "The Rise and Fall of the Congressional Caucus as a Machine for Nominating Candidates for the Presidency," in Leon Stein, ed., *The Caucus System in American Politics* (New York: Arno Press, 1974), 36; *Washington City Weekly Gazette*, March 16, 1816.

37. [John Armstrong,] *Exposition of the Motives for Opposing the Nomination of Mr. Monroe for the Office of President of the United States* (Washington, D.C.: Jonathan Elliot, 1816), 13, EAI, SS#37551.

38. Livermore, *Twilight of Federalism*, 27–28; Dixon Ryan Fox, *The Decline of Aristocracy in the Politics of New York, 1801–1840*, ed. by Robert V. Remini (New York: Harper & Row Publishers, 1965), 101, 173–74.

39. Robert Ernst, *Rufus King: American Federalist* (Chapel Hill: University of North Carolina Press, 1968), 345–346. The amendment was proposed by North Carolina, but Massachusetts offered an improved version. (See chapter 3.)

40. Ibid., 347; Fox, *Decline of Aristocracy*, 187–88.

41. Dwight to King, Feb. 10, 1816, King, ed., *King Correspondence*, 5:503.

42. Fox, *Decline of Aristocracy*, 189.

43. Ernst, *Rufus King*, 349–50; King to Bleecker Committee, March 2, 1816, *New York Evening Post*, March 13, 1816; King to Edward King, March 28, 1816, King, ed., *King Correspondence*, 6:17.

44. Oakley to King, March 29, 1816, Rufus King Papers, NYHS, vol. 15.

45. Irwin, *Tompkins*, 203–204. A doggerel appeared in the *Albany Argus*, April 20, 1816, that suggested King was disloyal during both the Revolutionary War and War of 1812.

46. See the list of toasts for the St. Patrick's Day celebration, *Albany Argus*, April 2, 1816. King's protest to the British is detailed in Fox, *The Decline of Aristocracy*, 78–79. King was also attacked by "Agricola," *Albany Argus*, April 5, 16, and his protest to the British is stressed negatively.

47. Irwin, *Tompkins*, 204–205; *New York Evening Post*, April 16, 1816.

48. Ernst, *Rufus King*, 204–205; Livermore, *Twilight of Federalism*, 31–32.

49. *New York Evening Post*, April 12, 1816; King to Gore, May 15, 1816, King Papers, NYHS, vol. 15.

50. King to D.B. Ogden, April 19, 1816, King, ed., *King Correspondence*, 5:530; King to Edward King, May 21, 1816, ibid., 5:537.

51. *Richmond Enquirer*, May 22, 1816.

52. *Daily National Intelligencer*, March 16, 1816; *Portsmouth* (NH) *Oracle*, March 23, 1816, *New York Evening Post*, March 19, 1816.

53. Monroe to Hay, July 3, 6 (quotation), 7, 1816, Monroe Papers, L.C.

54. *Niles' Weekly Register*, 10 (June 1, 1816), 217.

55. *United States Gazette*, May 22, 1816.

56. [Armstrong,] *Exposition of Motives*, 1–2.

57. Ibid., 5–8.

58. Evidence of Armstrong's authorship may be found in Skeen, *John Armstrong, Jr.*, 207–208.

59. A South Carolinian [Charles Pinckney], *Observations to shew the Propriety of the Nomination of Colonel James Monroe, to the Presidency of the United States by the Caucus in Washington, In Which a Full Answer is given to the Pamphlet entitled "Exposition of the Motives for Opposing the Nomination of Mr. Monroe as President of the United States"* (Charleston, SC: Office of the Southern Patriot, 1816. EAI, SS#38643.

60. *Muskingum Messenger*, June 13, 1816.

61. "At a Large and Respectable Meeting of the Federal Republicans of the Borough of Lancaster . . . on the 29th of September Ultimo," [Lancaster: n.p., 1816]. EAI, SS#37571. See also, "At a Meeting of the Federalists holden at New-Haven, October 1816 . . ." (New Haven: n.p., 1816). EAI, SS#37569.

62. Broadside, "March Meeting is at Hand!" (Salem: n.p., March 9, 1816), EAI, SS#38141a.

63. *Albany Argus*, March 19, 1816.

64. *As You Were! A Word of Advice to Straight-Haired Folks: Addressed to the Freemen of Connecticut, by One of their Number* (New Haven: T.G. Woodward, 1816), EAI, SS#36763, 1, 15. See also, a Federalist broadside in New York attacking Thomas Addis Emmett as a tool of the Clintonians. "Washington," *Independent Americans* (n.p., 1816), EAI, SS#37917.

65. William Darling, *An Oration Delivered Before the Washington Benevolent Society of Canaan, Columbia County, February 22d, 1816—Being the Birth Day of the Immortal Washington . . .* (Hudson: William L. Stone, 1816), EAI, SS#37390, 9, 11–12.

66. [William Plumer], *General Address to the Freemen of New Hampshire; or, the General Government and the Leaders of the New England Opposition Contrasted* (Concord: n.p., 1816), EAI, SS#37689, 2, 24, 27, 31, 35. Other examples of political broadsides include, "A Voter," *The Case Fairly Stated* [Lexington, KY: n.p., 1816], EAI, SS#37193, defending Henry Clay, despite his vote for the Compensation Act; and two appeals to voters (May 6, July 18) by John Ewing, *To the Citizens of Knox County* (Vincennes, IN: n.p., 1816), EAI, SS#37545.

67. John Kilbourn, *A Public Exposition; by John Kilbourn, of his Political Sentiments, in a Communication, Addressed to the People of Columbus, Ohio* (Columbus: Western Intelligencer Office, 1816), 4–5. Whether Kilbourn was related to the congressman from that district, James Kilbourne, is unknown.

68. Livermore, *Twilight of Federalism*, 29–30.

69. Turner, "Elections of 1816 and 1820," 1:307; Livermore, *Twilight of Federalism*, 34; "The Federal Party in 1816," PMHB, 6 (1882), 247–249.

70. Cited in *Boston Gazette*, March 28, 1816.

71. Cited in Turner, "Elections of 1816 and 1820," 1:307.

72. Speech of Randolph in House, Dec. 18, 1816, *Annals*, 14th Cong., 2nd Sess. (House), 332.

73. King to Gore, Nov. 5, 1816, King Papers, NYHS, vol. 15.

74. Fisk to Taylor, Aug. 2, 1816, Taylor Papers, NYHS.

75. Jackson to Monroe, Oct. 23, 1816, Moser, ed., *Papers of Andrew Jackson*, 4:70.

76. King to Christopher Gore, Nov. 22, 1816, King Papers, NYHS, vol. 15.

77. Quoted in Ernst, *Rufus King*, 352.

78. Gore to King, Dec. 20, 1816, King Papers, NYHS, vol 15.

79. *Annals*, 14th Cong., 2nd Sess. (House), 944–946. According to the House record, the Senate, back in its chamber, took up a motion from James Barbour (VA) supporting the right of Indiana to cast its electoral vote. He was supported by both Connecticut senators, Samuel W. Dana and David Daggett, and was opposed by George W. Campbell (TN) and Eligius Fromentin (LA). Before the decision was taken, however, word was received from the House that they were ready to resume the process, and Barbour withdrew his motion.

80. Ibid., 945–47.

81. Ibid., 948–50 (quotations on 948–49).

82. Gore to Rufus King, Jan. 16, 1817, King Papers, NYHS, vol. 15.

83. King to Christopher Gore, Jan. 2, 1817, ibid.

Epilogue

1. Richardson, ed., *Messages and Papers*, 2:10.

2. Bassett, *Correspondence of Andrew Jackson*, 2:266, 268 (entire letter 266–70).

3. Contemporary accounts of Monroe's tour include Richard Radcliffe, ed., *The President's Tour: A Collection of Addresses made to James Monroe, Esq. President of the United States on his Tour through the Northern and Middle States, A.D. 1817 . . .* (New Ipswich, N.H.: Salmon Wilder, 1822); [T.A. Wheelock ?] *A Narrative of a Tour of Observation, Made During the Summer of 1817, by James Monroe, President of the United States, through the North-Eastern and North-Western Departments of the Union: With a View to the Examination of their Several Military Defences* (Philadelphia: S.A. Mitchell & H. Ames, 1818); Samuel P. Waldo, *The Tour of James Monroe, President of the United States, Through the Northern and Eastern States, in 1817; His Tour in the Year 1818; Together with a Sketch of His Life*, 2nd ed. (Hartford, CN: Silas Andrus, 1820). A convenient summary of the tour is found in Noble E. Cunningham, Jr., *The Presidency of James Monroe* (Lawrence: University Press of Kansas, 1996), 30–40.

4. Gore to King, May 15, 1817, Rufus King Papers, NYHS, vol. 15.

5. Christopher Gore to Rufus King, July 8, 1817, King, ed., *King Correspondence*, 6:78.

6. Livermore, *Twilight of Federalism*, 34.

7. Sullivan, *An Oration*, 22.

8. 8. King to Christopher Gore, Nov. 5, 1816, Rufus King Papers, NYHS, vol. 15.

9. King to [Christopher Gore ?], June 26, 1816, ibid.

10. Norman K. Risjord, "The Virginia Federalists," *The Journal of Southern History*, 33 (Nov. 1967), 512–517.

11. Livermore, *Twilight of Federalism*, 268.

Bibliographical Essay

Primary Sources

This work is based very heavily on primary sources, as the endnotes attest. Perhaps the most useful collection was the Early American Imprint series, which was published for the American Antiquarian Society (Worcester, Massachusetts) by the Readex Microprint Corporation. This series includes almost all known extant publications in the early American period and is based on the bibliographical checklist compiled by Ralph R. Shaw and Richard H. Shoemaker (New York, 1958–1966). The work was begun by Charles Evans, and his bibliography had been completed to 1799 (13 vols.) before his death. The American Antiquarian Society completed the years 1799 and 1800, but they dropped the project for economic reasons. Approximately twenty years passed before the project was resumed by Shaw and Shoemaker in 1958. By 1997 the project had been completed through 1846, and the number of descriptive entries was approximately 200,000. The collection is extremely valuable for its inclusion of the books and the pamphlet literature of the period. With the exception of the tedious sermon literature often devoted to arcane theological points (but a rich source for some future researcher), all of the literature for 1816 was consulted, and much of this work is based on that research.

All of the published congressional debates of the Fourteenth Congress, compiled by the editors of the Washington, D.C., newspaper, *Daily National Intelligencer*, Joseph Gales (House) and William Seaton (Senate), were read. It should be understood that not everything that appears in the compilation known as the *Annals of Congress of the United States . . .*, 42 vols. (Washington, D.C., 1834–1856) is a verbatim transcription. Congressmen and senators often gave Gales and Seaton "polished" copies of their speeches after delivery. Nevertheless, this is a valuable source for the historian.

A third valuable resource was the *American State Papers*, which is broken down into various categories. Those most useful for this study include: *Military Affairs*, 7 vols. (Washington, D.C., 1832–1861); *Finance*, 5 vols. (Washington, D.C., 1832–1859); *Commerce and Navigation*, 2 vols. (Washington, D.C., 1832–1834); *Naval Affairs*, 3 vols. (Washington, D.C., 1834–1860); and *Miscellaneous*, 1 vol. (Washington, D.C., 1834).

Newspapers also served as an important tool to understand the myriad developments of 1816. Probably the most valuable was the quasi-administration paper in Washington, D.C., published by Gales and Seaton, the *Daily National Intelligencer*. Gales exchanged newspapers with several hundred editors and frequently printed excerpts from them. Next most valuable was *Niles' Weekly Register*, the closest thing to a news magazine for that period. Hezekiah Niles published his magazine in Baltimore, and he strove to take a national perspective and to be a journal of record. Many other newspapers were valuable sources. In no particular order, they would include: the *Richmond* (VA) *Enquirer*; the *Albany* (NY) *Argus*; the Annapolis *Maryland Gazette*; the *Charleston* (SC) *Courier*; the *New York Evening Post*; the Boston *Columbian Centinel*; the Hartford *Connecticut Courant*; the Philadelphia *United States Gazette*; the Lexington (KY) *Kentucky Gazette*; the *Pittsburgh Gazette*; the *Nashville* (TN) *Gazette*; and the *Scioto Gazette* (Chillicothe, OH). Many other newspapers were consulted in the course of this study, which may be found in the notes.

The personal papers of prominent individuals were also consulted. Particularly useful were the Rufus King Papers and the John W. Taylor Papers in the New York Historical Society; the James Monroe Papers in the New York Public Library; and collections of papers of James Madison, James Monroe, Andrew Jackson, Henry Clay, John C. Calhoun, William H. Crawford, and Richard M. Johnson in the Manuscript Division of the Library of Congress, Washington, D.C.

Many of the collections of leading figures of the period are also available on microfilm, and the Papers of Daniel Webster (Dartmouth College, Hanover, NH) and Timothy Pickering (Massachusetts Historical Society, Boston, MA) were consulted in this form. Published collections of many participants in the events of this time are also available. There are two sets of Jackson papers: John S. Bassett, ed., *Correspondence of Andrew Jackson*, 6 vols. (Washington, D.C.,1926–1933), and a modern version, Harold D. Moser, ed., *The Papers of Andrew Jackson*, 5 vols. to date (Knoxville, 1980–). See also, Charles R. King, ed., *The Life and Correspondence of Rufus King*, 6 vols. (New York 1894–1900); Stanislaus M. Hamilton, ed., *The Writings of James Monroe*, 7 vols. (1901, reprint New York, 1969); James F. Hopkins et al., eds., *The Papers of Henry Clay*, 11 vols. (Lexington, KY, 1959–1992); W. Edwin Hemphill, et al., eds., *The Papers of John C. Calhoun*, 26 vols. to date (Columbia, SC, 1959–); Gaillard Hunt, ed., *The Writings of James Madison*, 9 vols. (New York, 1900–1910); Paul L. Ford, ed., *The Writings of Thomas Jefferson*, 10 vols. (New York, 1892–1899); Noble E. Cunningham, ed., *Circular Letters of Congressmen to Their Constituents, 1789–1829*, 3 vols. (Chapel Hill, NC, 1978); and James D. Richardson, ed., *A Compilation of the Messages and Papers of the Presidents, 1789–1897*, 10 vols. (Washington, D.C., 1897–1900).

Secondary Sources

The so-called Era of Good Feelings (1815–1829) has not received the attention it deserves from historians. Textbooks generally sweep from the War of 1812 to the Age of Jackson in a few pages, suggesting that little of importance occurred in these years, except for the disturbing slavery controversy in Missouri in 1820–1821. It is also noted that the Jacksonian period was ushered in by the "rise of the common man," but exactly why that phenomenon occurred is often left very vague in these textbooks. It is hoped that this work is a contribution to the beginning of an understanding of this much misunderstood and neglected period of American history. The last volume of Henry Adams's magisterial nine volume study, *History of the United States During the Administrations of Jefferson and Madison*, 9 vols. (New York, 1889–1991) is good for understanding the postwar period. There are two studies of this time by George Dangerfield: *The Era of Good Feelings* (New York, 1952); and *The Awakening of American Nationalism, 1815–1828* (New York, 1965), but while both works are beautifully written, there is much that Dangerfield did not understand about this era, and there is a need to update his interpretations. His coverage of the postwar years is particularly thin. Shaw Livermore, Jr., *The Twilight of Federalism: The Disintegration of the Federalist Party, 1815–1830* (Princeton, 1962) is useful, but his interpretations are also in need of revision. Norman K. Risjord, *The Old Republicans, Southern Conservativism in the Age of Jefferson* (New York, 1968), is helpful for an understanding of one wing of the Republican party. David Hackett Fischer, *The Revolution of American Conservativism: The Federalist Party in the Era of Jeffersonian Democracy* (New York, 1965), sets the stage for the demise of the Federalist Party. Richard P. McCormick, *The Second Party System: Party Formation in the Jacksonian Era* (Chapel Hill, 1966), shows the development of the new party system after the collapse of Federalism.

A contemporary (and controversial) work of this period that had great influence was Mathew Carey, *The Olive Branch: or Faults on Both Sides, Federal and Democratic . . .* 7th ed. (Middlebury, VT, 1816). Kendrick Charles Babcock, *The Rise of American Nationality, 1811–1819* (New York, 1906), part of the old American Nation Series, is of marginal value, and Gaillard Hunt, *Life in America One Hundred Years Ago* (New York, 1914), while it has some interesting information, does not focus much on 1816. A recent study by Noble E. Cunningham, Jr., *The Presidency of James Monroe* (Lawrence, KS, 1996), in the American Presidency Series, is very useful and has a convenient summary of the Monroe tour of 1817.

Biographies of participants in the events of this era are also a valuable resource. Among them are William Cabell Bruce, *John Randolph of Roanoke, 1773–1833*, 2 vols. (New York, 1922); and a perverse, but fun, biography in the American Statesmen Series by Henry Adams, *John Randolph* (Boston, 1908). Other biographies are Charles M. Wiltse, *John C. Calhoun, Nationalist, 1782–1828*, vol. 1 of 3 vols. (Indianapolis, 1944); Glyndon G. Van Deusen, *The Life of Henry Clay* (Boston, 1937); Robert V. Remini, *Henry Clay: Statesman for the Union* (New York 1991); Alvin Laroy Duckett, *John Forsyth: Political Tactician* (Athens, GA, 1962); Marquis James, *Andrew Jackson: The Border Captain* (New York, 1933); Robert V. Remini, *Andrew Jackson and the Course of American Empire, 1767–1821* (New York, 1977); Harry Ammon, *James Monroe: The Quest for National Identity* (New York, 1971); Chase Mooney, *William H. Crawford* (Lexington, KY, 1974); Robert V. Remini, *Daniel Webster* (New York, 1997); Evan D. Cornog, *The Birth of Empire: De Witt Clinton and the American*

Experience, 1769–1828 (New York, 1998); Lamont D. Thomas, *Paul Cuffe: Black Entrepreneur and Pan-Africanist* (Urbana, 1988); Richard G. Stone, *Hezekiah Niles as an Economist* (Baltimore, 1933); and Kenneth W. Rowe, *Matthew Carey: A Study in American Economic Development* (Baltimore, 1933).

On the weather of 1816, there are many articles in the journalistic vein, such as Charles M. Wilson, "The Year Without a Summer," *American History Illustrated,* 5 (June 1970); G.S. Fichter, "Eighteen-hundred-and-froze-to-death: Snow-filled summer of 1816," *Science Digest,* 69 (Feb. 1971), 62–66; H.E. Landsberg and J.M. Albert, "Summer of 1816 and Volcanism," *Weatherwise,* 27 (April 1974); and Henry and Elizabeth Stommel, "The Year Without a Summer," *Scientific American,* 240 (June 1979), 176–86. The most useful study was Willis I. Milham, "The Year 1816: The Causes of Abnormalities," *Monthly Weather Review,* 52 (Dec. 1824), 563–70. Emmanuel Le Roy Ladurie, *Times of Feast, Times of Famine: A History of Climate Since the Year 1000* (Garden City, NY, 1971), has coverage of Europe's weather in 1816. A contemporary account that has valuable information on the effects of the summer's weather is David Thomas, *Travels through the Western Country in the Summer of 1816 . . .* (Auburn, NY, 1819).

Despite the obvious importance of the nationalistic legislation of 1816, there is no systematic study of the subject, unless one counts a single chapter in Henry Adams' last volume on the Madison Administration. The tariff is a much neglected subject. The best work is more than a century old, F.W. Taussig, *The Tariff History of the United States* (1892, reprint New York, 1964). An article by Norris W. Preyer, "Southern Support of the Tariff of 1816: A Reappraisal," *The Journal of Southern History,* 25 (Aug. 1959), 306–22, sheds some light on Southern motives on this measure. The Bank of the United States has received more coverage, but the rechartering of the BUS in 1816 is rarely analyzed. The old standard work on the Second BUS is Ralph C.H. Catterrall, *The Second Bank of the United States* (Chicago, 1903). Bray Hammond, *Banks and Politics in America, From the Revolution to the Civil War* (Princeton, 1957), is an outstanding work on banking and politics in early America. Raymond Walters, Jr., "The Origins of the Second Bank of the United States," *The Journal of Political Economy,* 53 (June 1945), 115–31, covers the circumstances that led to the adoption of the second BUS, and Leon

M. Schur, "The Second Bank of the United States and the Inflation after the War of 1812," *The Journal of Political Economy*, 68 (April 1960), 118–34, is informative on the early tribulations of the second bank.

John Lauritz Larson, "'Bind the Republic Together': The National Union and the Struggle for a System of Internal Improvements," *The Journal of American History*, 74 (Sept. 1987), 363–87, provides an excellent background for the Bonus Bill. His recent study, *Internal Improvement: National Public Works and the Promise of Popular Government in the Early United States* (Chapel Hill, 2001) is a valuable analysis of this important issue in the early republic. A good general survey of transportation developments in this period is George Rogers Taylor, *The Transportation Revolution, 1815–1860* (New York, 1957). An earlier work on the same period is Balthasar Henry Meyer, *History of Transportation in the United States before 1860* (Forge Village, MA, 1948). Also useful is Carter Goodrich, *Government Promotion of American Canals and Railroads, 1800–1890* (New York, 1960), and an edited work by the same author, *Canals and American Economic Development* (New York, 1961). On turnpikes, see Karl Raitz, ed., *The National Road* (Baltimore, 1996), Philip D. Jordan, *The National Road* (Indianapolis, 1948), and Joseph A. Durrenberger, *Turnpike: A Study of the Toll Road Movement in the Middle Atlantic States and Maryland* (1931, reprint Cos Cob, CN, 1968). On canals, a good overview of the literature may be found in Ronald E. Shaw, "Canals in the Early Republic: A Review of Recent Literature," *Journal of the Early Republic*, 4 (Summer 1984), 117–42. An older survey is Alvin F. Harlow, *Old Towpaths: The Story of the American Canal Era* (1954, reprint Port Washington, 1964). A case study is Ralph D. Gray, *The National Waterway: A History of the Chesapeake and Delaware Canal* (Urbana, 1967). For the Erie Canal, Ronald E. Shaw, *Erie Water West: A History of the Erie Canal* (Lexington, KY, 1966) is excellent. Also useful on the Erie Canal are George E. Condon, *Stars in the Water: The Story of the Erie Canal* (New York, 1974), and Carol Sheriff, *The Artificial River: The Erie Canal and the Paradox of Progress, 1817–1862* (New York, 1996).

Fourth of July celebrations are described in several works, such as Len Travers, *Celebrating the Fourth: Independence Day and the Rites of Nationalism in the Early Republic* (Amherst, 1997). Other useful studies include David Waldstreicher, *In the Midst of Perpetual Fetes:*

The Making of American Nationalism, 1776–1820 (Chapel Hill, 1997); Susan Davis, *Parades and Power: Street Theater in Nineteenth Century Philadelphia* (Philadelphia, 1986); Mary Ryan, "The American Parade: Representations of the Nineteenth-Century Social Order," in Lynn Hunt, ed., *The New Cultural History* (Berkeley, 1989); and Andrew Burstein, *America's Jubilee: How in 1826 a Generation Remembered 50 Years of Independence* (New York, 2001).

National defense policies in the post-War of 1812 period have been surprisingly neglected. Two articles focus on this period: Brian W. Beltman, "Territorial Commands of the Army: The System Refined but not Perfected, 1815–1821," *Journal of the Early Republic*, 11 (Summer 1991), 185–218, and Michael S. Fitzgerald, "'Nature Unsubdued': Diplomacy, Expansion and the American Military Buildup of 1815–1816," *Mid-America*, 77 (Winter 1995), 5–32. Although it is nearly a century old, Emory Upton, *The Military Policy of the United States* (1904, reprinted New York, 1968), still has value today. General histories touching on the period include Russell F. Weigley, *History of the United States Army* (1967, reprint Bloomington, IN, 1984), Edward M. Coffman, *The Old Army: A Portrait of the American Army in Peacetime, 1784–1898* (New York, 1986), and C. Joseph Bernardo and Eugene H. Bacon, *American Military Policy: Its Development Since 1775* (Harrisburg, PA, 1961). Leonard D. White, *The Jeffersonians: A Study in Administrative History, 1801–1829* (New York, 1951) is an excellent administrative history that covers the military well. Studies of the navy in the post-war period include: Craig L. Symonds, *Navalists and Anti-Navalists: The Naval Policy Debate in the United States, 1785–1827* (Newark, DE, 1980); K. Jack Bauer, "Naval Shipbuilding Programs, 1794–1860," *Military Affairs*, 19 (Spring 1965), 33–36; and Kenneth J. Hagan, *This People's Navy: The Making of American Sea Power* (New York, 1991). Also helpful are Charles O. Paullin, *Paullin's History of Naval Administration, 1775–1911* (1906–1914, reprint Annapolis, MD, 1968) and Harold Sprout and Margaret Sprout, *The Rise of American Naval Power, 1776–1918* (1939, reprint Annapolis, MD, 1967).

The Dartmouth College case has been well covered by Francis N. Stites, *Private Interest and Public Gain: The Dartmouth College Case, 1819* (Amherst, MA, 1972). Also valuable is Richard N. Current, "The Dartmouth College Case," in John A. Garraty, ed., *Quarrels That Have Shaped the Constitution* (New York, 1962). An older study is John M. Shirley, *The Dartmouth College Causes and the Supreme Court of the United States* (1895, reprint New York, 1971). Also useful is Lynn W. Turner, *William Plumer of New Hampshire, 1759–1850* (Chapel Hill, 1962). The standard work on Maine's separation from Massachusetts is Ronald F. Banks, *Maine Becomes a State: The Movement to Separate Maine from Massachusetts, 1785–1820* (Middletown, CT, 1970).

Humanitarian reform has been richly covered by historians. For an overview of the social reform movements in the early American republic, the best general survey is still Alice Felt Tyler, *Freedom's Ferment: Phases of American Social History from the Colonial Period to the Outbreak of the Civil War* (Minneapolis, 1944). A more recent work is Ronald G. Walters, *American Reformers, 1815–1860* (New York, 1978). Capital punishment and the ritual of public executions is effectively dealt with in Louis P. Masur, *Rites of Execution: Capital Punishment and the Transformation of American Culture, 1776–1865* (New York, 1989). The best study on alcoholism in the early republic is William J. Rorabaugh, *The Alcoholic Republic: An American Tradition* (New York, 1979). Sabbatarianism has been efficiently covered by Richard R. John in an article, "Taking Sabbatarianism Seriously: The Postal System, the Sabbath, and the Transformation of American Political Culture," *Journal of the Early Republic* 10 (Winter 1990), 517–567, and by his book, *Spreading the News: The American Postal System from Franklin to Morse* (Cambridge, MA, 1998). The standard treatment of the peace movement is Merle Curti, *The American Peace Crusade, 1813–1860* (Durham, NC, 1929). Henry O. Dwight, *The Centennial History of the American Bible Society* (New York, 1916), is an unsatisfactory work, full of inaccuracies. Much better is Clifford S. Griffin, *Their Brother's Keepers: Moral Stewardship in the United States, 1800–1865* (New Brunswick, NJ, 1960), which is also an excellent survey of the humanitarian impulse.

Little has been written about the quiet period in the anti-slavery movement from 1808 to 1831. A background for the early stages of the movement is Winthrop Jordan, *White Over Black: American Attitudes toward the Negro, 1550–1812* (Chapel Hill, NC, 1968). Also valuable are William W. Freehling, "The Founding Fathers and Slavery," *American Historical Review*, 77 (Oct. 1972), 81–91, and Paul Finkelman, *Slavery and the Founders: Race and Liberty in the Age of Jefferson* (Armonk, NY, 1996). Literally hundreds of articles have been written that deal with the colonization movement. The most useful for this study have been P.J. Staudenraus, *The African Colonization Movement, 1816–1865* (New York. 1961); Charles I. Foster, "The Colonization of Free Negroes, in Liberia, 1816–1835," *Journal of Negro History*, 38 (Jan. 1953), 41–66; Henry Noble Sherwood, "The Formation of the American Colonization Society," *Journal of Negro History*, 2 (July 1917), 209–28; Douglas R. Egerton, "'Its Origin is Not a Little Curious': A New Look at the American Colonization Society," *Journal of the Early Republic*, 5 (Winter 1985), 463–80; and Henry Noble Sherwood, "Paul Cuffe," *Journal of Negro History*, 8 April 1923), 153–229.

The election of 1816 has been largely dismissed by historians as unimportant. Lynn W. Turner's article in Arthur Schlesinger, Jr., ed., *History of American Presidential Elections, 1789–1968*, 4 vols. (New York 1971), is the only one that combines two elections—that of 1816 and 1820. In addition to the biographies cited earlier, see J.E.D. Shipp, *Giant Days, or, The Life and Times of William H. Crawford* (Americus, GA, 1909), Ray W. Irwin, *Daniel D. Tompkins: Governor of New York and Vice President of the United States* (New York, 1968), and Holmes Alexander, *The American Talleyrand: The Career and Contemporaries of Martin Van Buren, Eighth President* (New York, 1935). On the nominating caucus, consult C.S. Thompson, "The Rise and Fall of the Congressional Caucus as a Machine for Nominating Candidates for the Presidency," in Leon Stein, ed., *The Caucus System in American Politics* (New York, 1965), and M. Ostrogorski, "The Rise and Fall of the Nominating Caucus, Legislative and Congressional," *American Historical Review*, 5 (Dec. 1899), 253–83. Also useful are Charles S. Sydnor, "The One Party Period of American History," *American Historical Review*, 51 (April 1946), 439–51, and Michael Wallace, "Changing Concepts of Party in the United States: New York, 1815–1828," *American Historical Review*, 74 (Dec. 1968), 453–91.

Index